A Facsimile Edition
of the
Dead Sea Scrolls

VOLUME II

A Facsimile Edition

of the

Dead Sea Scrolls

Prepared with

an Introduction

and Index

by

Robert H. Eisenman

and

James M. Robinson

VOLUME II

BIBLICAL ARCHAEOLOGY SOCIETY

Washington, DC

1991

Library of Congress Number 91-058627
ISBN 1-880317-02-8 (Volume II)
ISBN 1-880317-00-1 (Set)
©1991
Biblical Archaeology Society
3000 Connecticut Avenue, NW
Washington, DC 20008

Table of Contents

Volume I

Volume II

Plates
908–1785

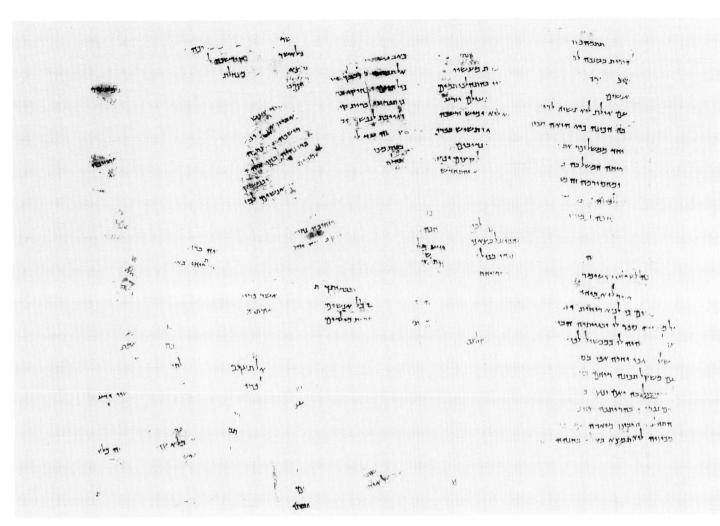

PLATE 908

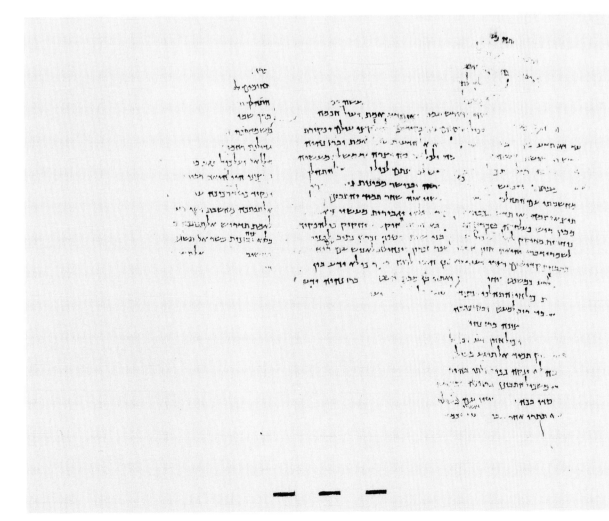

PLATE 909

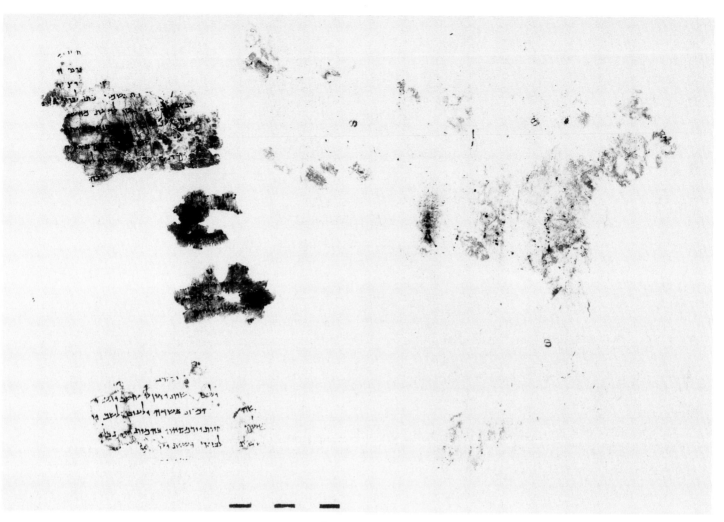

PLATE 910

PLATE 911

PLATE 912

PLATE 913

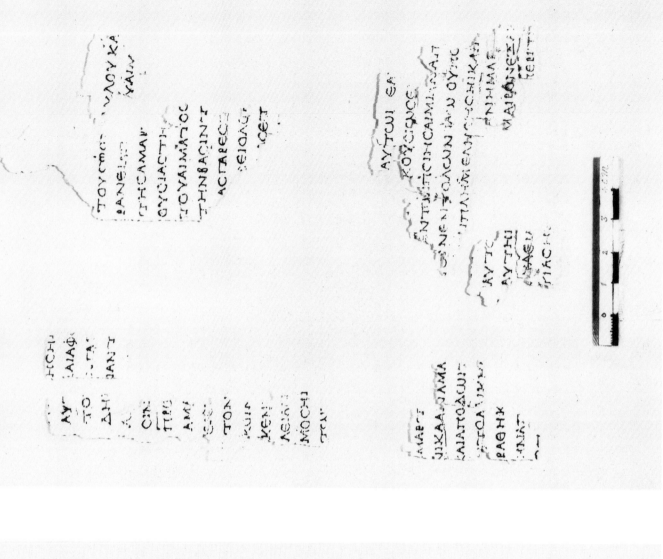

PLATE 915

PLATE 914

PLATE 916

PLATE 917

PLATE 918

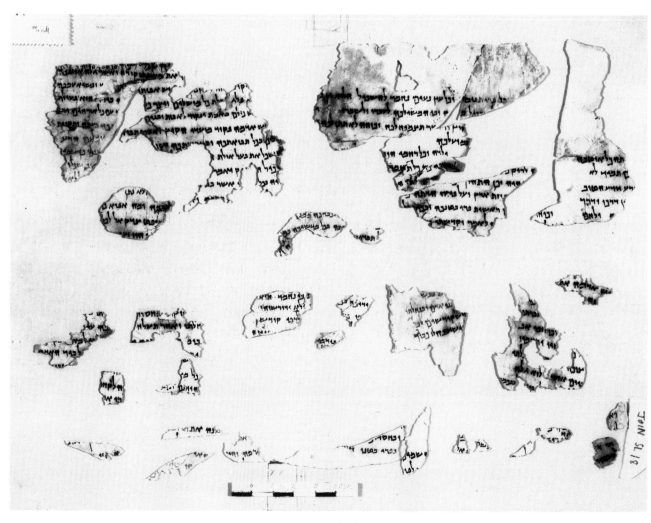

PLATE 919

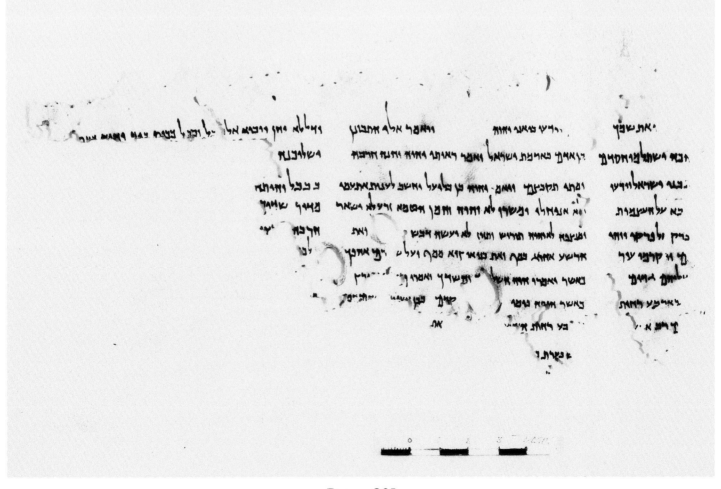

PLATE 920

PLATE 921

PLATE 922

PLATE 923

PLATE 955

PLATE 954

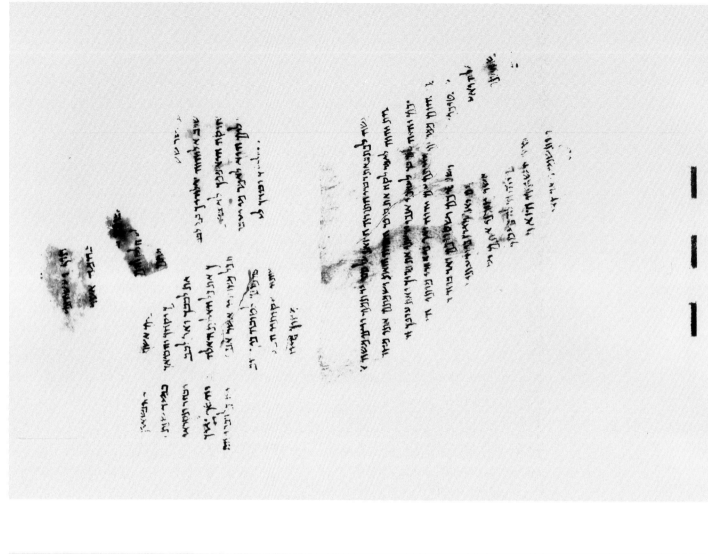

PLATE 957

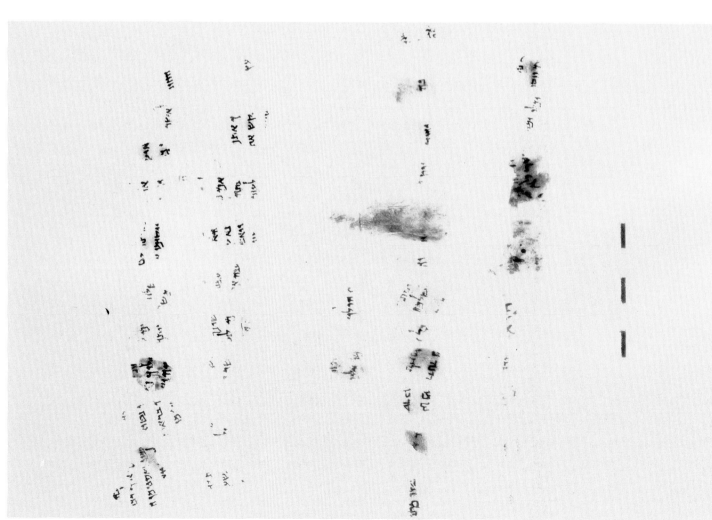

PLATE 956

PLATE 959

PLATE 958

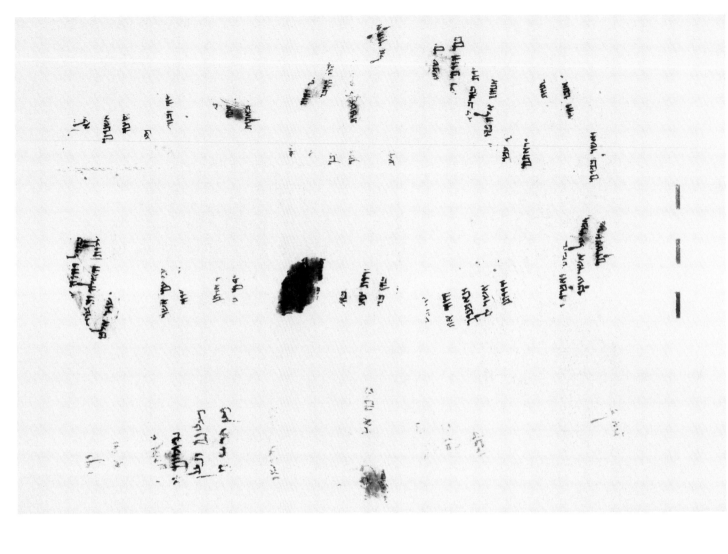

PLATE 961

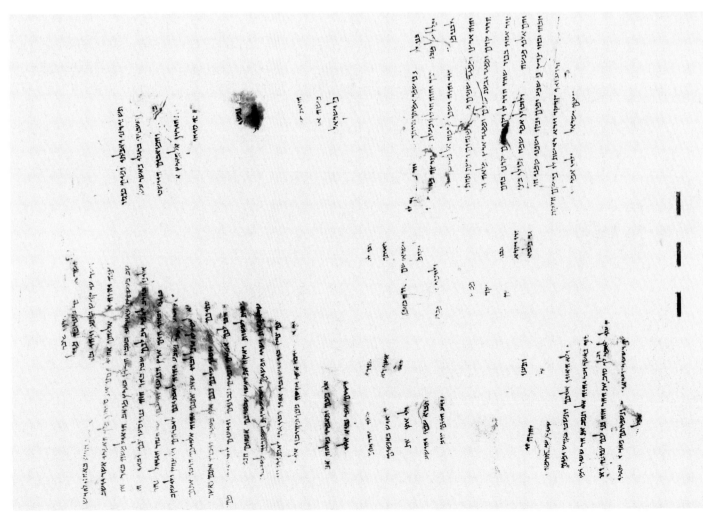

PLATE 960

PLATE 963

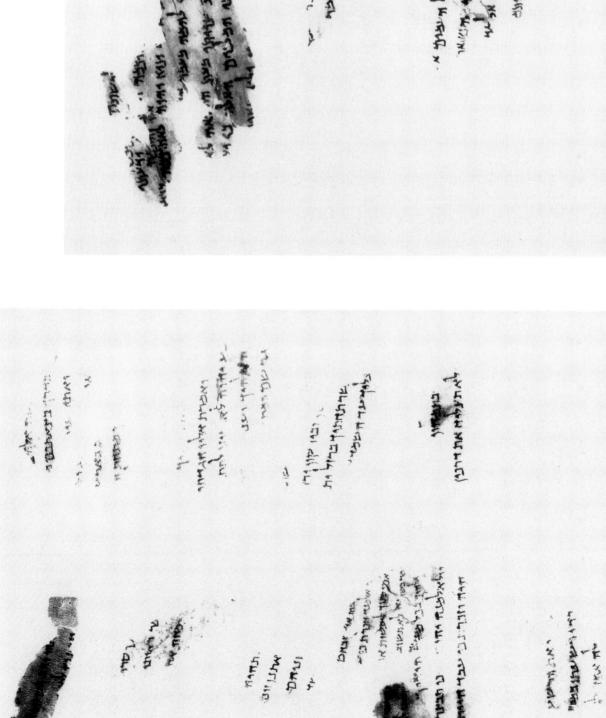

PLATE 962

Plate 965

Plate 964

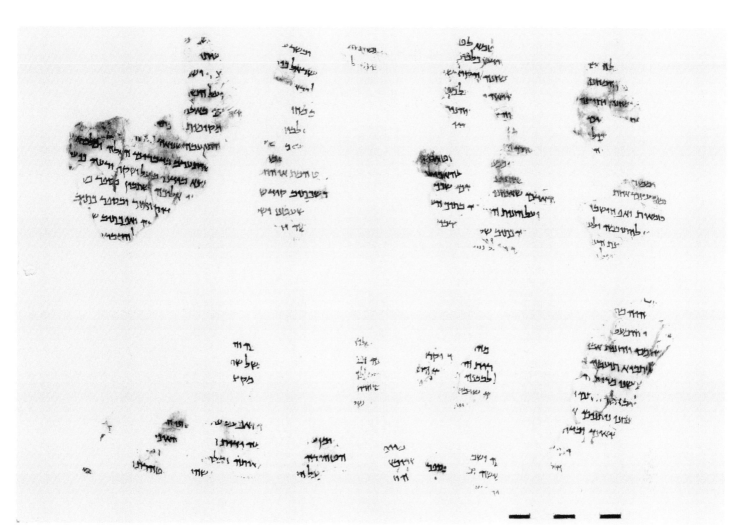

PLATE 966

PLATE 967

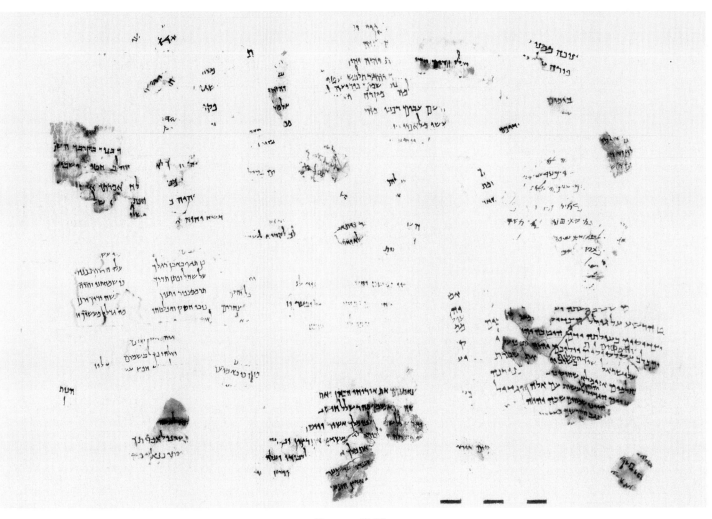

PLATE 968

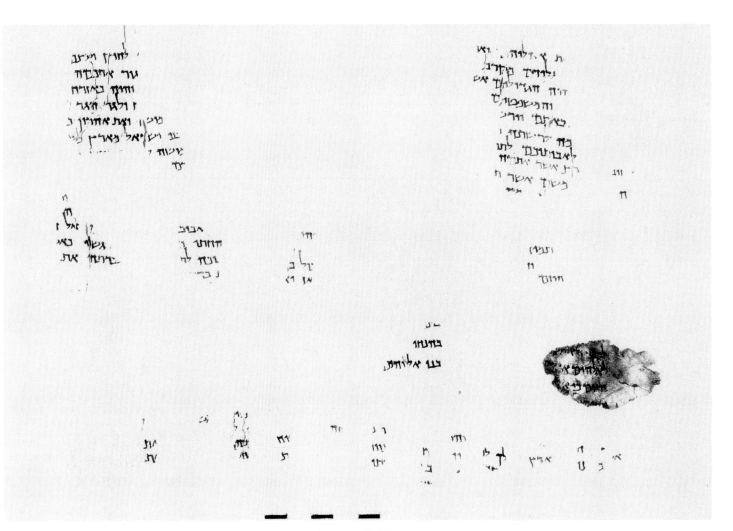

PLATE 969

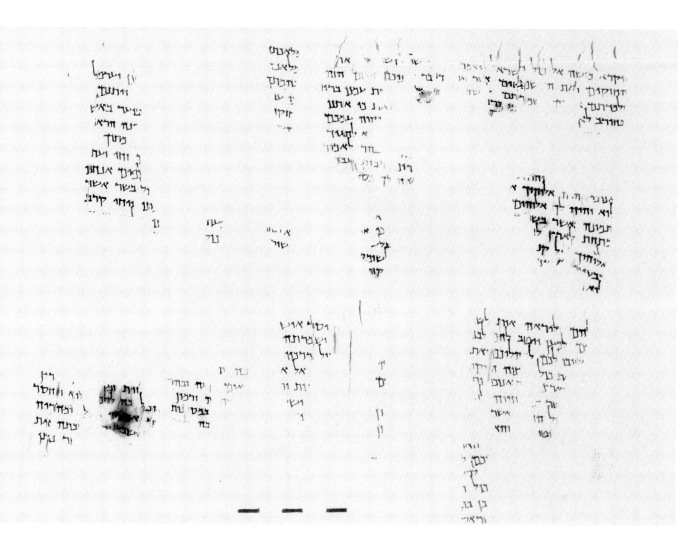

PLATE 970

PLATE 971

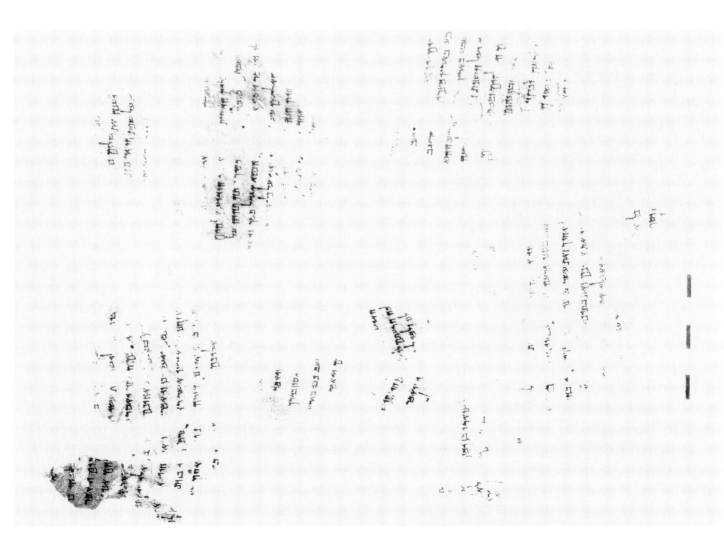

PLATE 972

PLATE 973

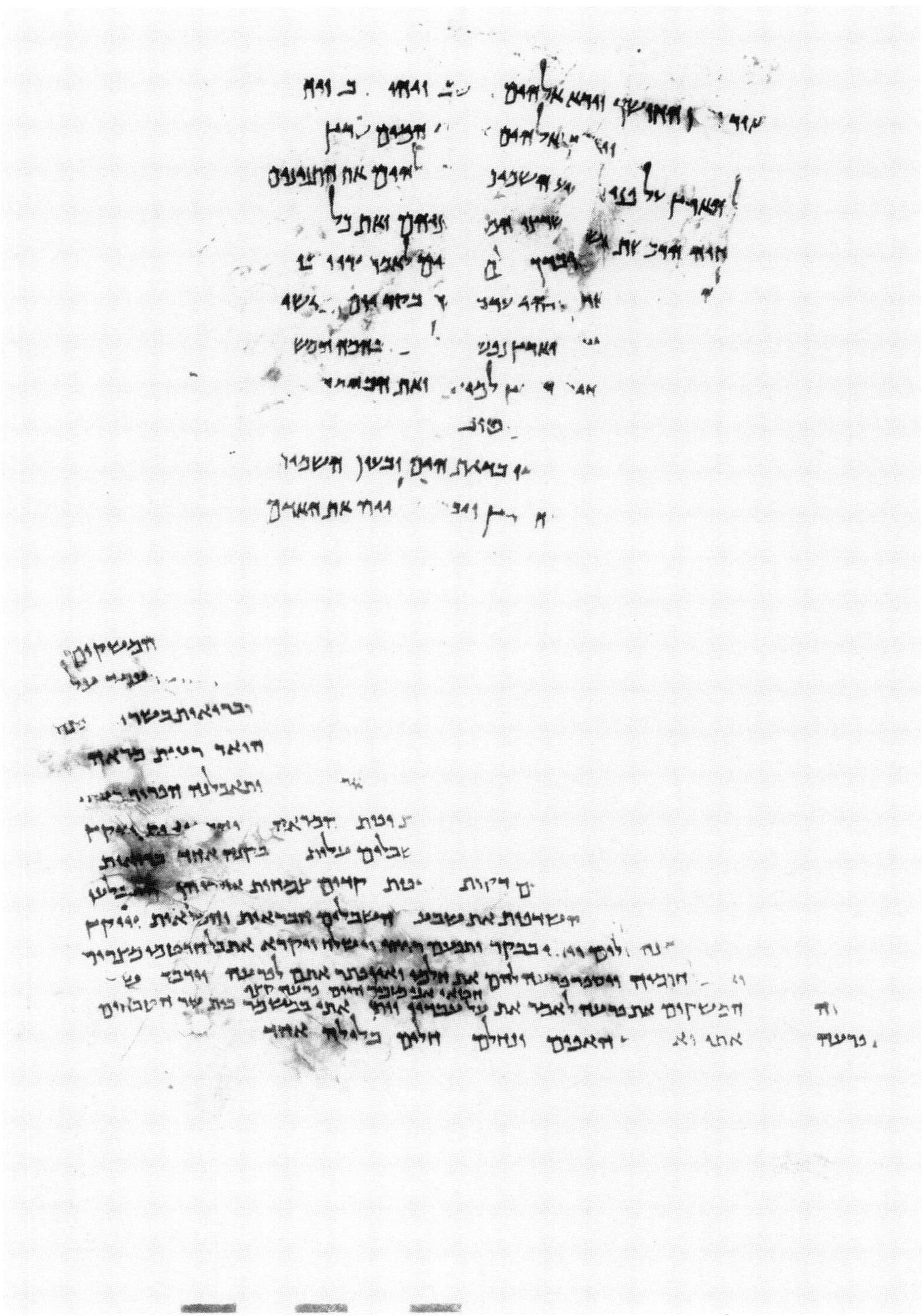

Plate 974

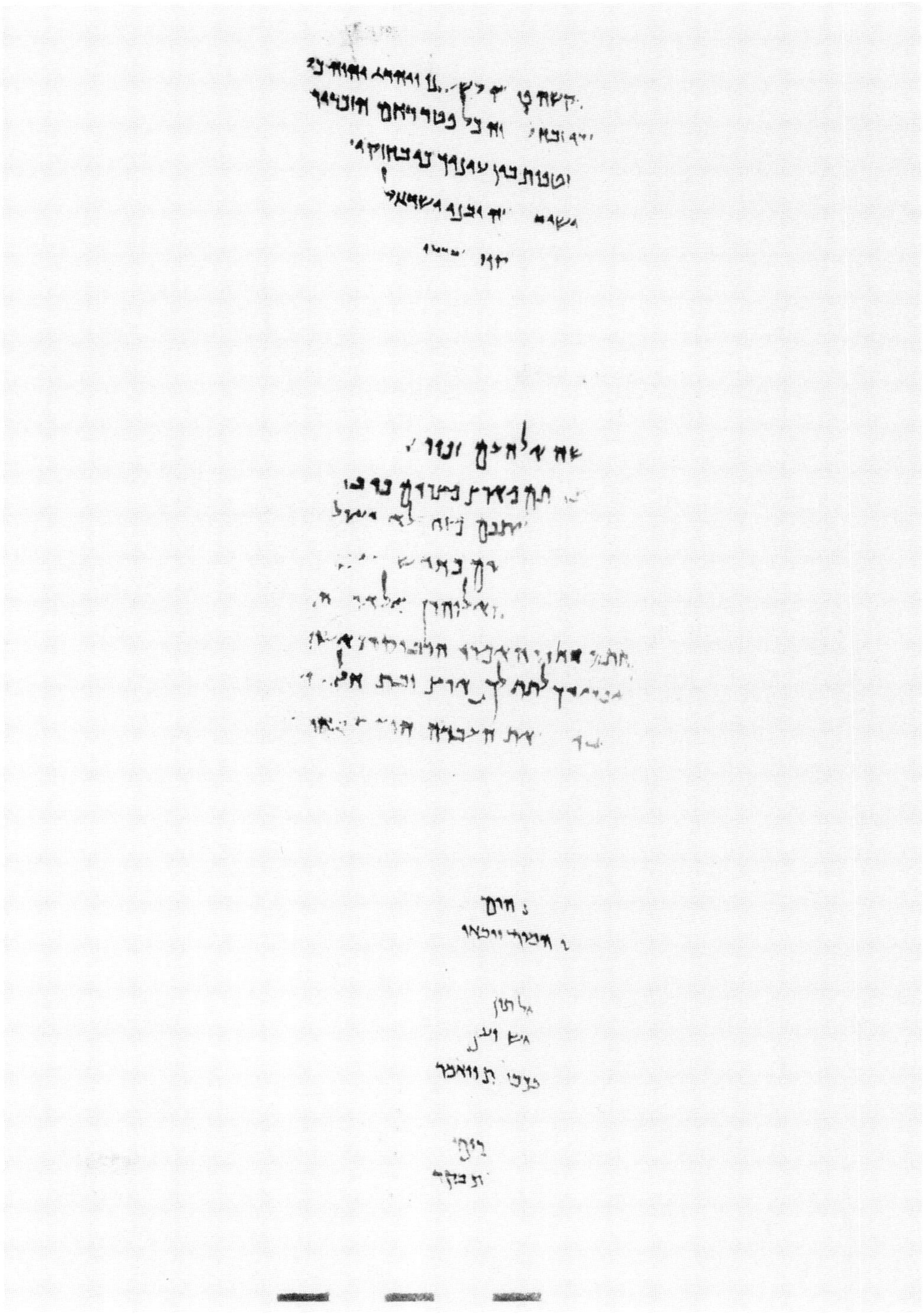

Plate 975

PLATE 977

PLATE 976

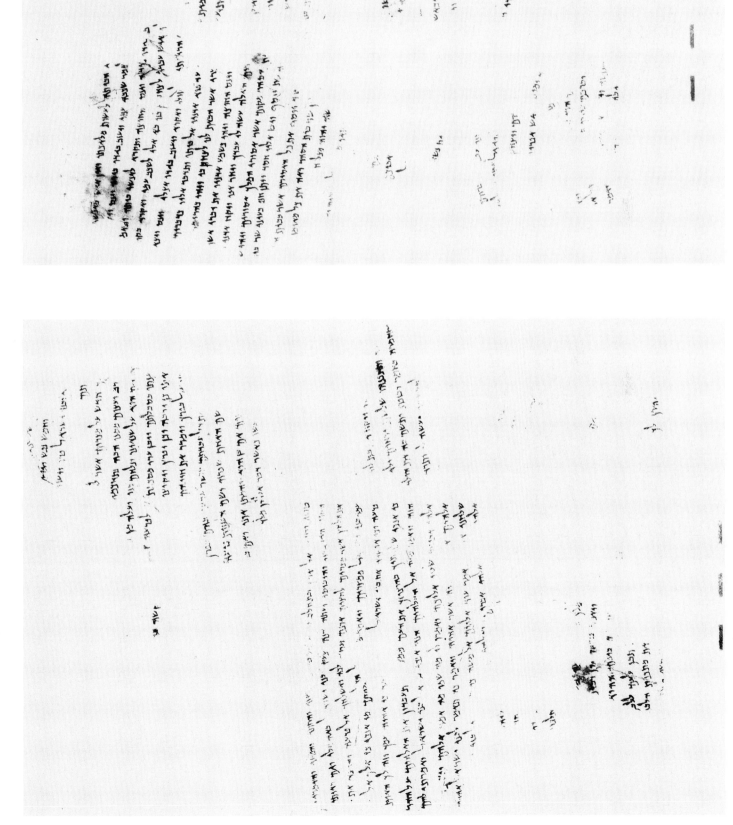

PLATE 978

PLATE 979

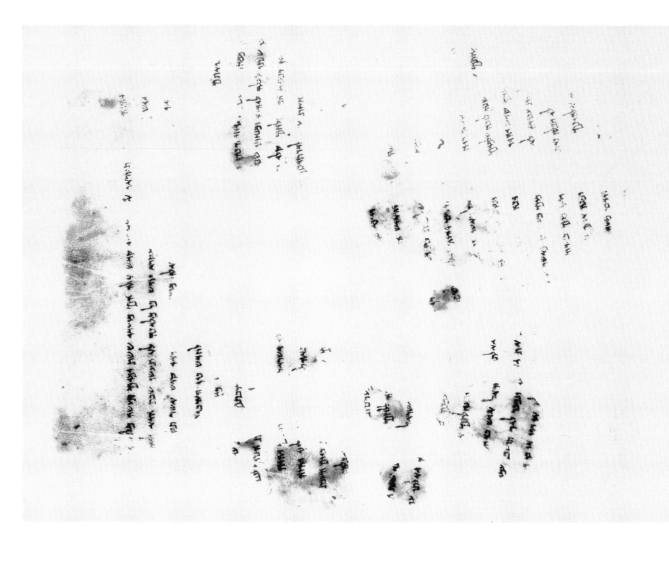

PLATE 981

PLATE 980

PLATE 983

PLATE 982

PLATE 985

PLATE 984

PLATE 986

PLATE 987

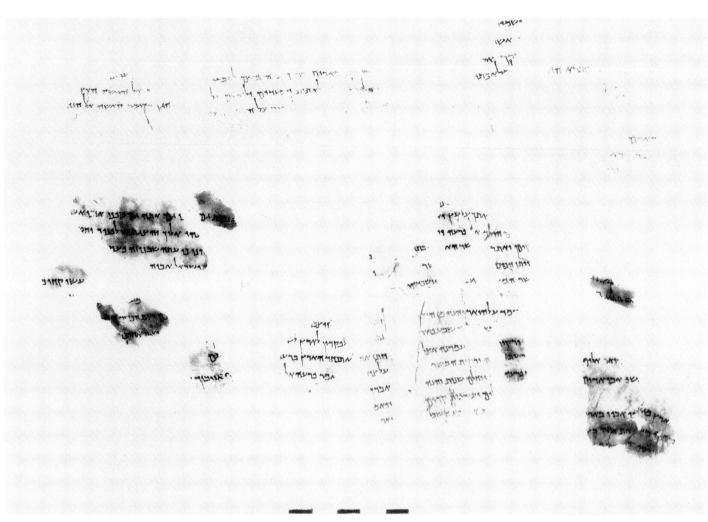

PLATE 988

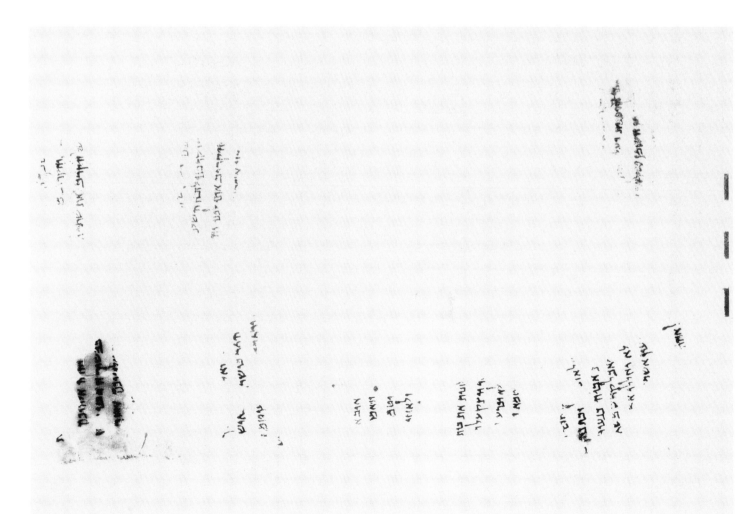

PLATE 989

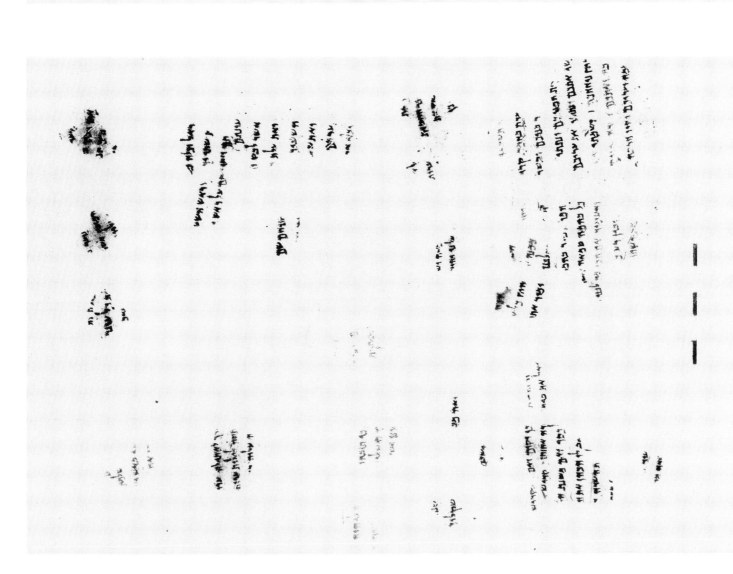

PLATE 991

PLATE 990

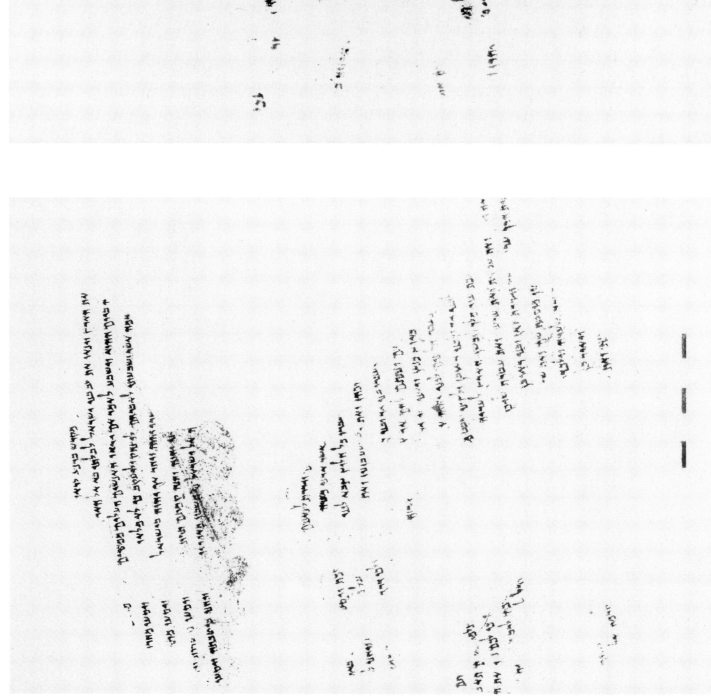

PLATE 992

PLATE 993

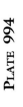

PLATE 995

PLATE 994

PLATE 996

PLATE 997

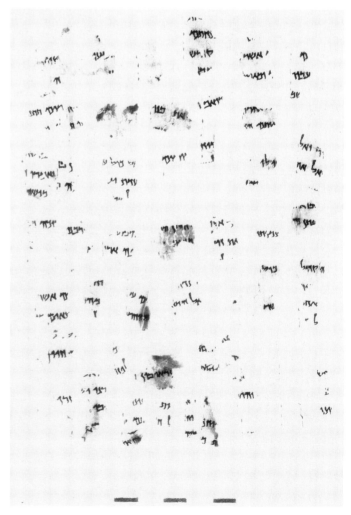

PLATE 998

PLATE 1000

PLATE 999

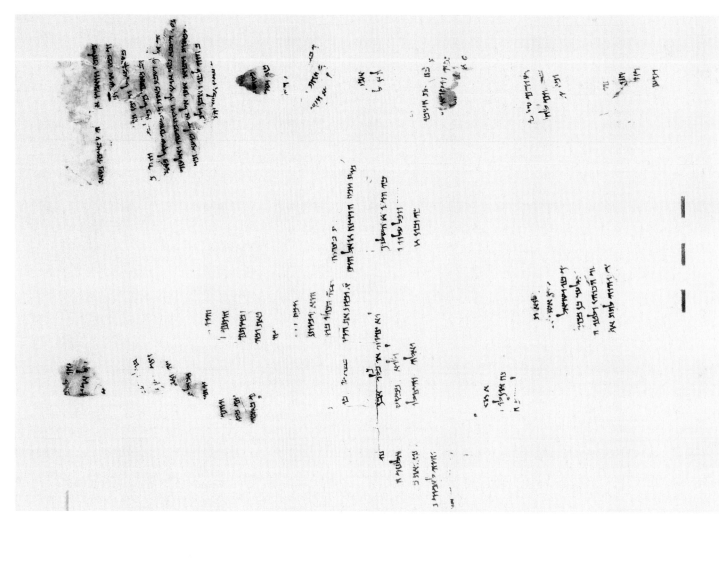

PLATE 1002

PLATE 1001

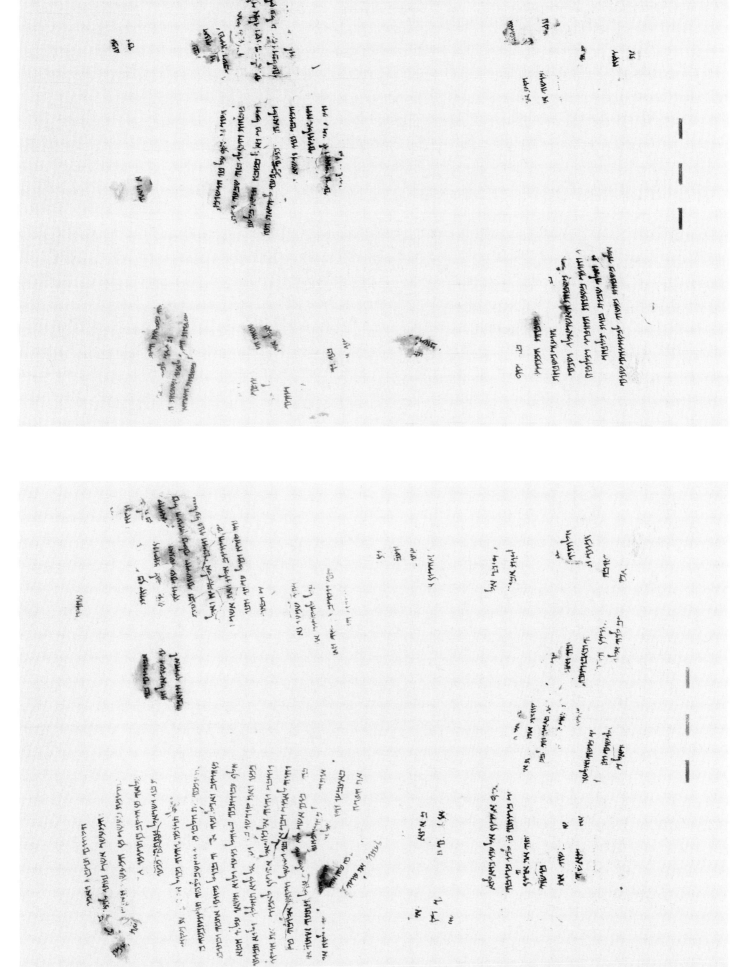

PLATE 1003

PLATE 1004

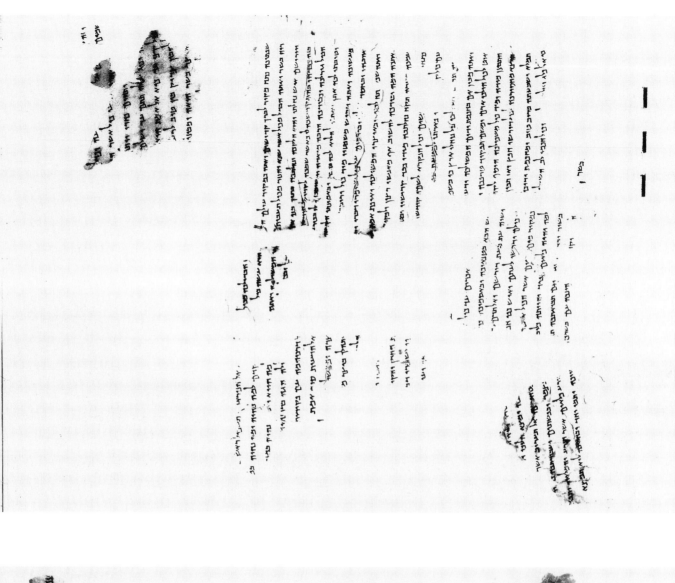

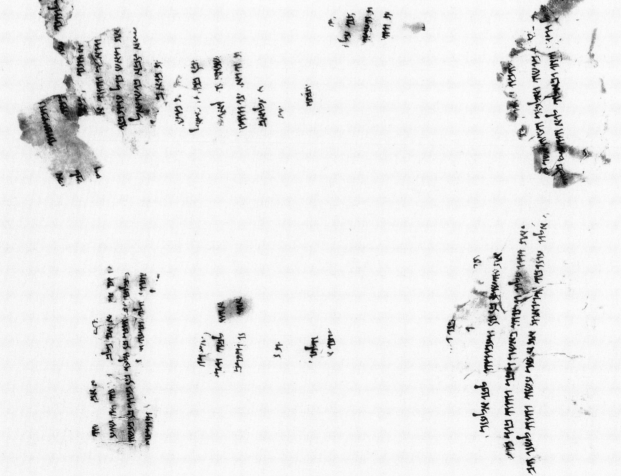

PLATE 1006

PLATE 1005

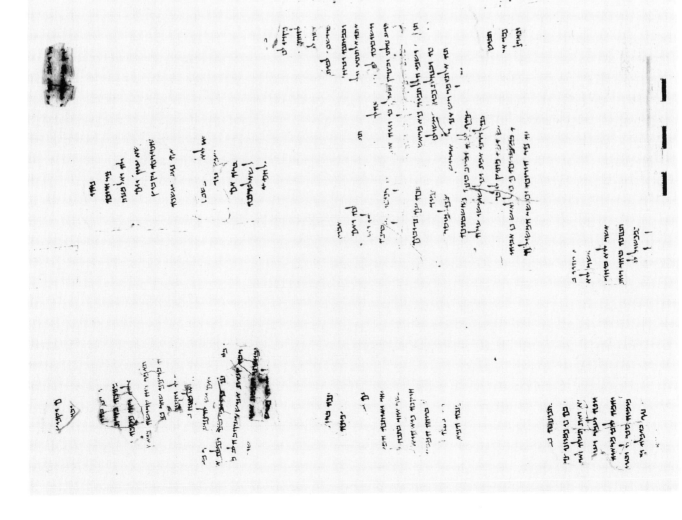

PLATE 1008

PLATE 1007

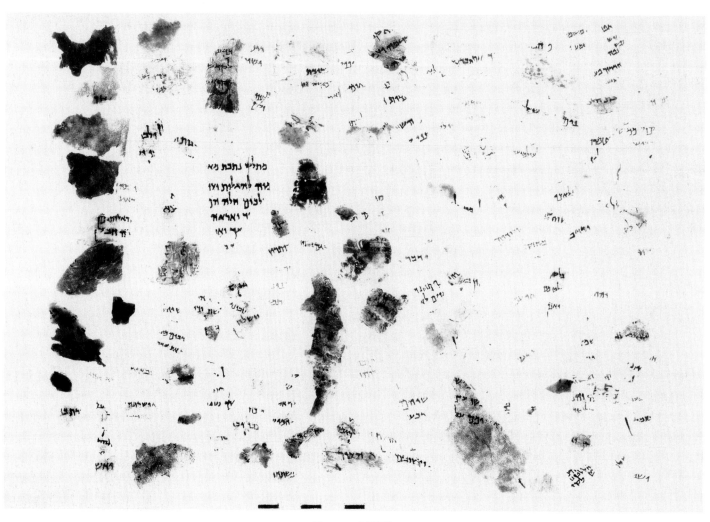

PLATE 1009

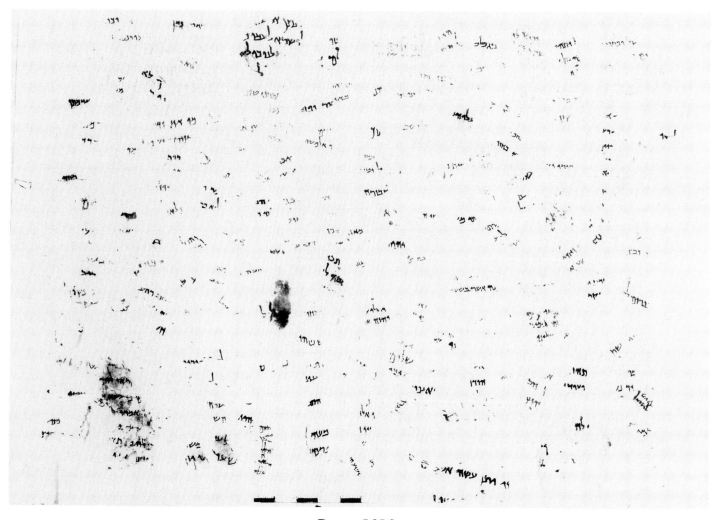

PLATE 1010

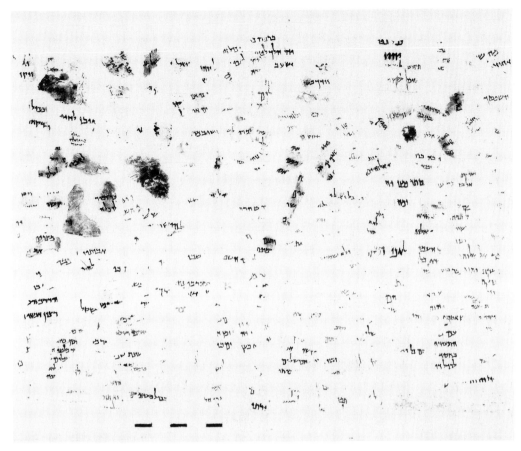

PLATE 1011

PLATE 1012

PLATE 1013

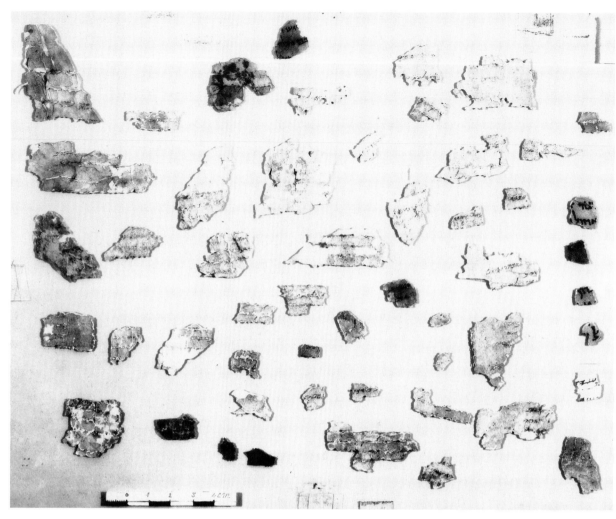

PLATE 1014

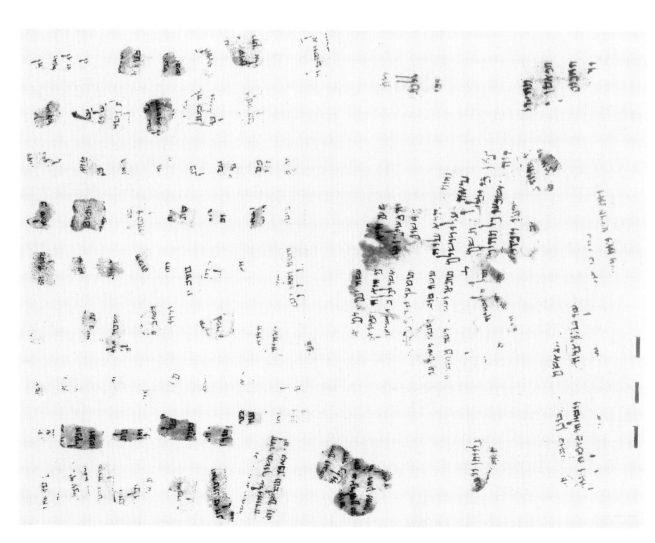

PLATE 1015

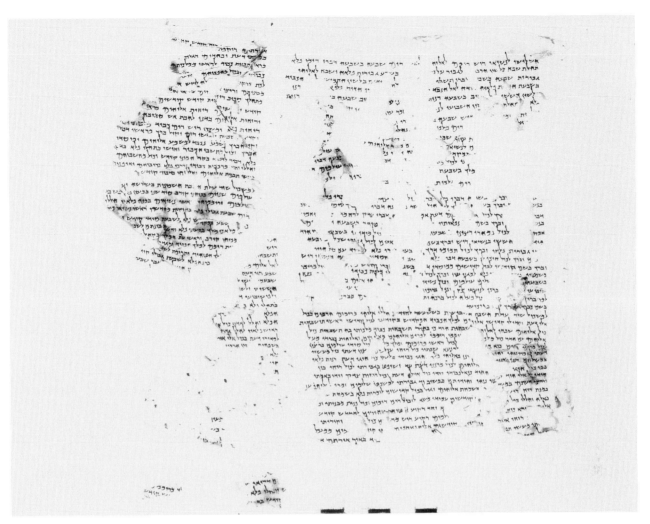

PLATE 1016

PLATE 1017

PLATE 1018

PLATE 1019

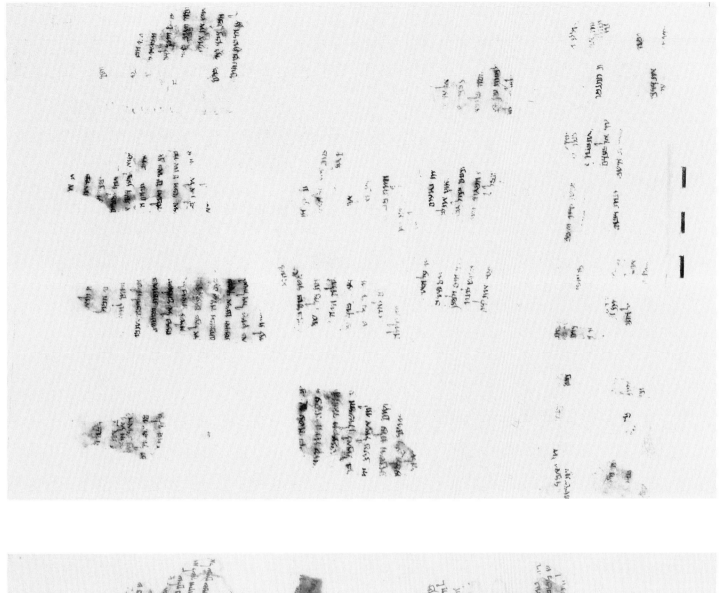

PLATE 1029

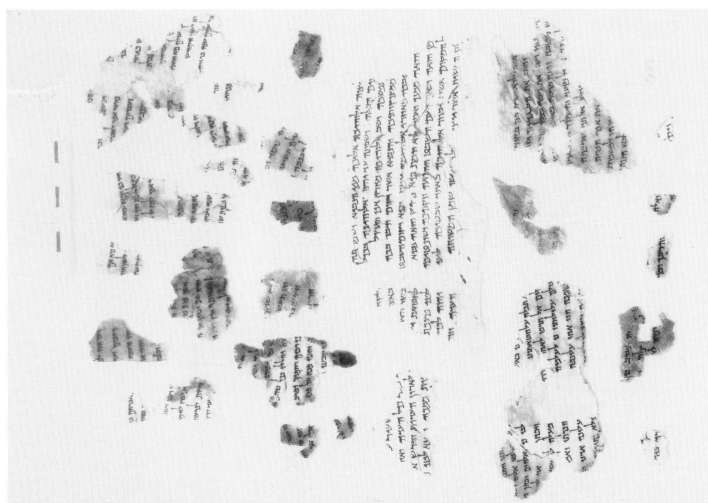

PLATE 1028

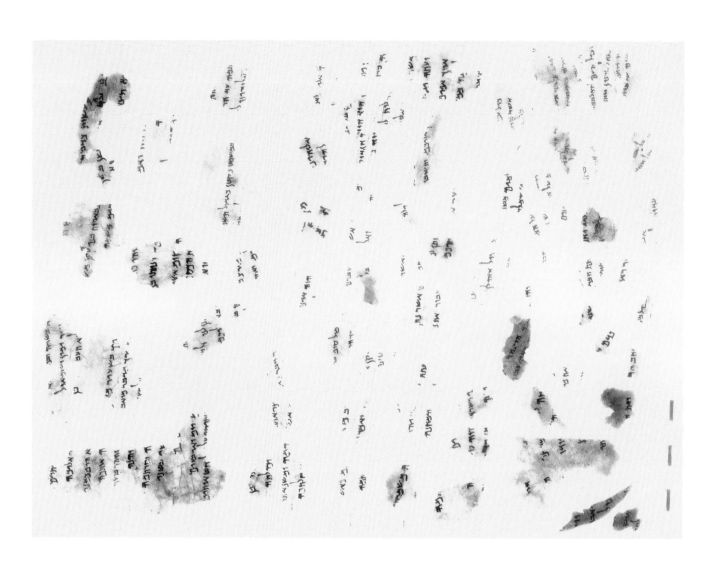

PLATE 1031

PLATE 1030

PLATE 1033

PLATE 1032

PLATE 1034

PLATE 1035

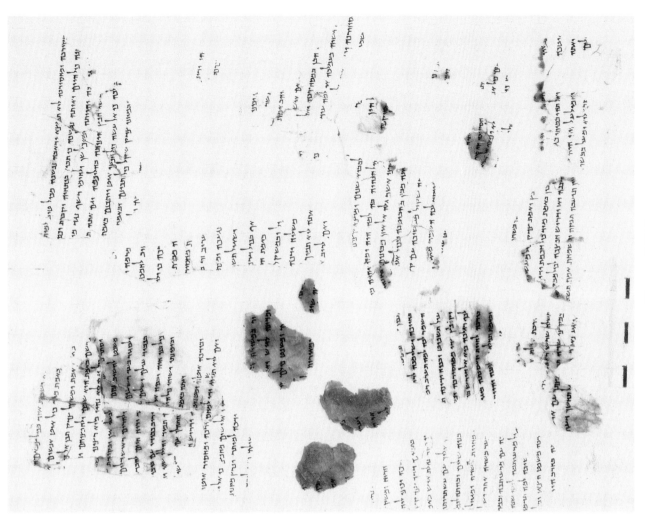

PLATE 1036

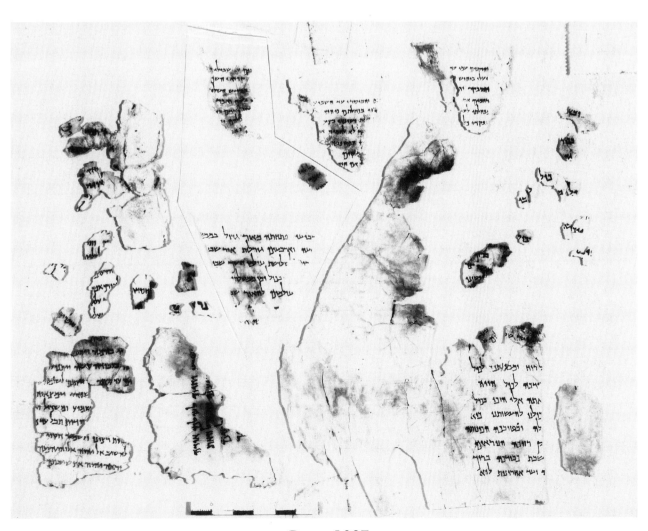

PLATE 1037

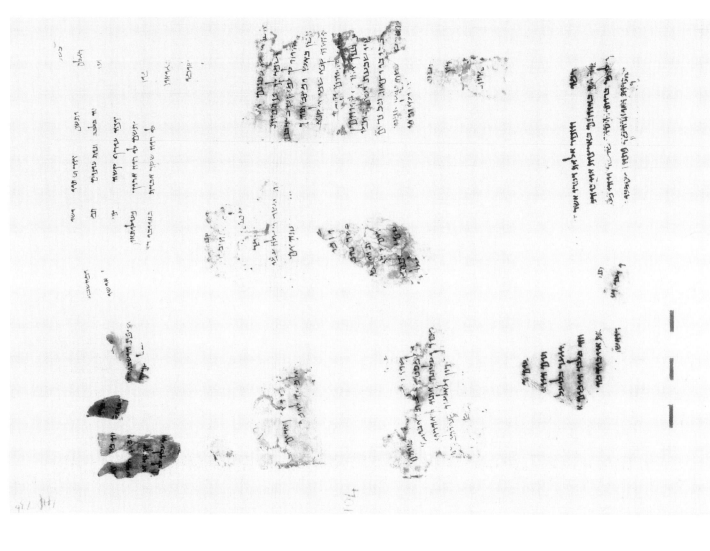

PLATE 1039

PLATE 1038

PLATE 1041

PLATE 1040

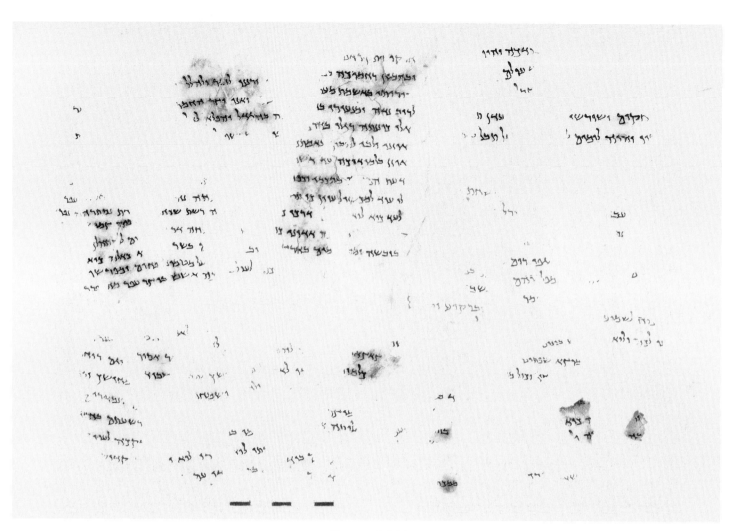

PLATE 1042

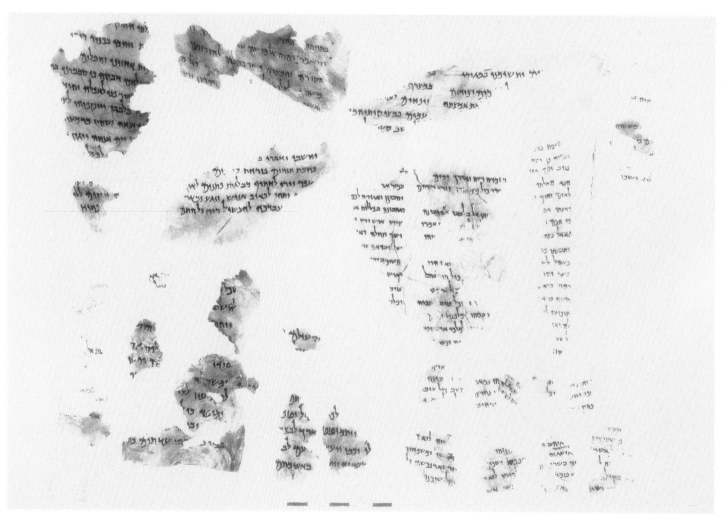

PLATE 1043

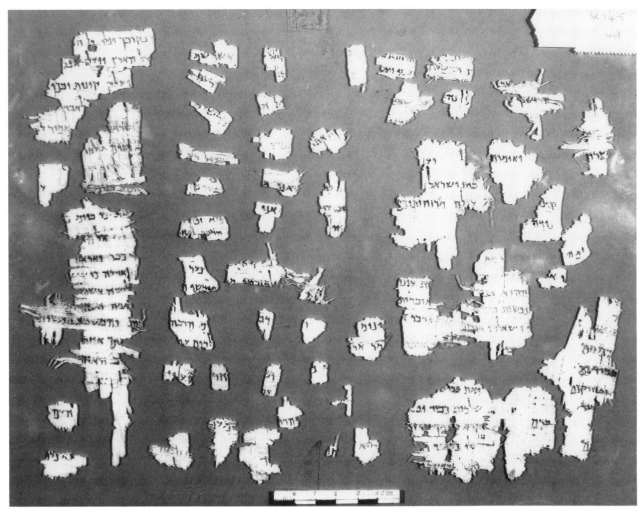

PLATE 1044

PLATE 1045

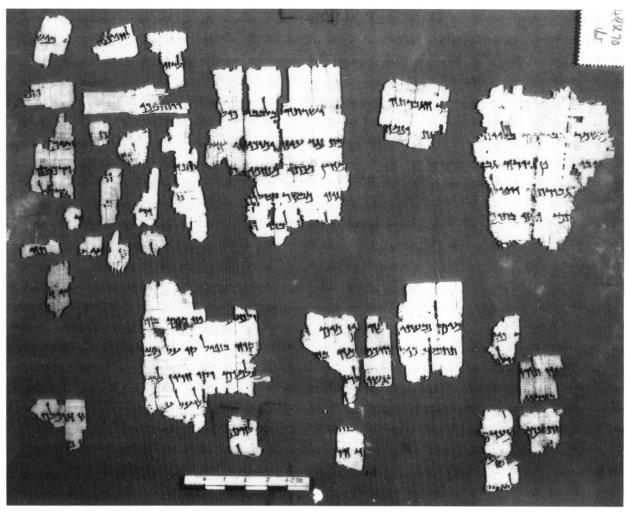

PLATE 1046

PLATE 1047

PLATE 1048

PLATE 1049

PLATE 1051

PLATE 1050

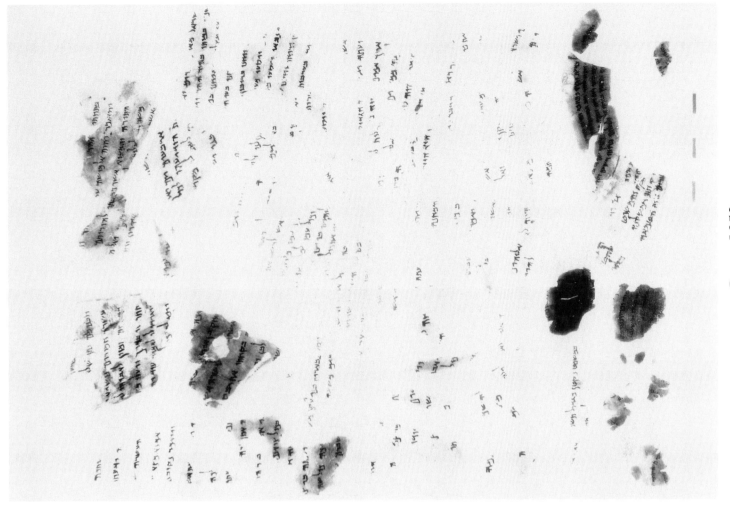

PLATE 1053

PLATE 1052

PLATE 1054

PLATE 1055

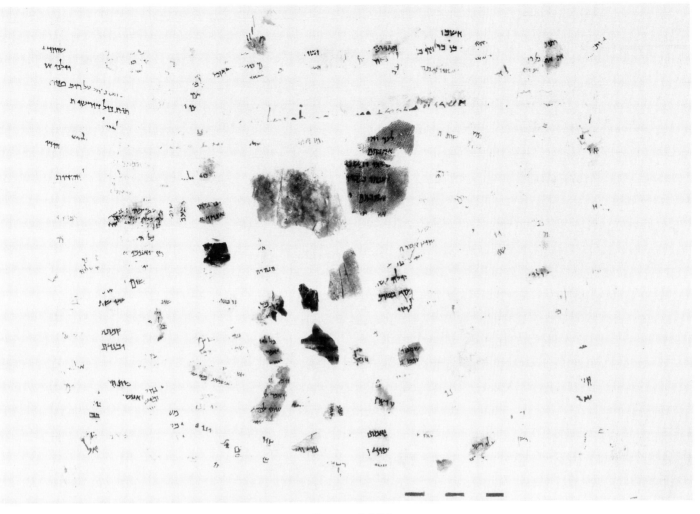

PLATE 1056

PLATE 1057

PLATE 1058

PLATE 1059

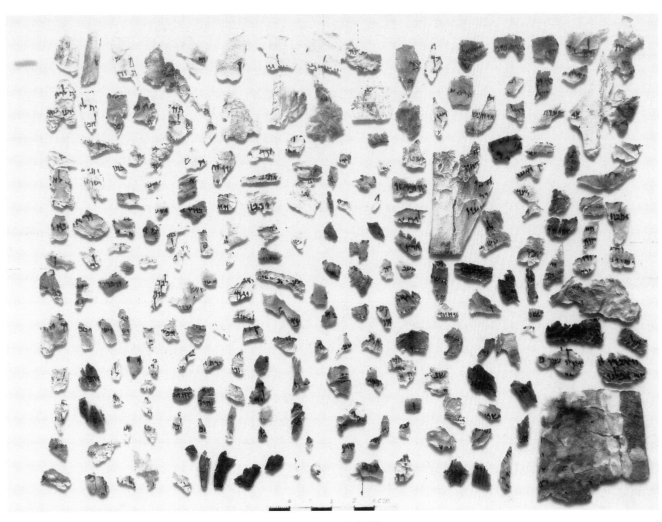

PLATE 1060

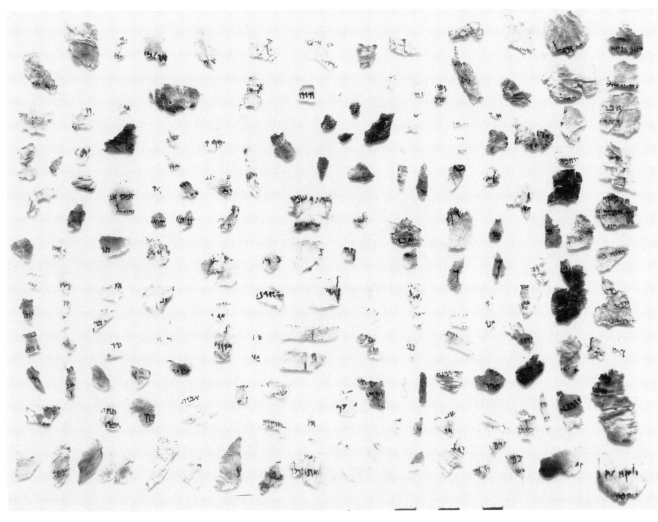

PLATE 1061

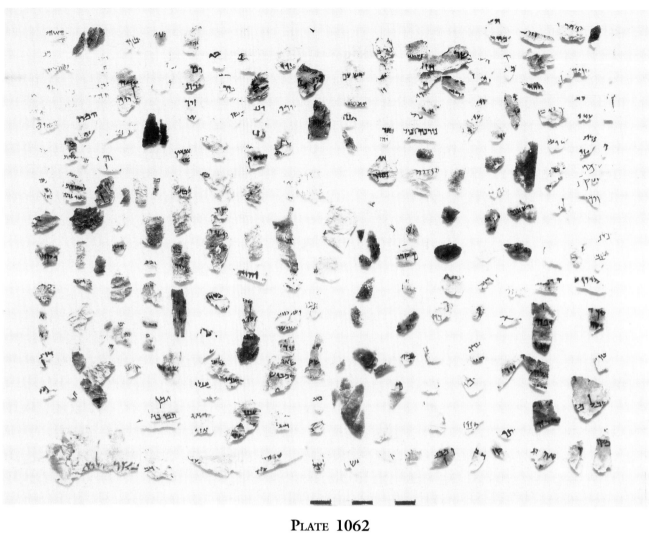

PLATE 1062

PLATE 1063

PLATE **1088**

PLATE **1089**

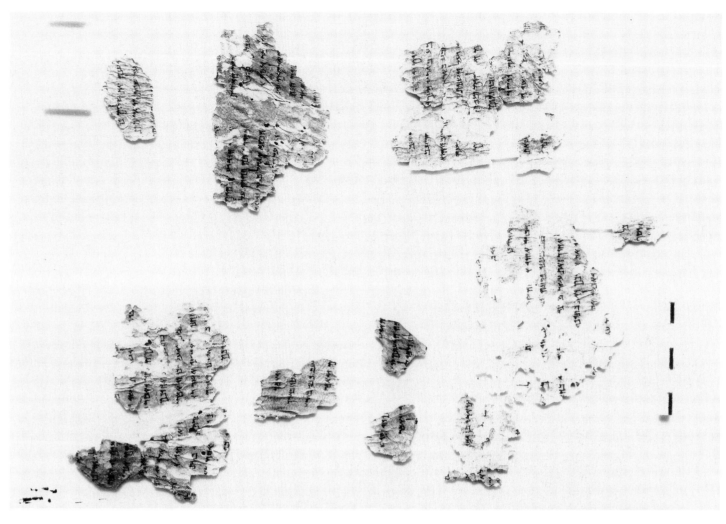

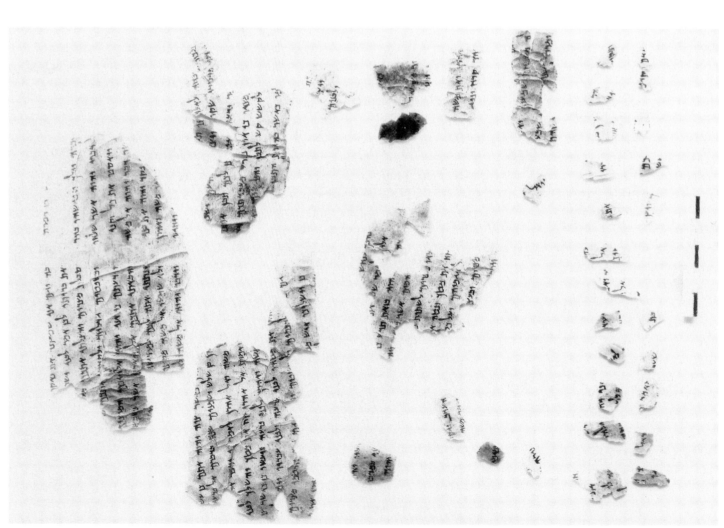

PLATE 1091

PLATE 1090

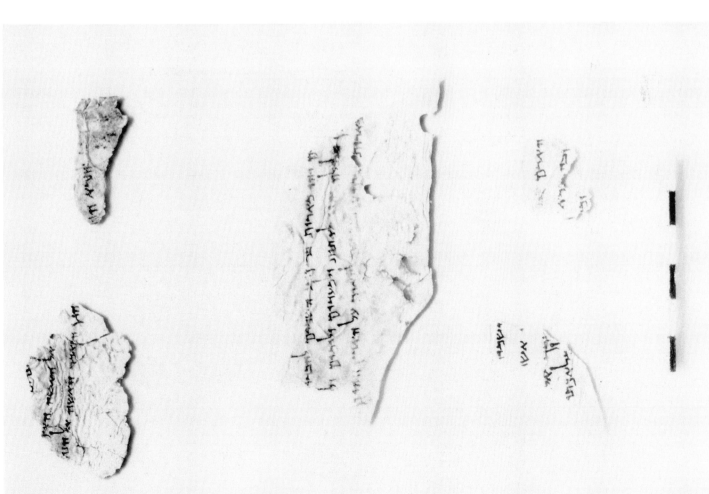

PLATE 1093

PLATE 1092

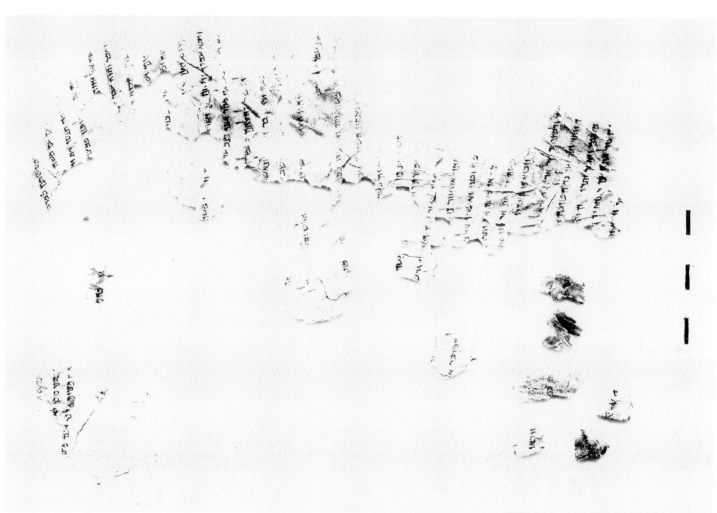

PLATE 1095

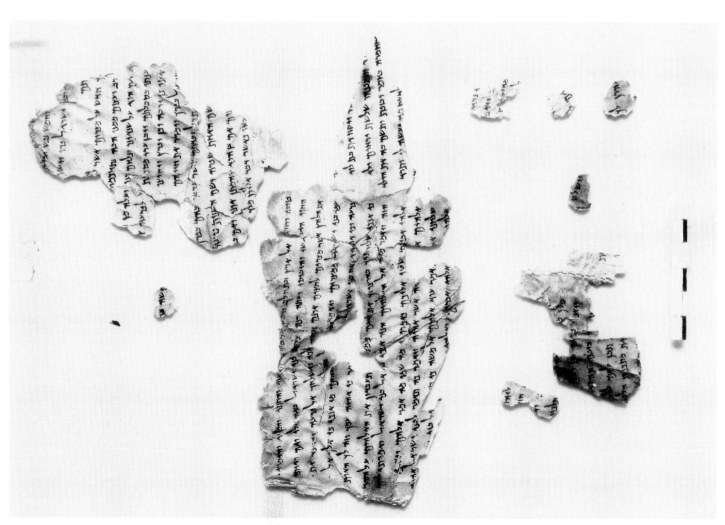

PLATE 1094

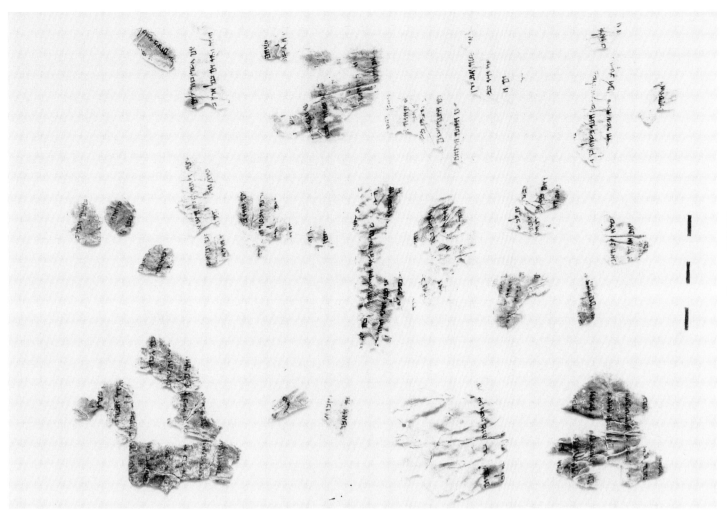

Plate 1097

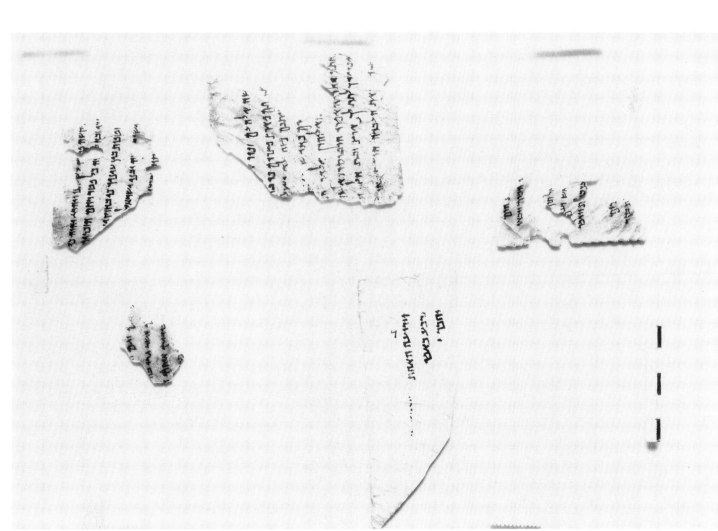

Plate 1096

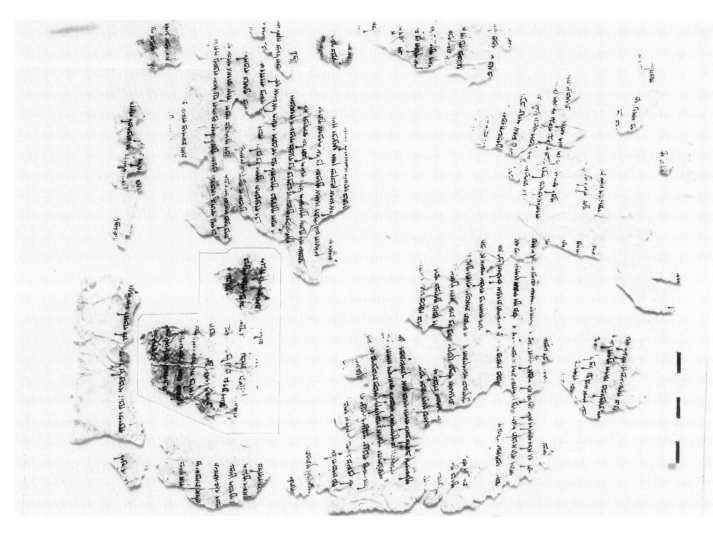

PLATE 1099

PLATE 1098

PLATE 1100

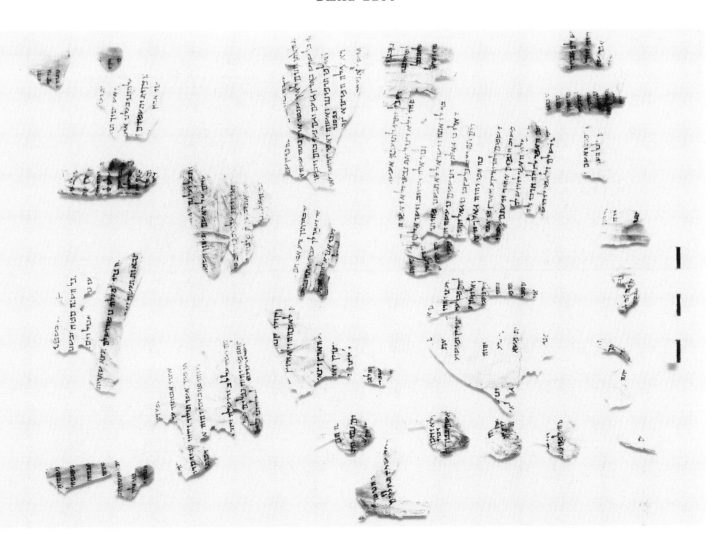

PLATE 1101

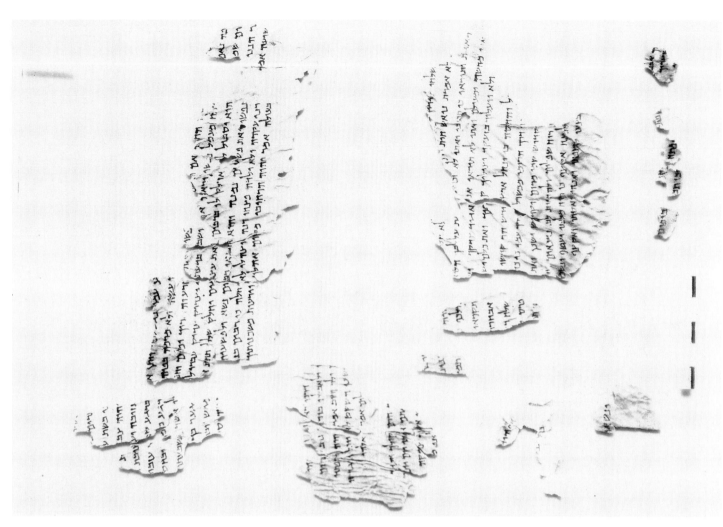

Plate 1102

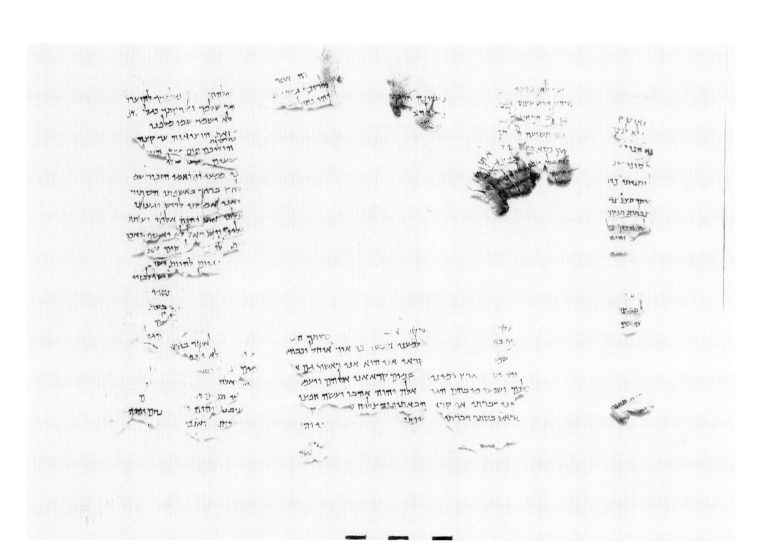

Plate 1103

PLATE 1104

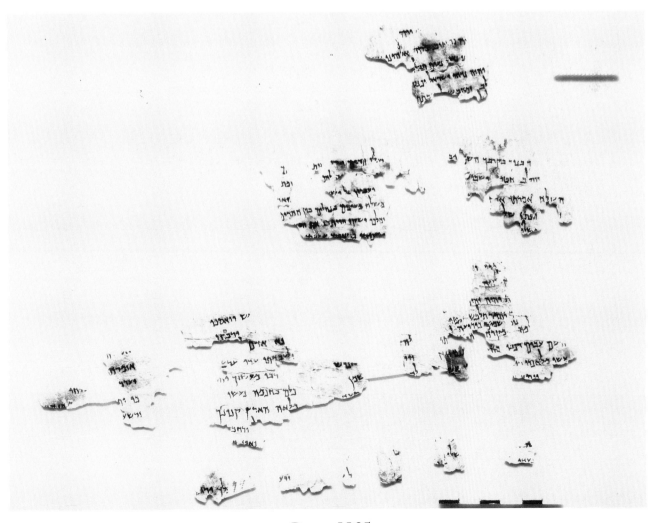

PLATE 1105

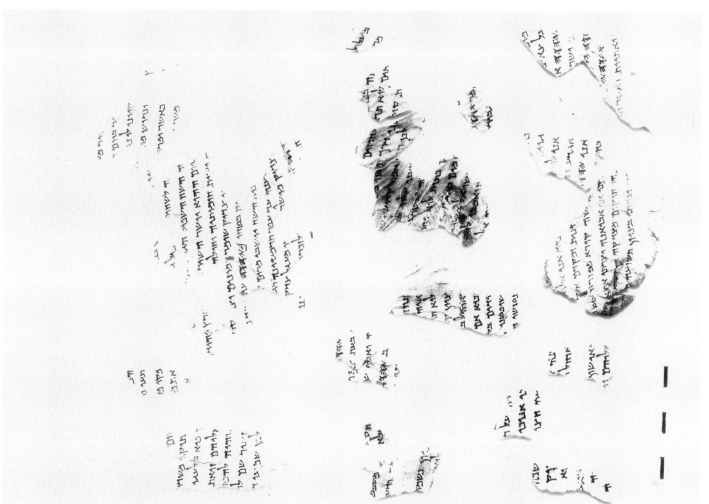

PLATE 1106

PLATE 1107

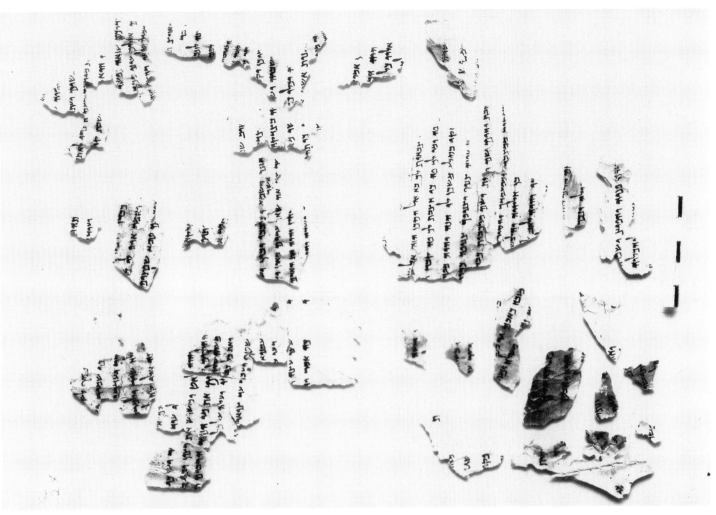

PLATE 1108

PLATE 1109

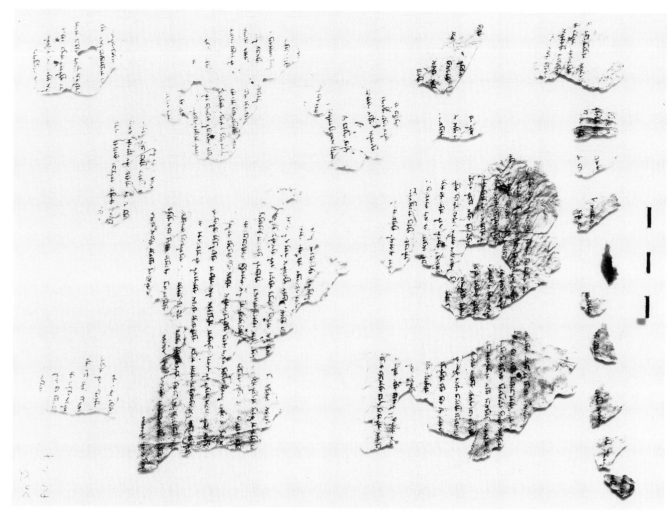

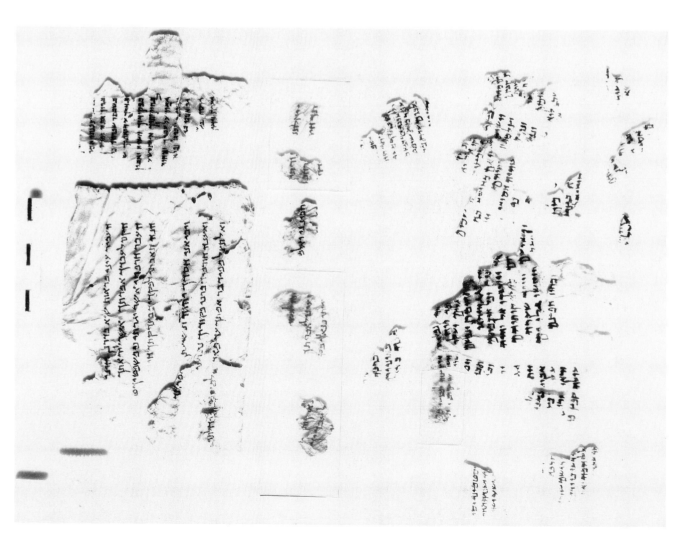

PLATE 1111

PLATE 1110

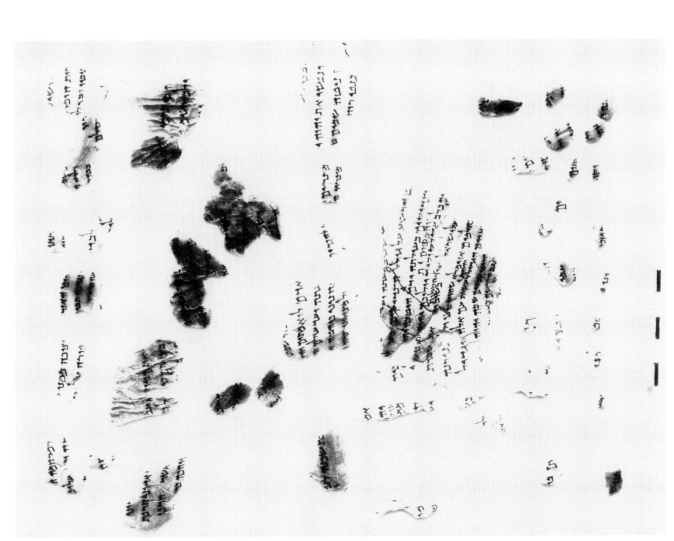

PLATE 1113

PLATE 1112

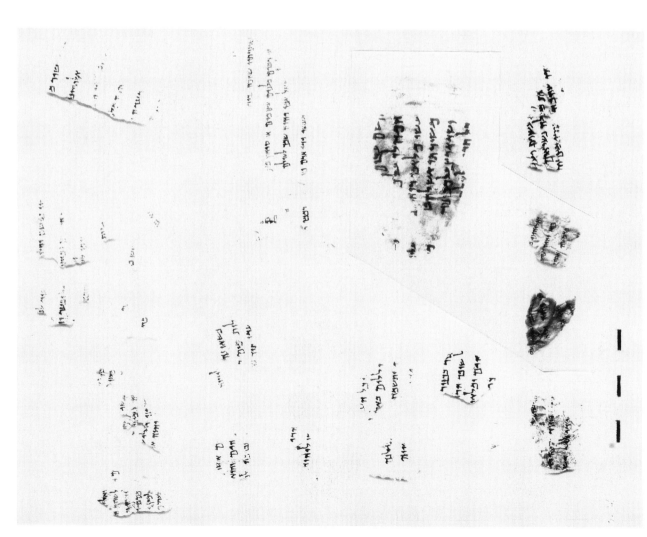

PLATE 1115

PLATE 1114

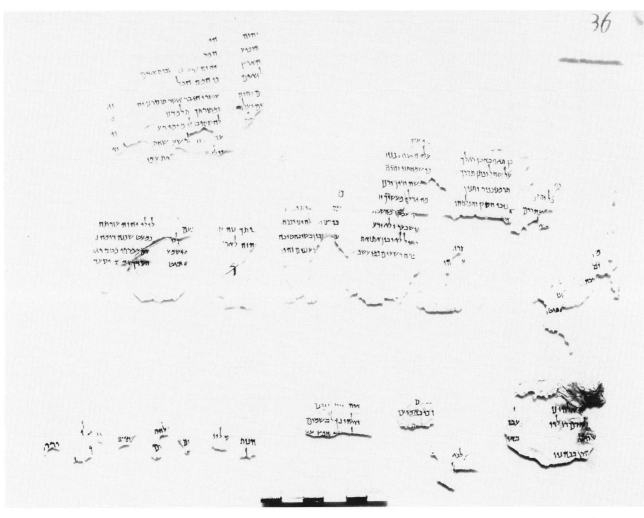

PLATE 1116

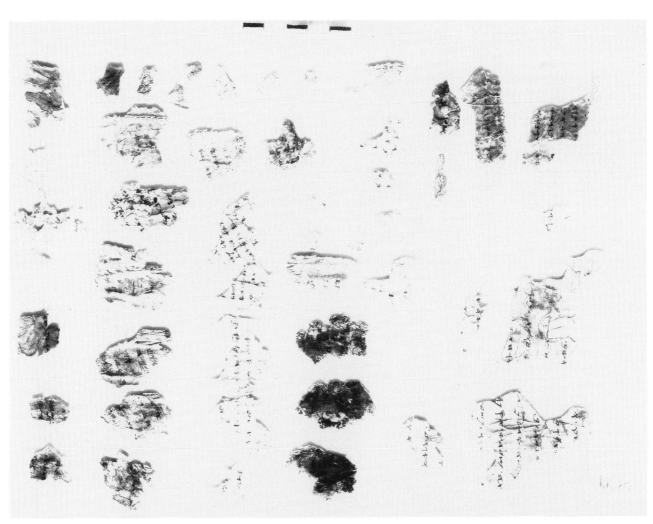

PLATE 1117

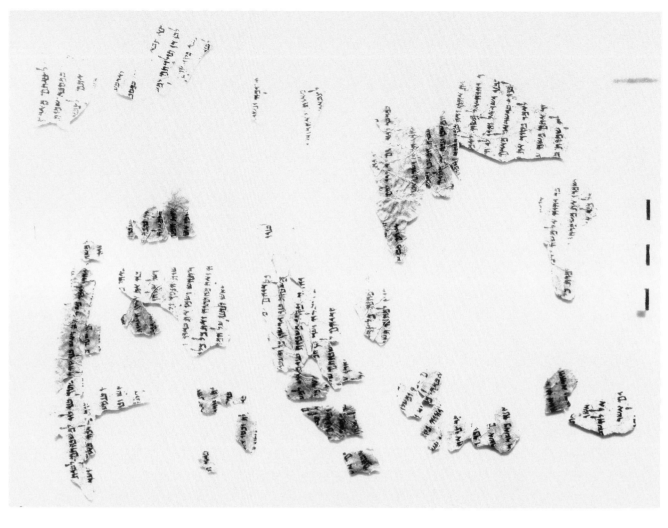

PLATE 1119

PLATE 1118

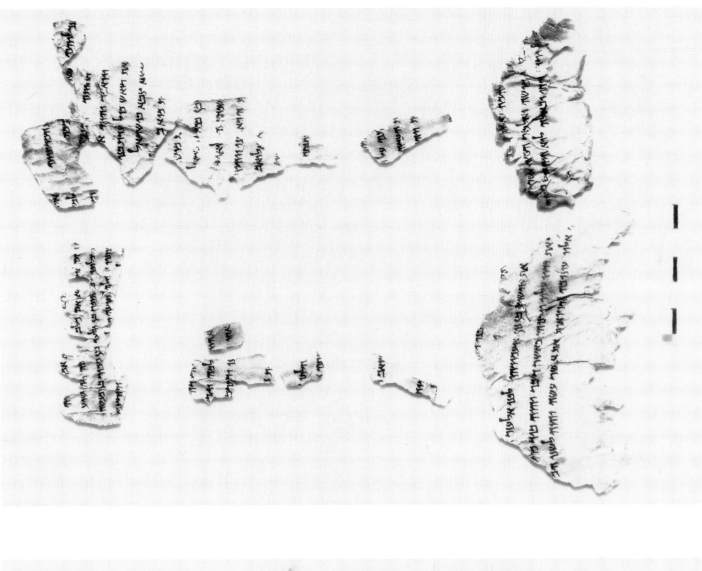

PLATE 1121

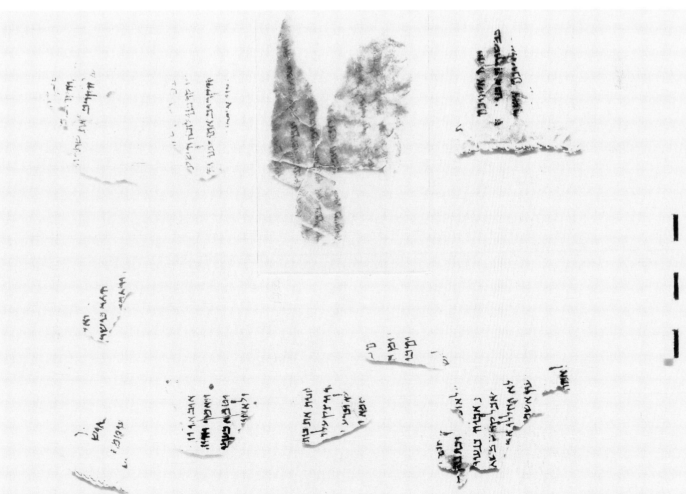

PLATE 1120

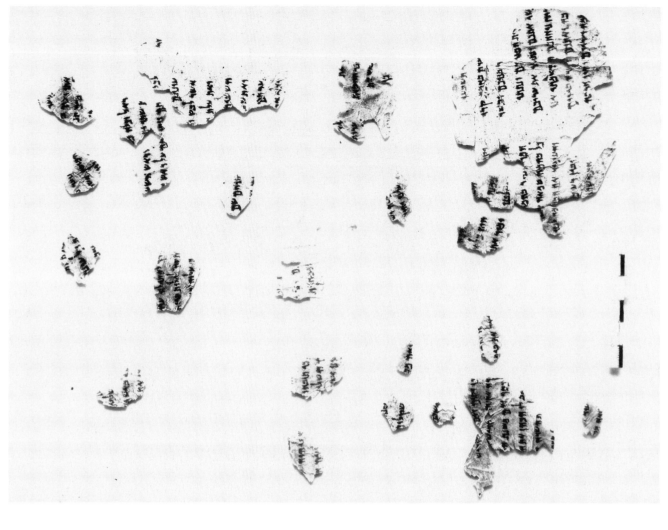

PLATE 1123

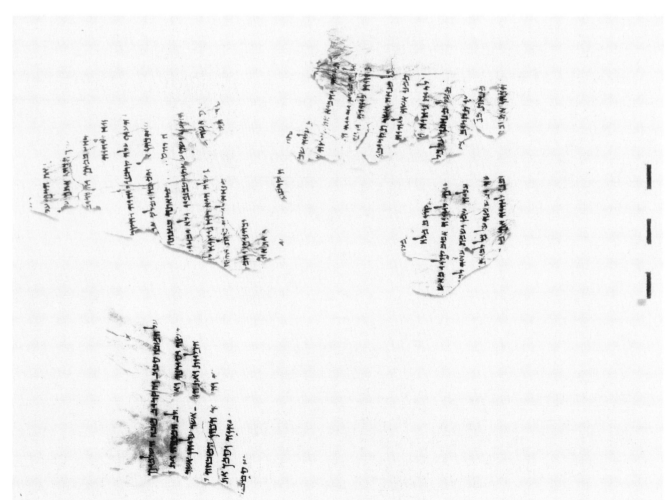

PLATE 1122

PLATE 1125

PLATE 1124

PLATE 1127

PLATE 1126

PLATE 1129

PLATE 1128

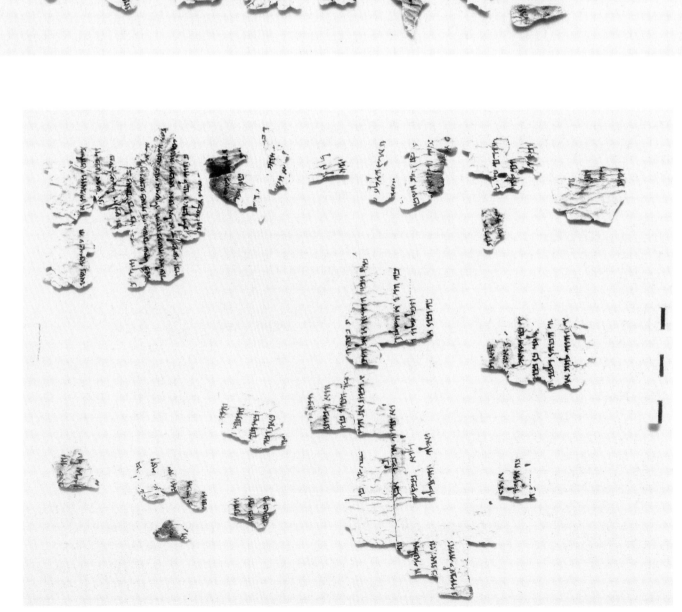

PLATE 1131

PLATE 1130

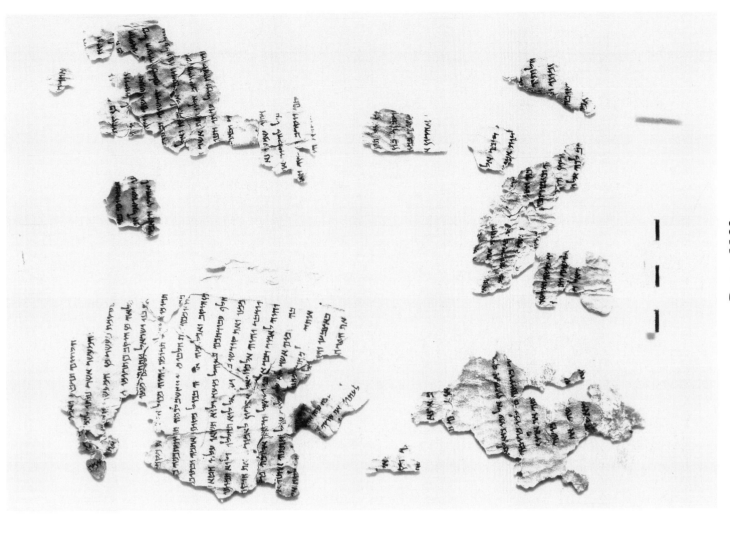

PLATE 1133

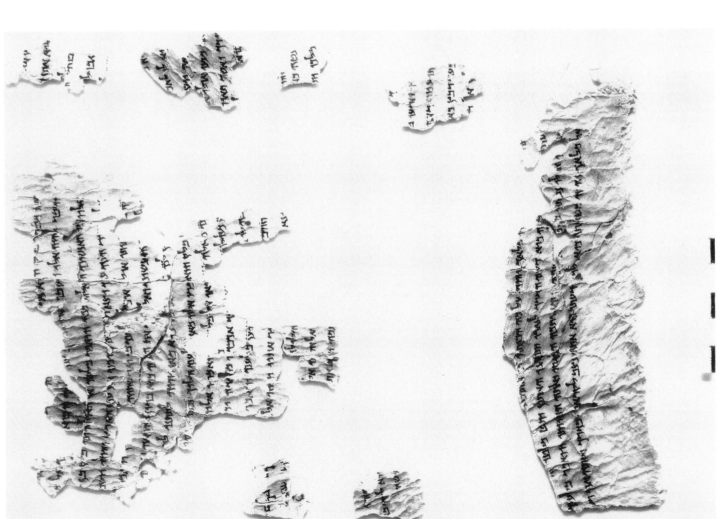

PLATE 1132

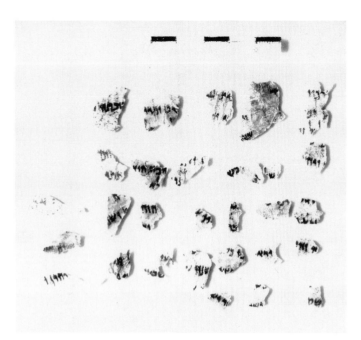

PLATE 1134

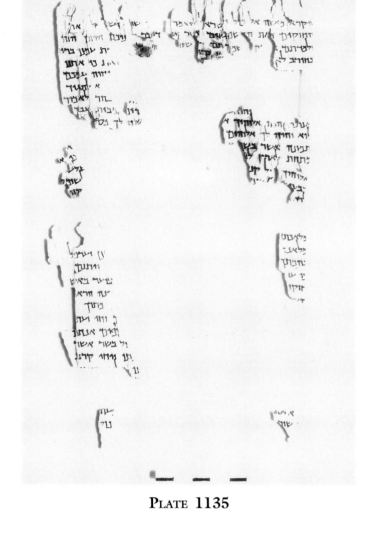

PLATE 1135

PLATE 1136

PLATE 1137

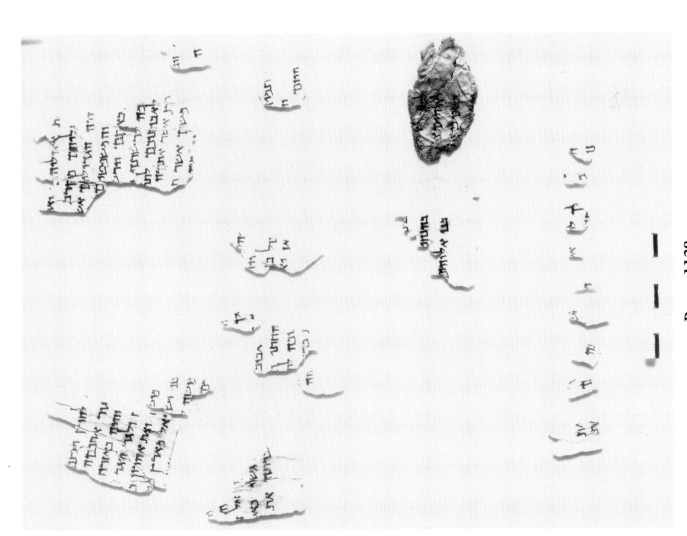

Plate 1139

Plate 1138

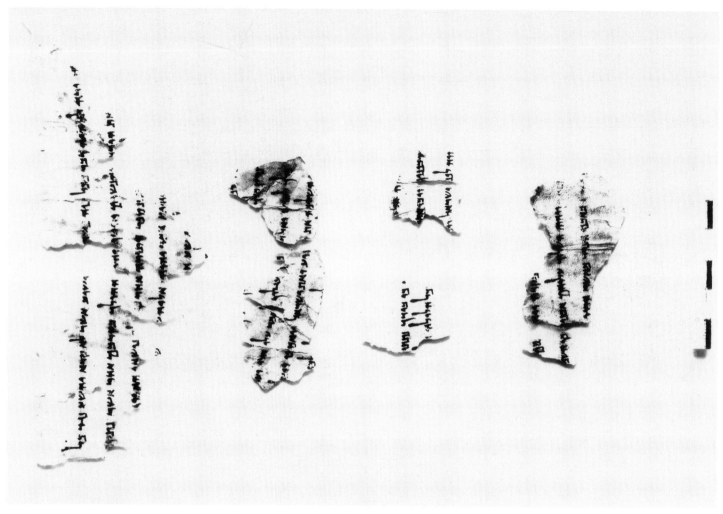

PLATE 1141

PLATE 1140

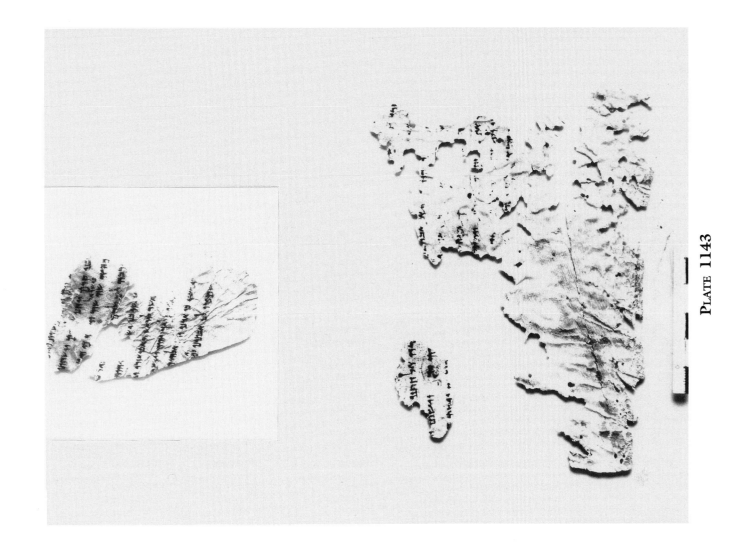

Plate 1143

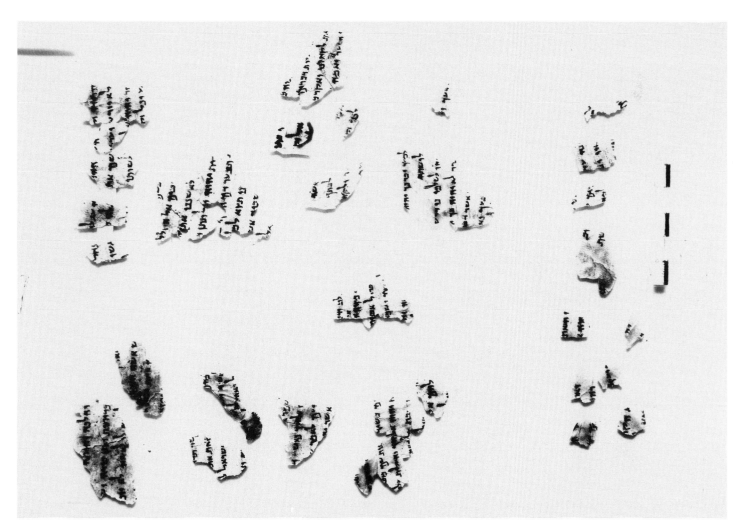

Plate 1142

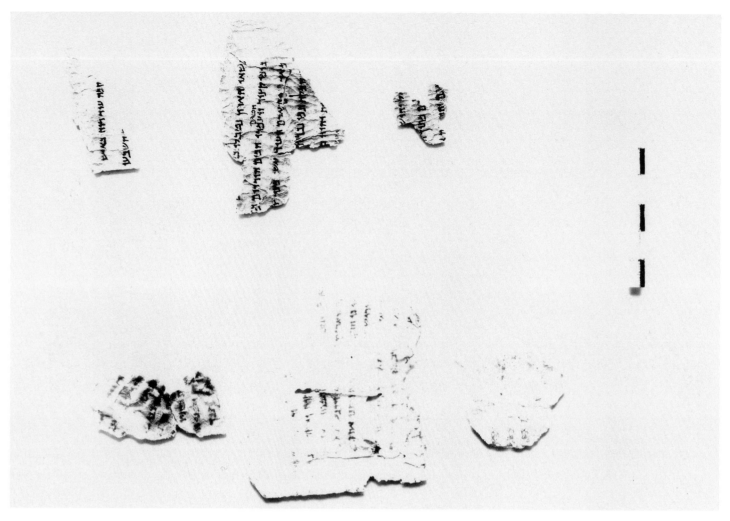

PLATE 1145

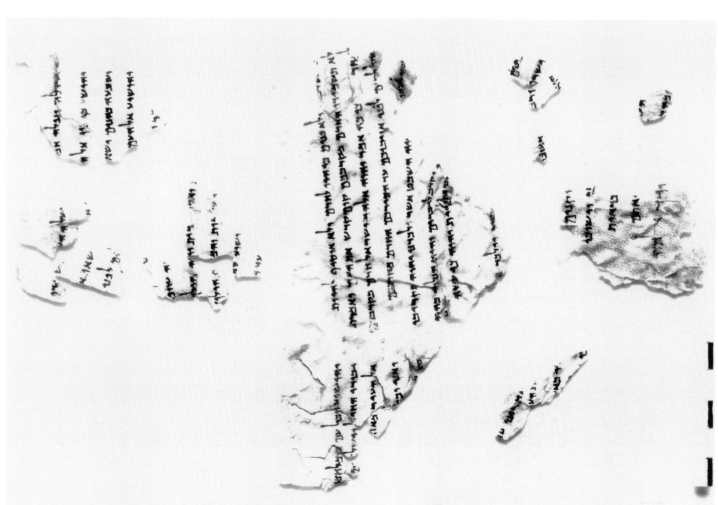

PLATE 1144

PLATE 1147

PLATE 1146

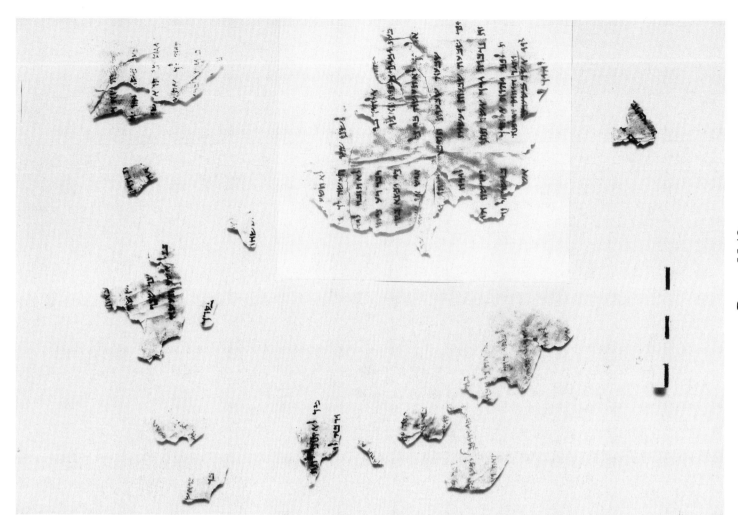

PLATE 1149

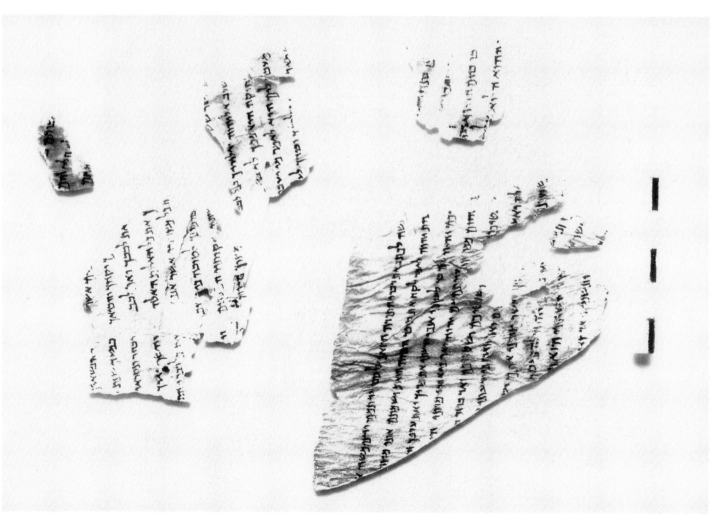

PLATE 1148

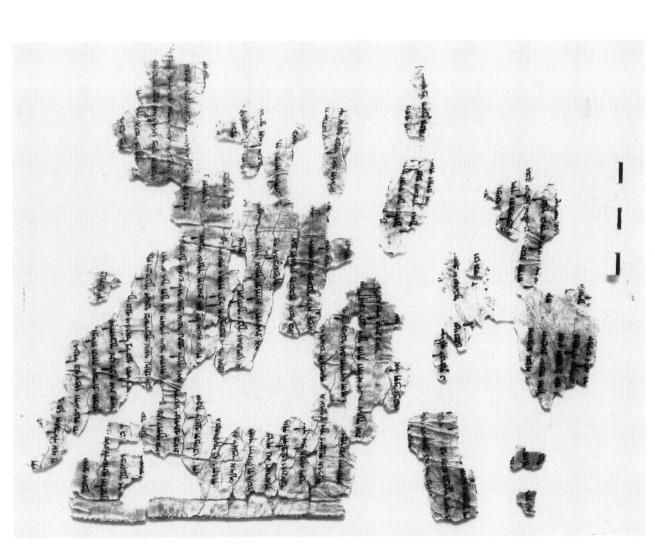

PLATE 1151

PLATE 1150

PLATE 1153

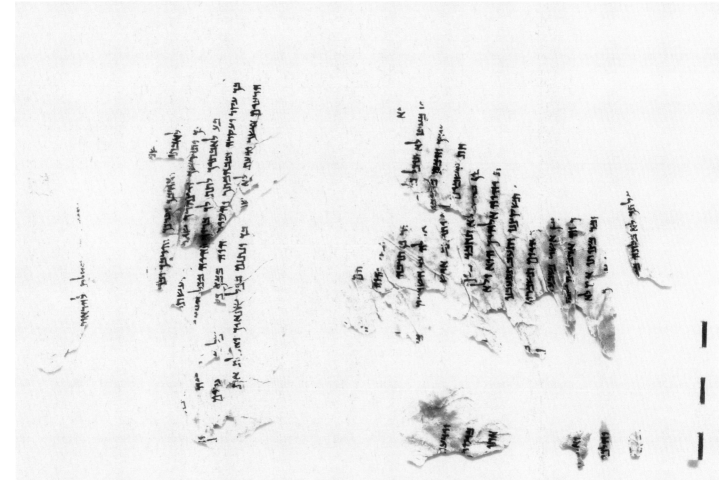

PLATE 1152

PLATE 1154

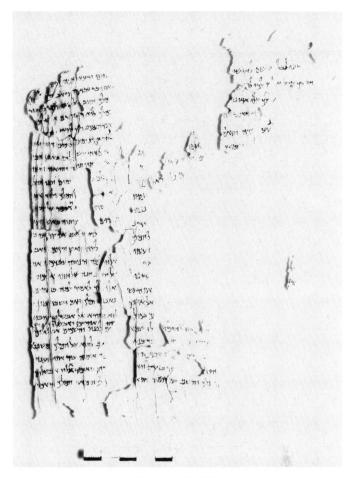

PLATE 1155

PLATE 1156

PLATE 1158

PLATE 1157

PLATE 1160

PLATE 1159

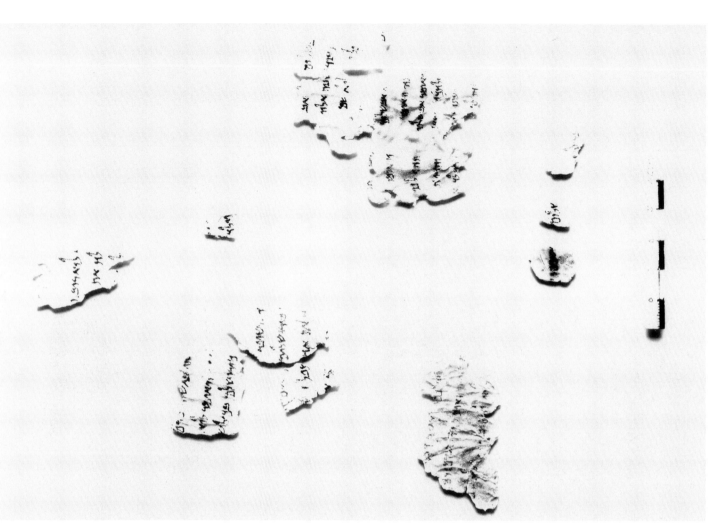

PLATE 1161

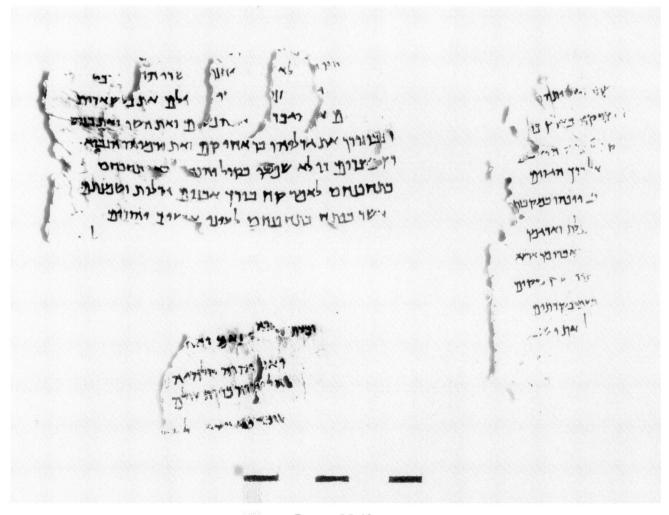

PLATE 1162

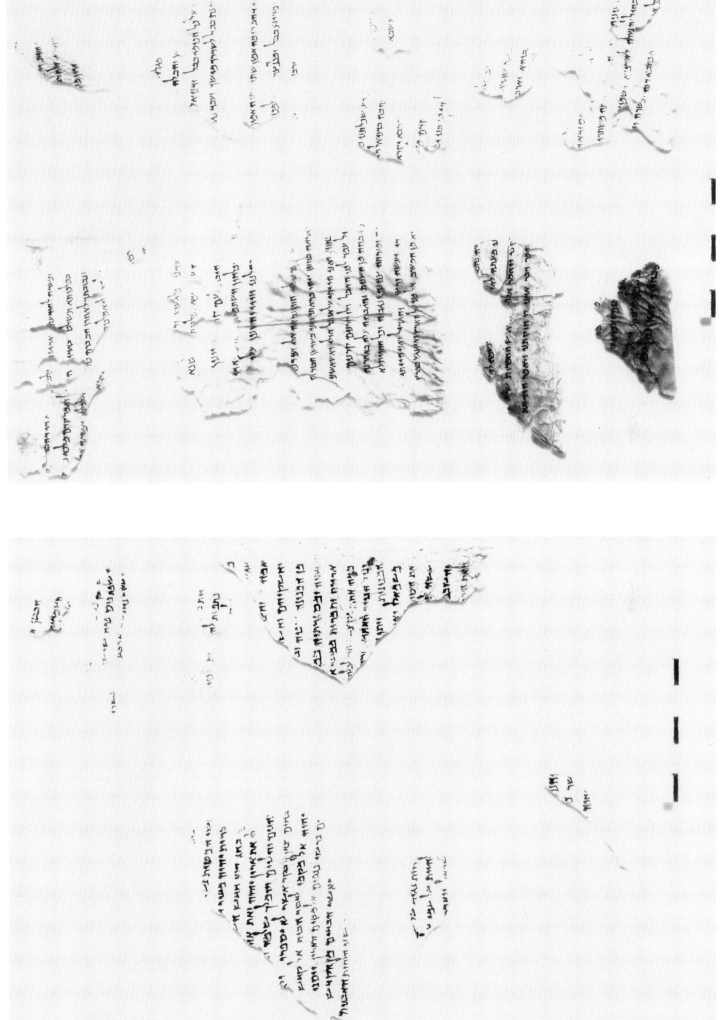

PLATE 1164

PLATE 1163

PLATE 1166

PLATE 1165

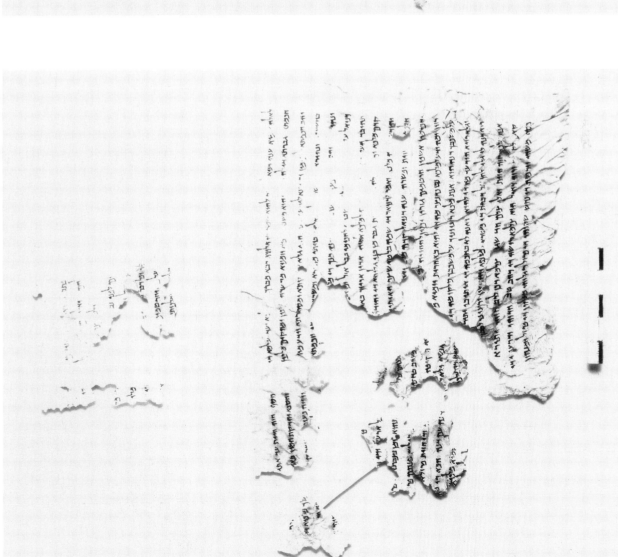

PLATE 1168

PLATE 1167

Plate 1170

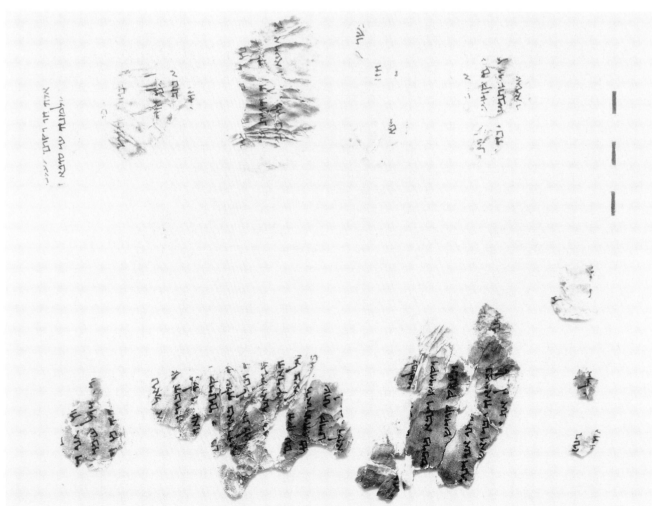

Plate 1169

PLATE 1171

PLATE 1172

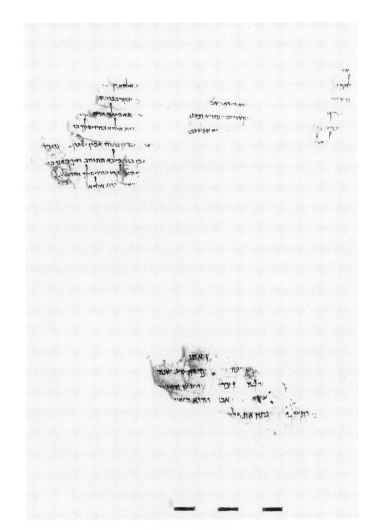

PLATE 1173

PLATE 1174

PLATE 1175

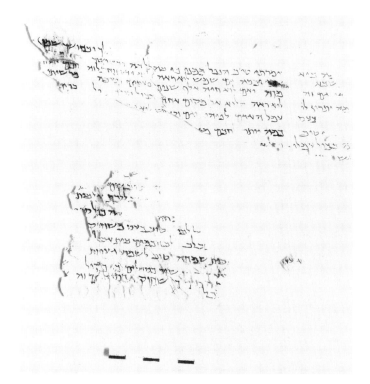

PLATE 1176

PLATE 1177

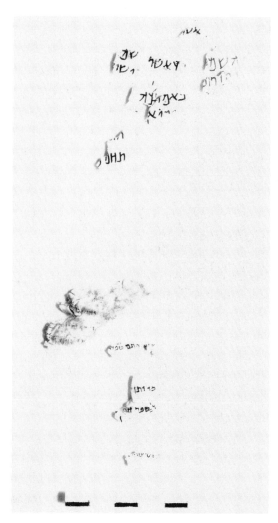

PLATE 1178

PLATE 1179

PLATE 1180

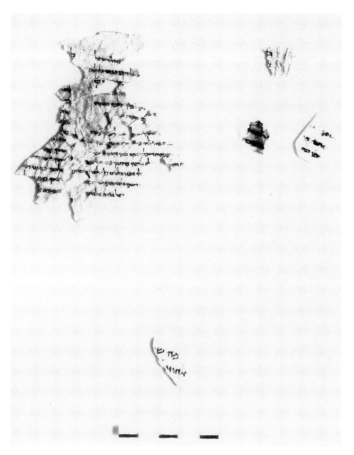

PLATE 1181

PLATE 1182

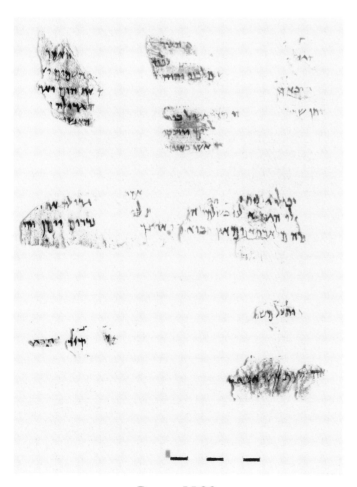

PLATE 1183

PLATE 1184

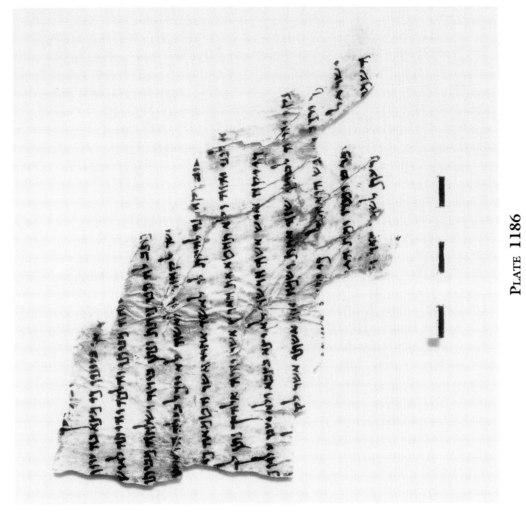

PLATE 1186

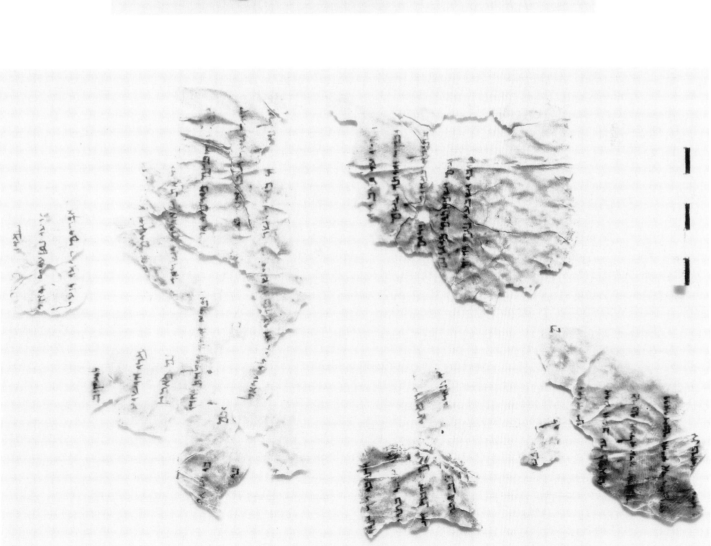

PLATE 1185

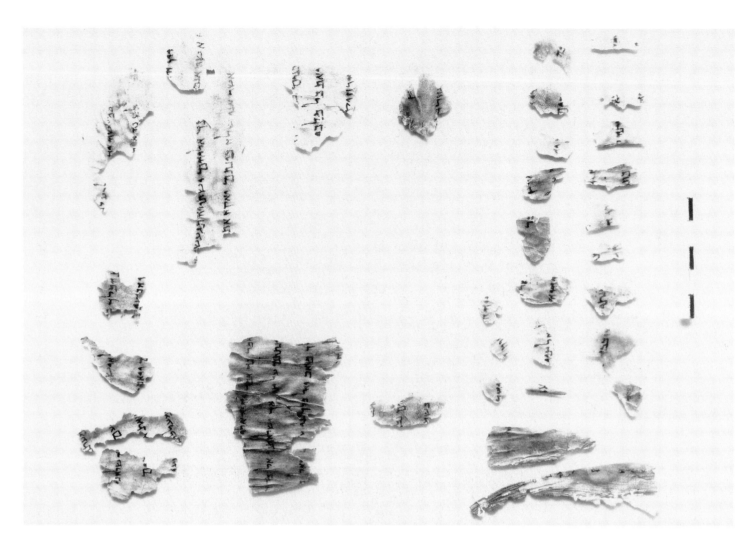

PLATE 1188

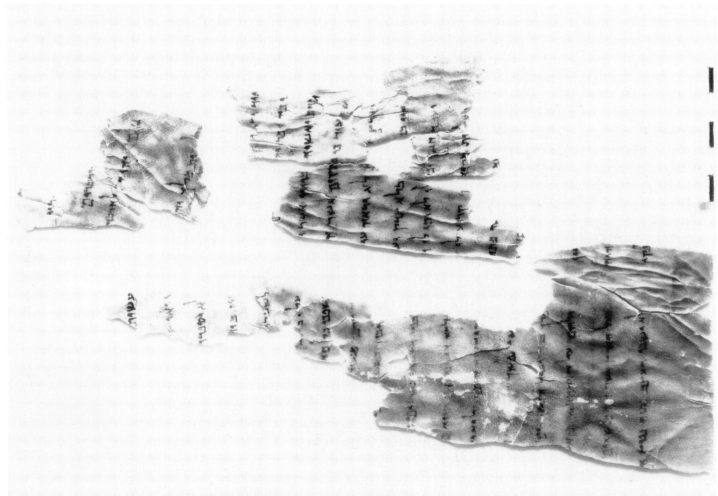

PLATE 1187

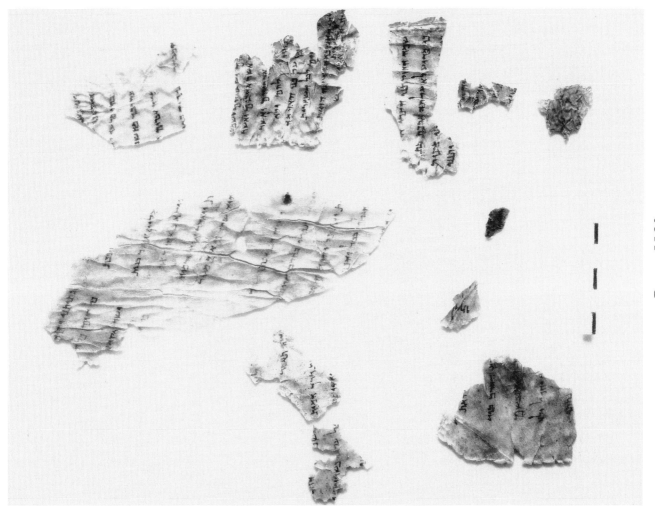

Plate 1190

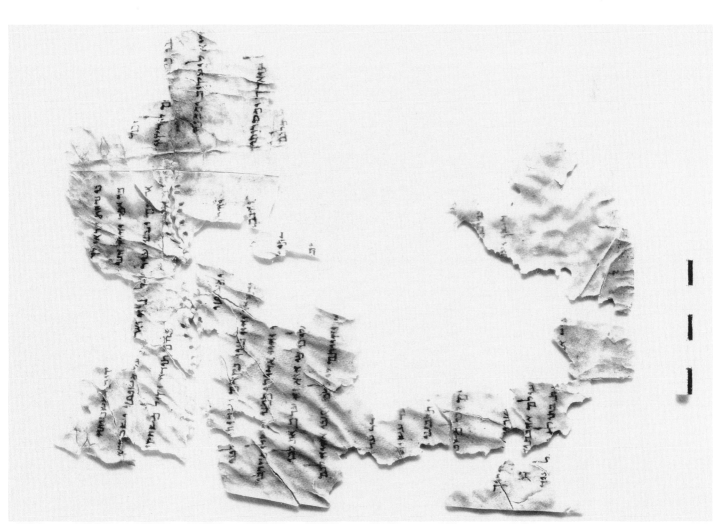

Plate 1189

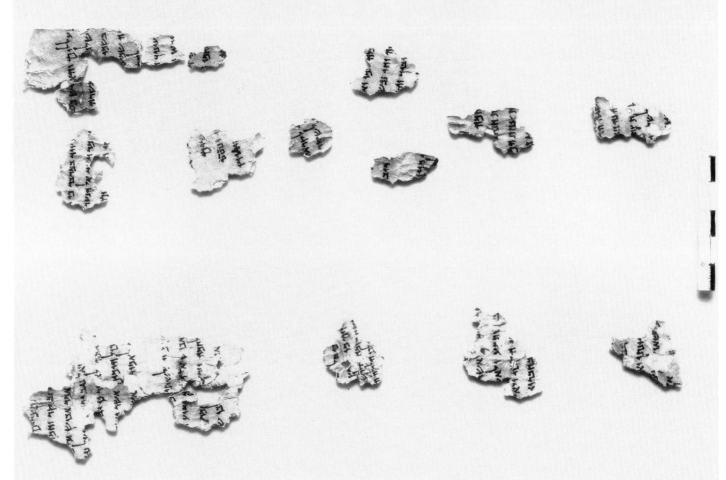

PLATE 1192

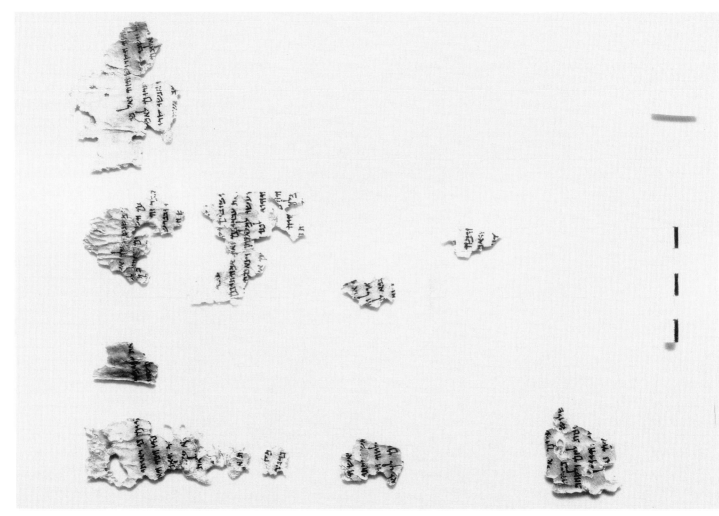

PLATE 1191

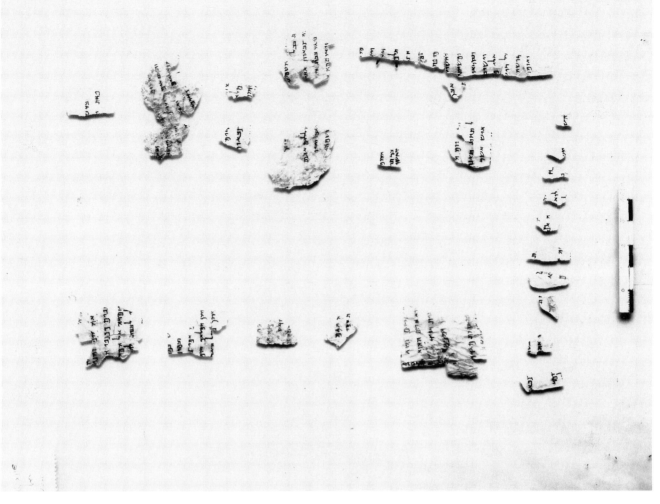

PLATE 1194

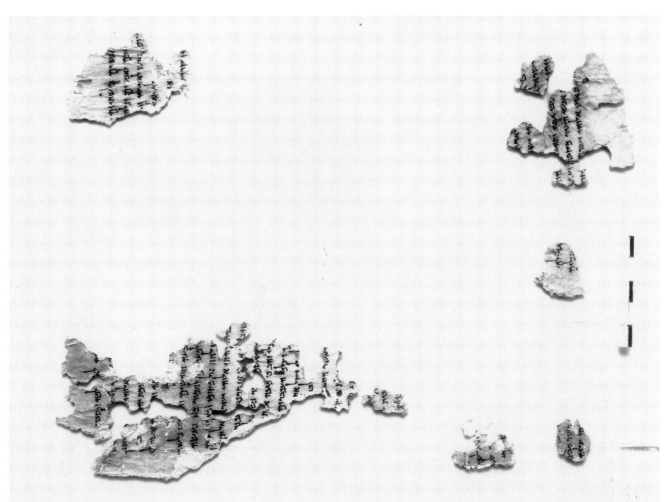

PLATE 1193

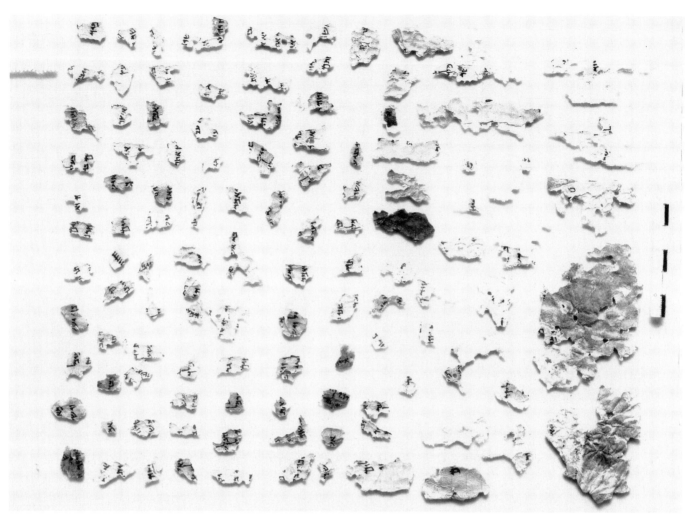

PLATE 1196

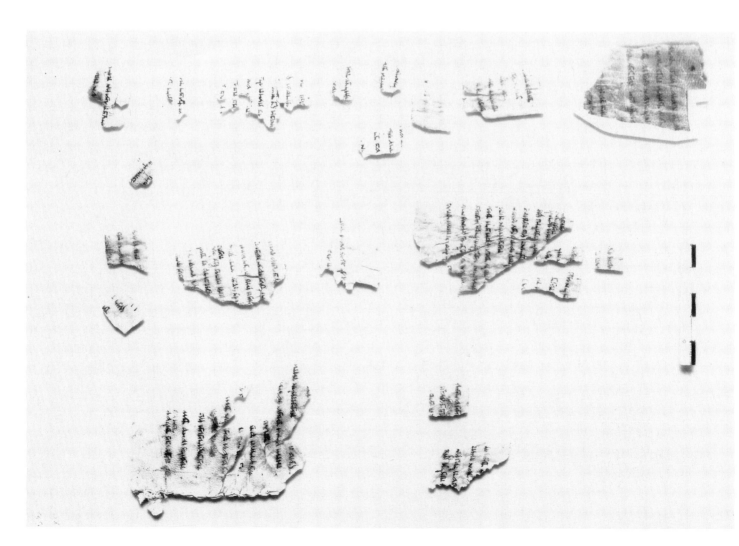

PLATE 1195

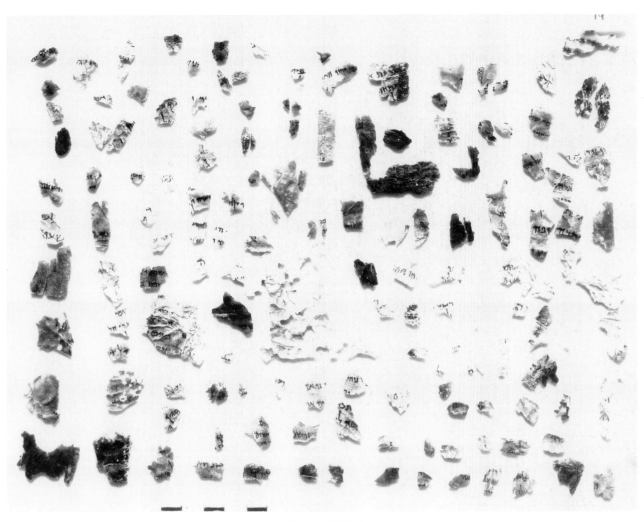

PLATE 1226

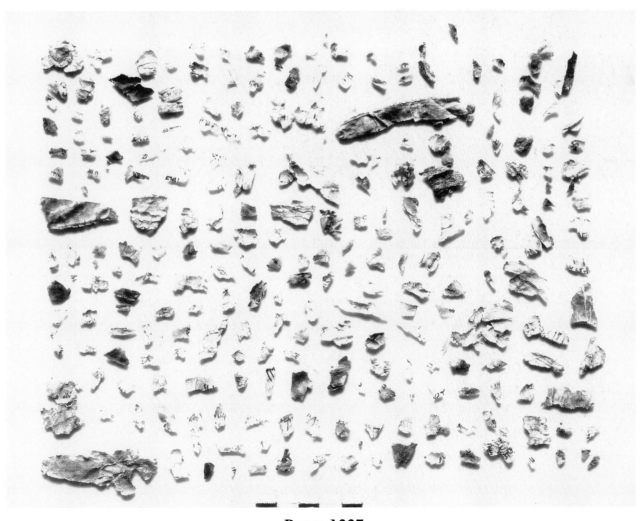

PLATE 1227

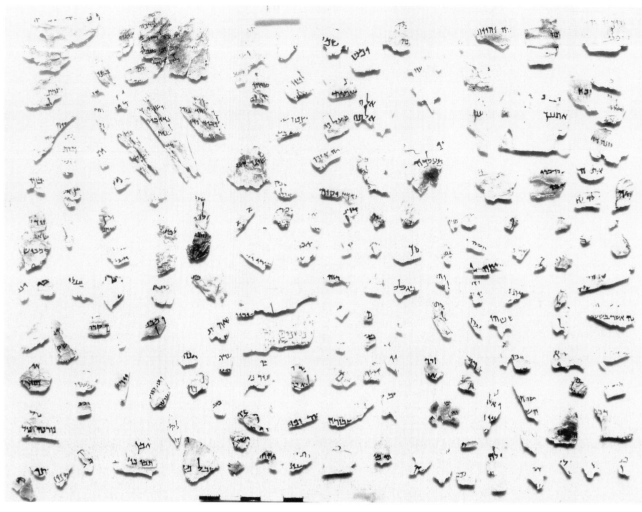

PLATE 1228

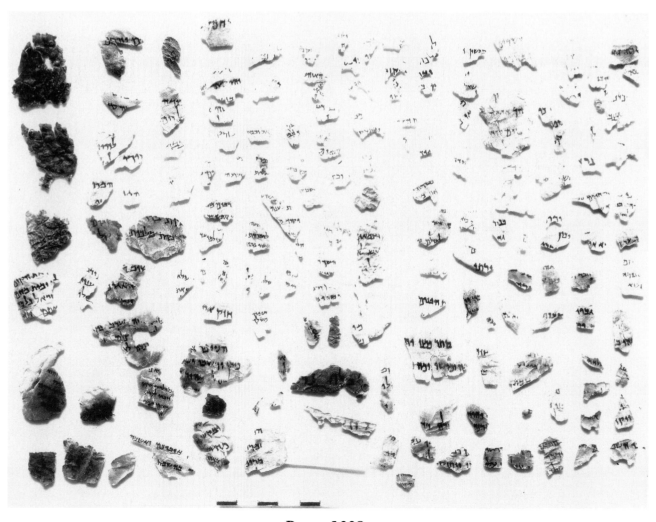

PLATE 1229

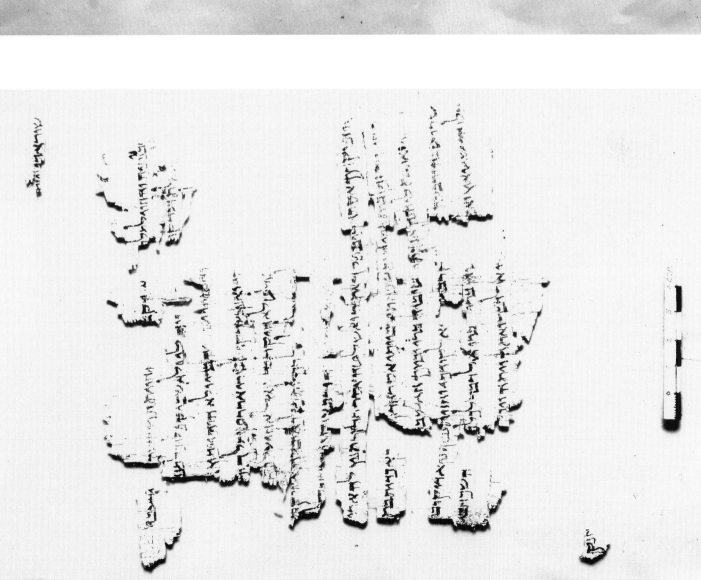

PLATE 1231

PLATE 1230

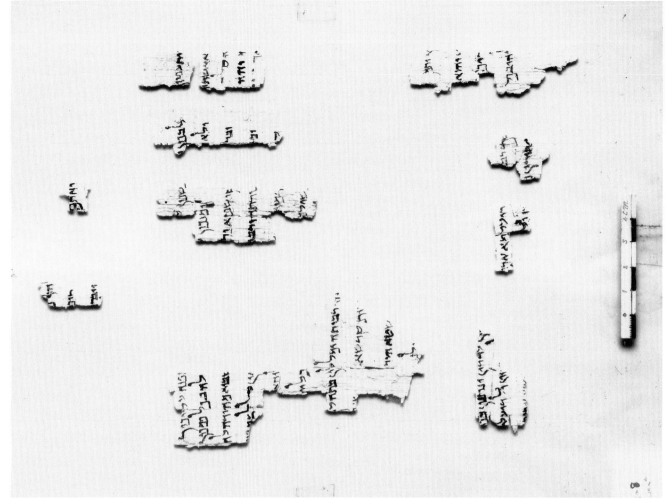

PLATE **1233**

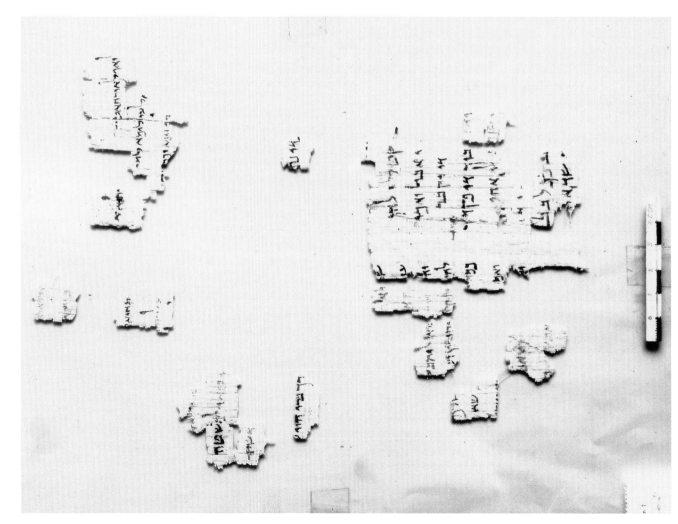

PLATE **1232**

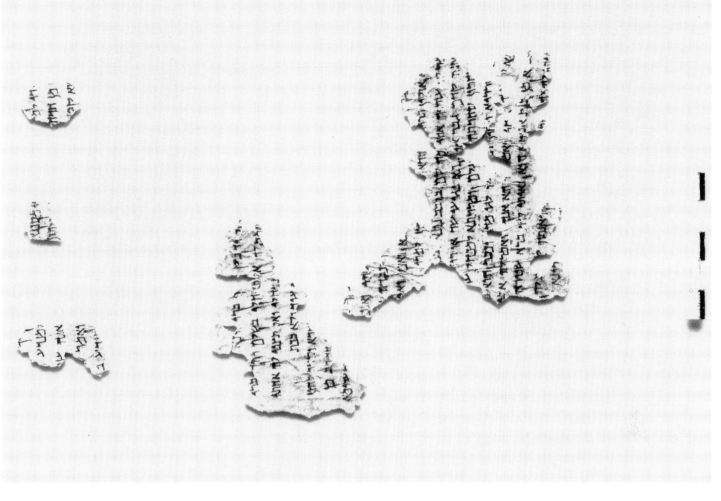

PLATE 1235

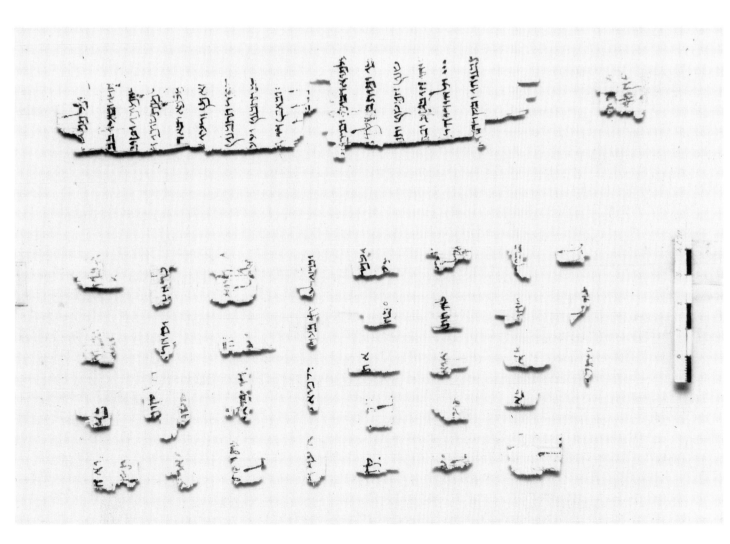

PLATE 1234

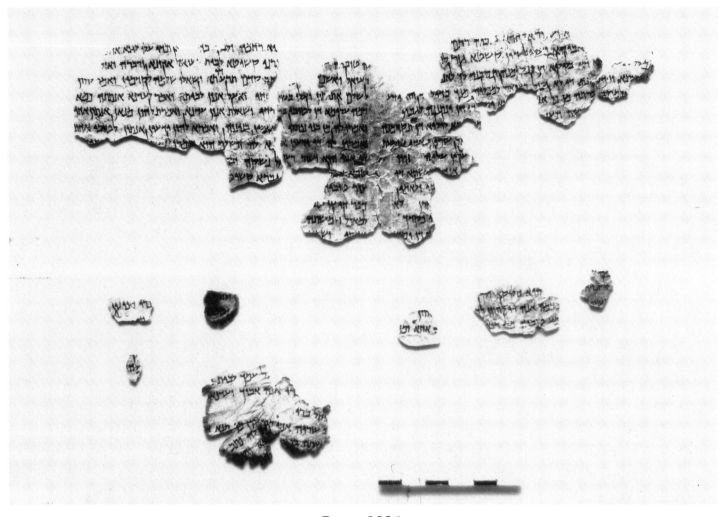

PLATE 1236

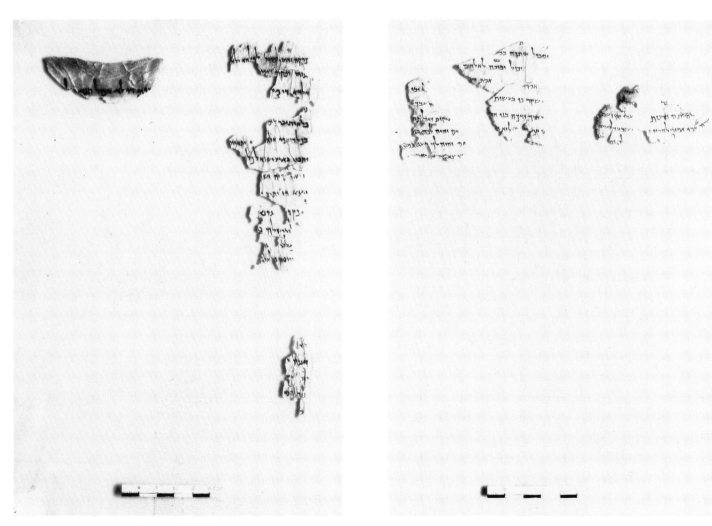

PLATE 1237

PLATE 1238

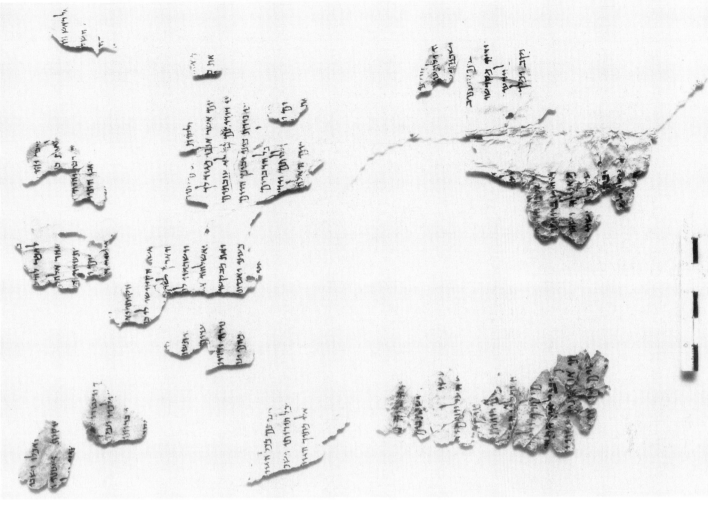

PLATE 1240

PLATE 1239

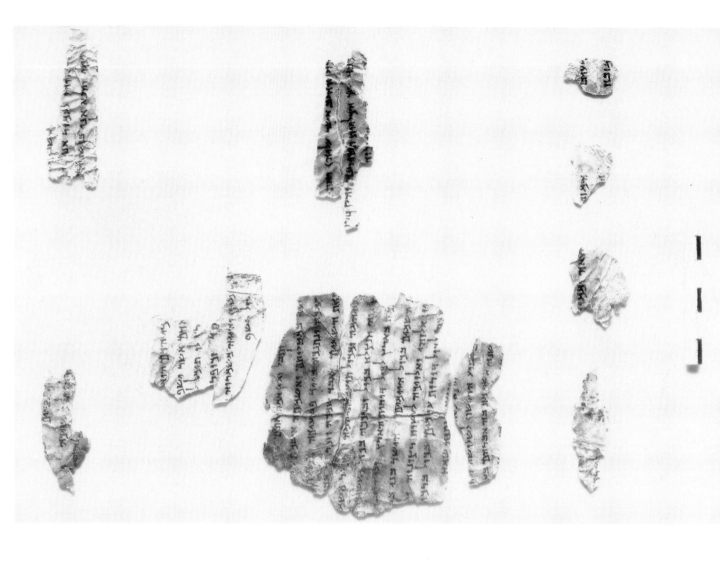

PLATE 1242

PLATE 1241

PLATE 1244

PLATE 1243

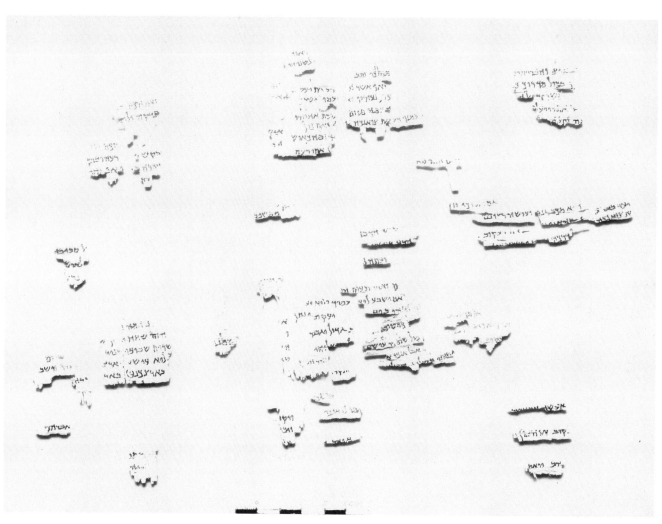

PLATE 1245

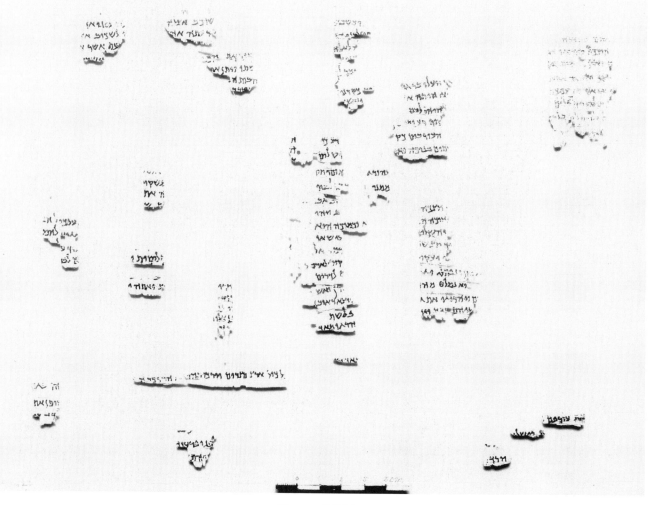

PLATE 1246

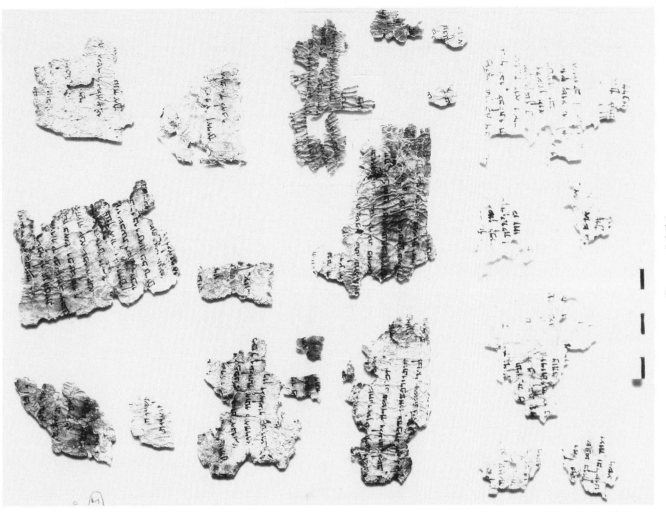

PLATE 1256

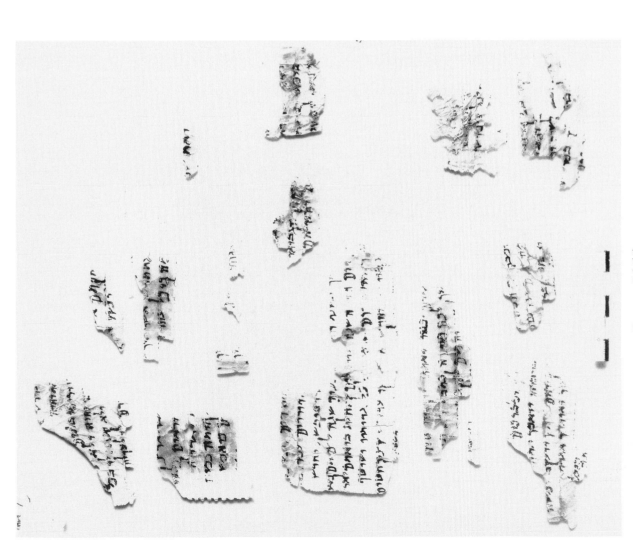

PLATE 1255

Plate 1258

Plate 1257

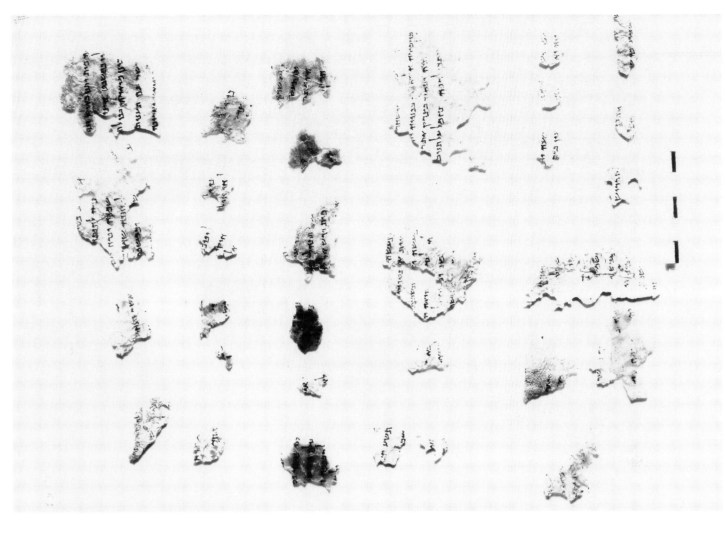

PLATE 1260

PLATE 1259

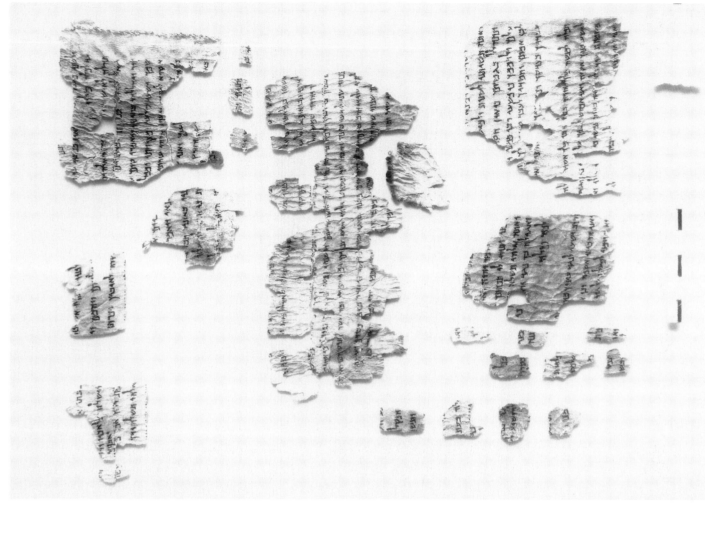

PLATE 1262

PLATE 1261

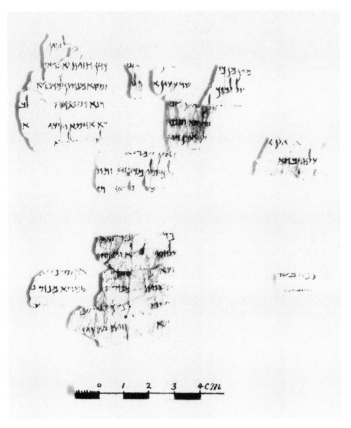

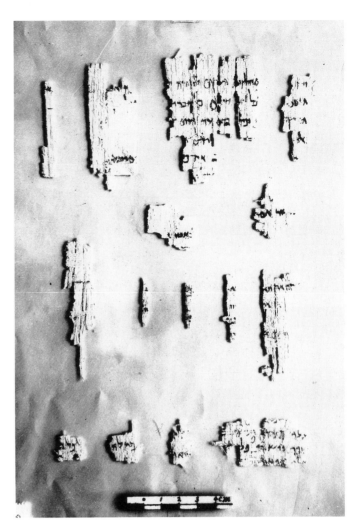

PLATE 1296

PLATE 1297

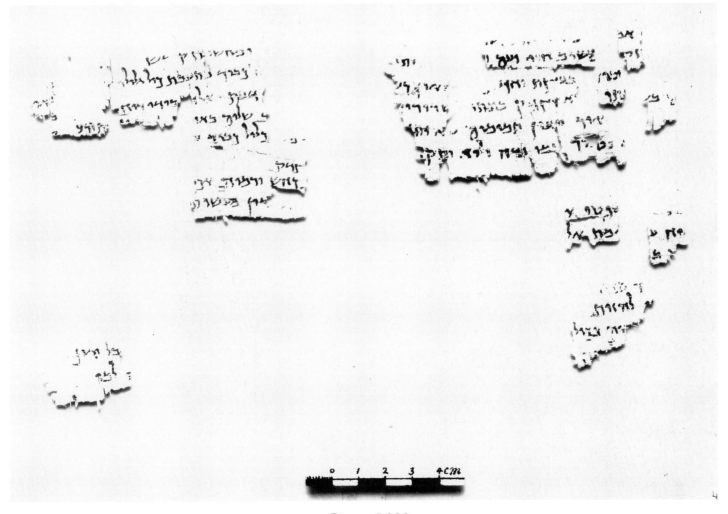

PLATE 1298

PLATE 1299

PLATE 1300

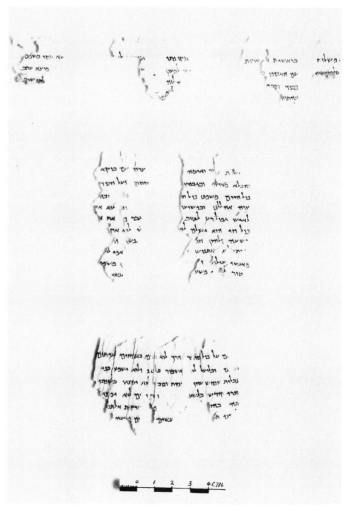

PLATE 1301

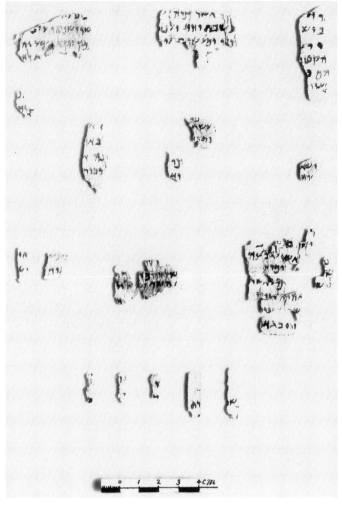

Plate 1302

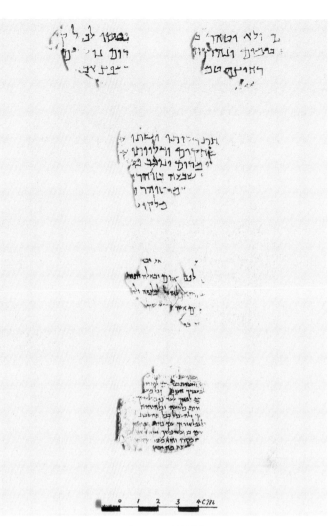

Plate 1303

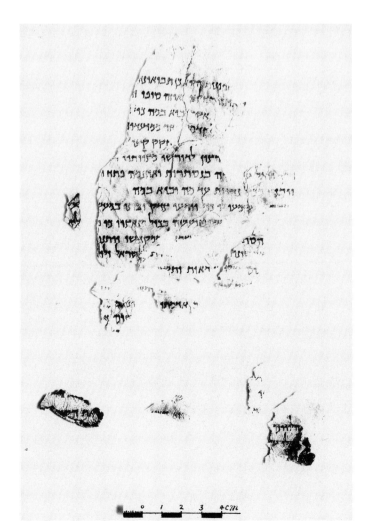

Plate 1304

Plate 1305

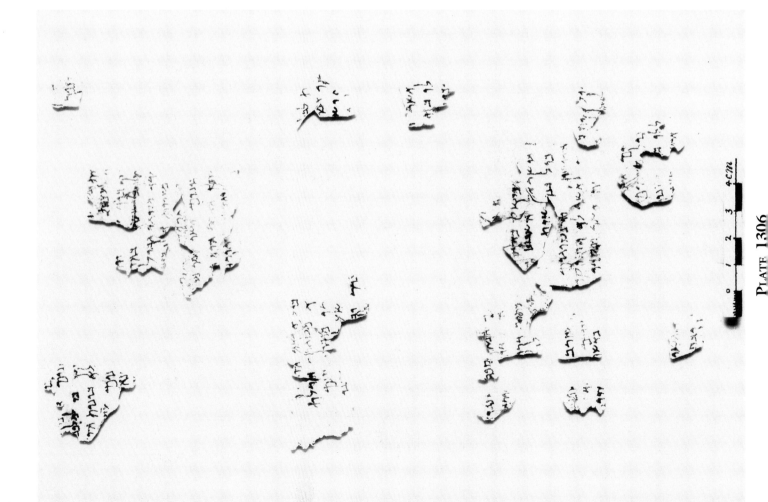

PLATE 1307

PLATE 1306

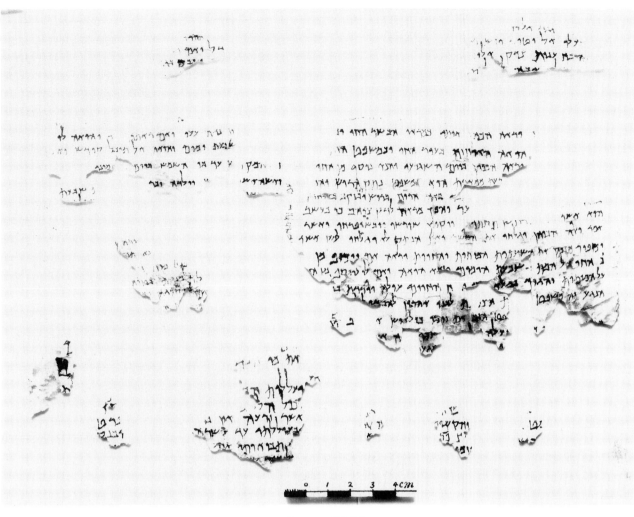

PLATE 1308

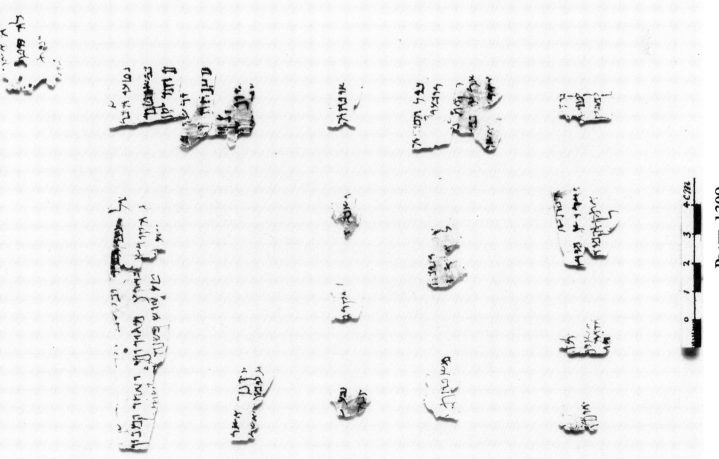

PLATE 1309

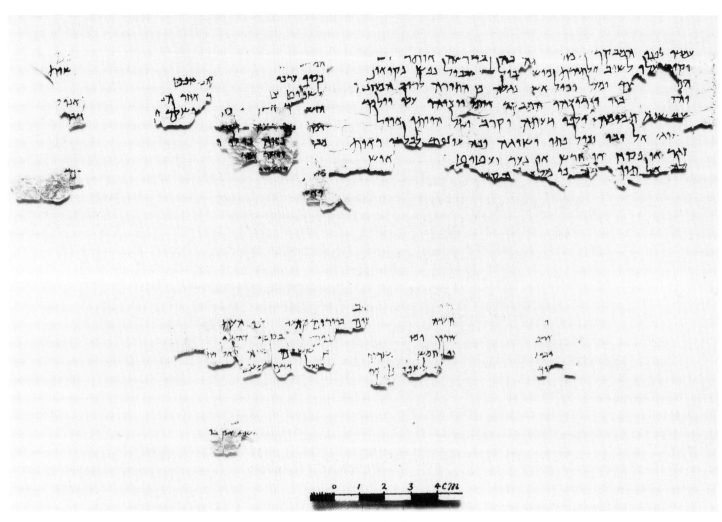

PLATE 1310

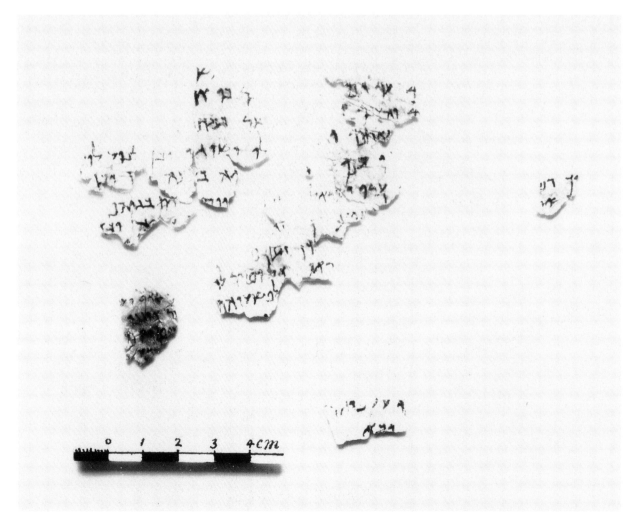

PLATE 1311

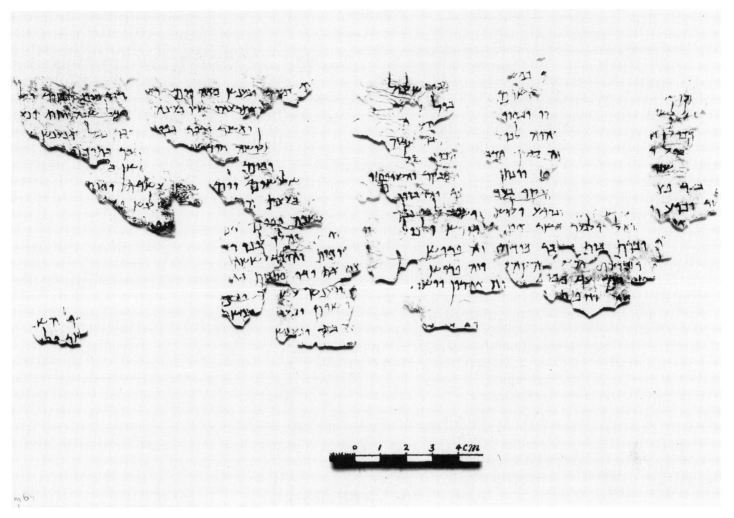

PLATE 1312

PLATE 1313

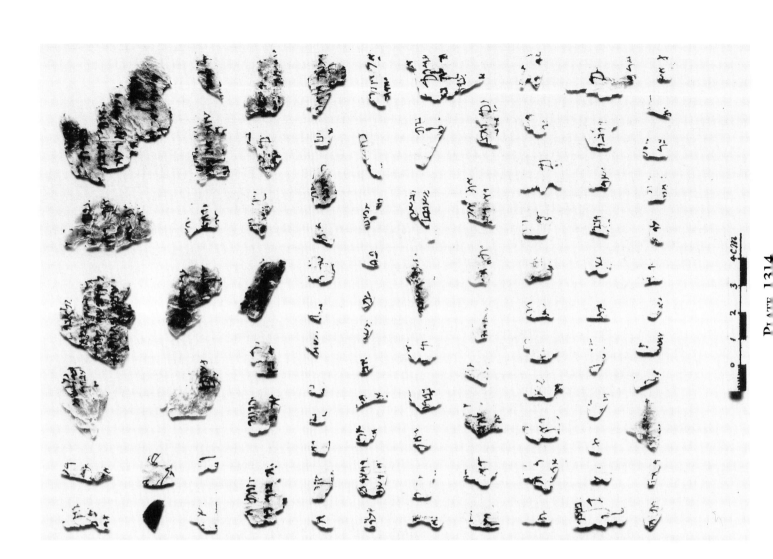

PLATE 1314

PLATE 1315

PLATE 1316

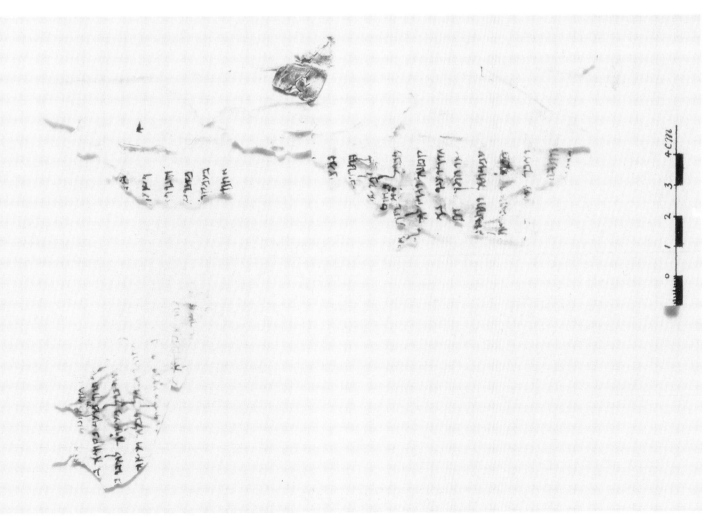

PLATE 1317

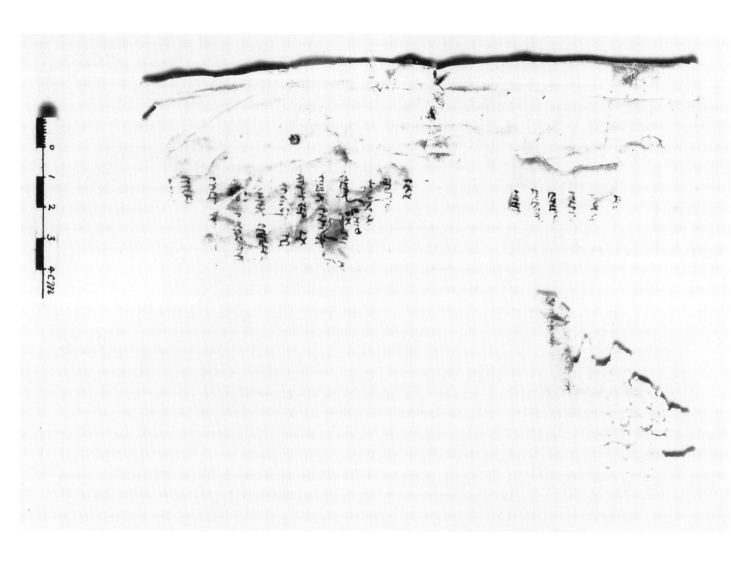

PLATE 1318

PLATE 1319

PLATE 1320

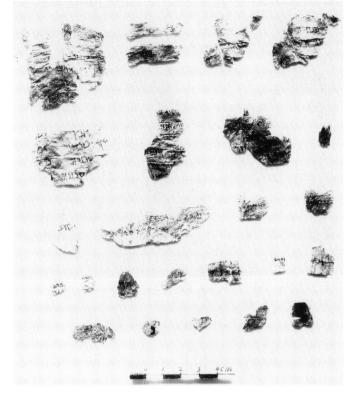

PLATE 1321

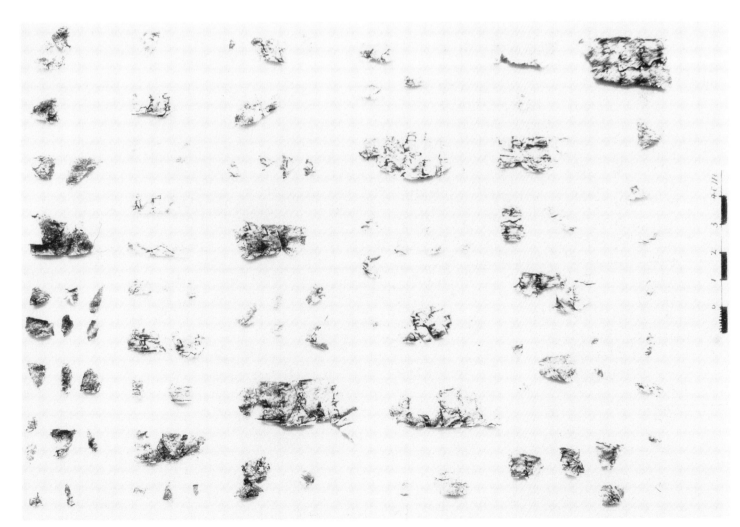

PLATE 1322

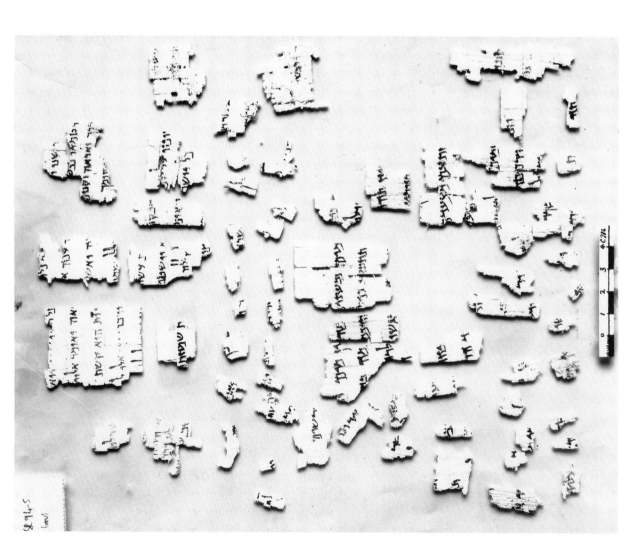

PLATE 1324

PLATE 1323

PLATE 1325

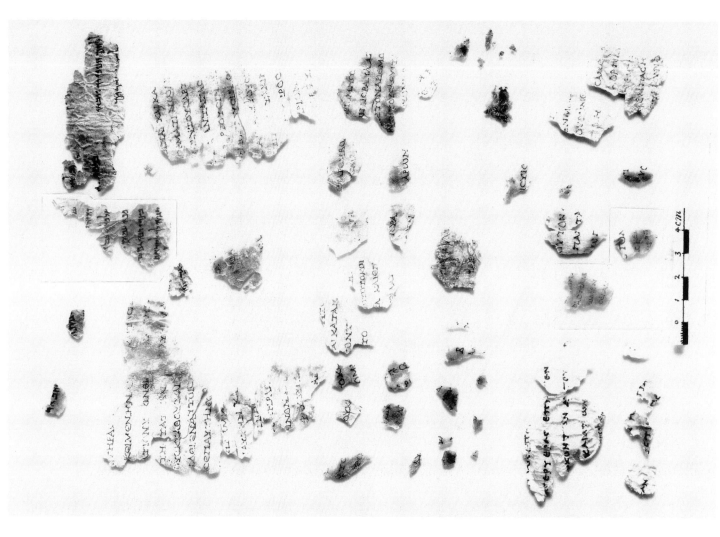

PLATE 1327

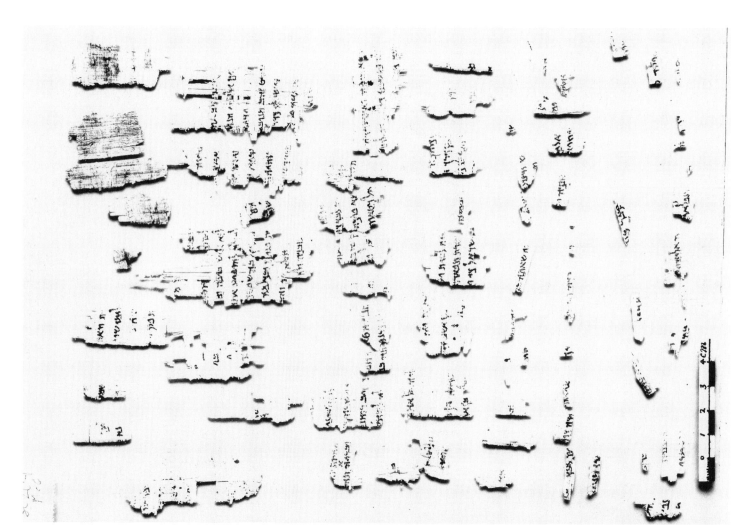

PLATE 1326

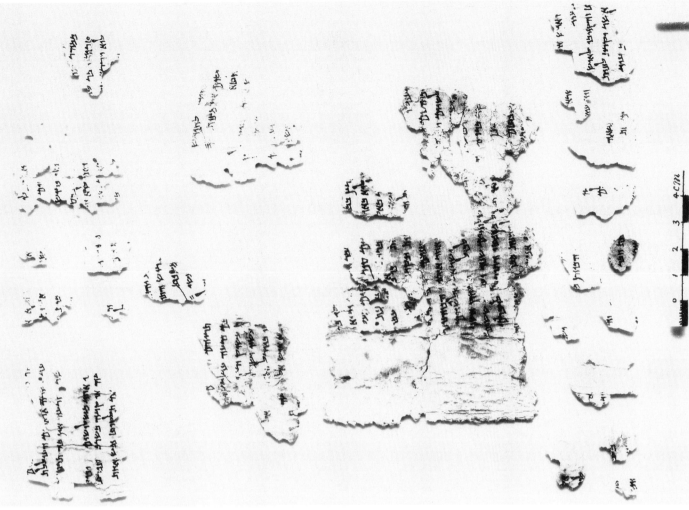

PLATE 1328

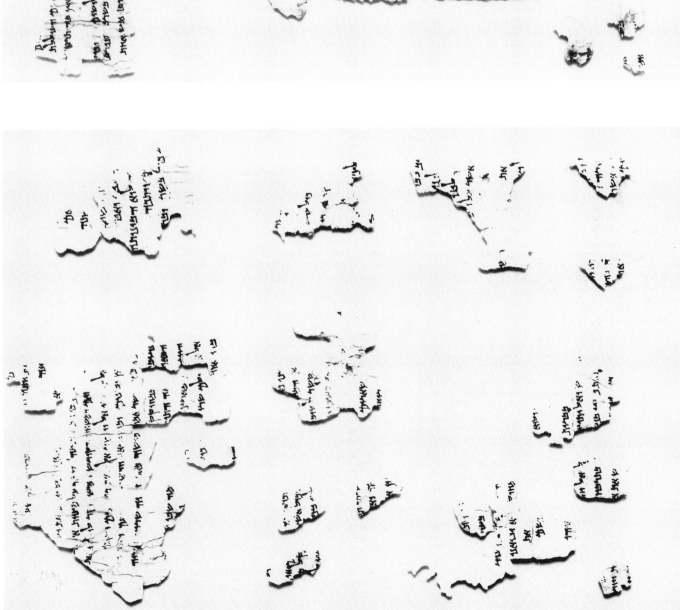

PLATE 1329

PLATE 1330

PLATE 1331

PLATE 1332

PLATE 1334

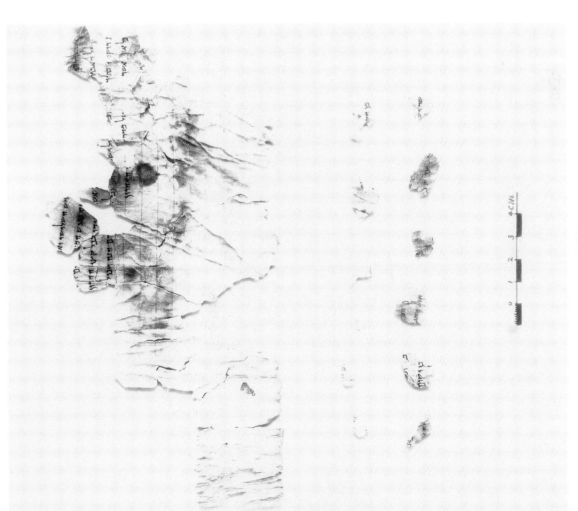

PLATE 1333

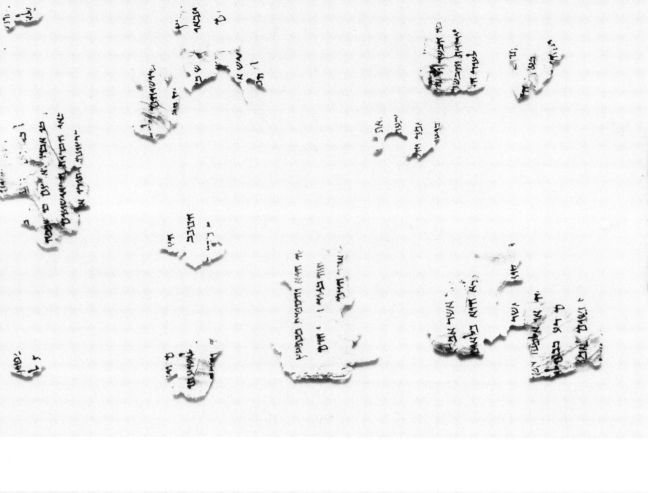

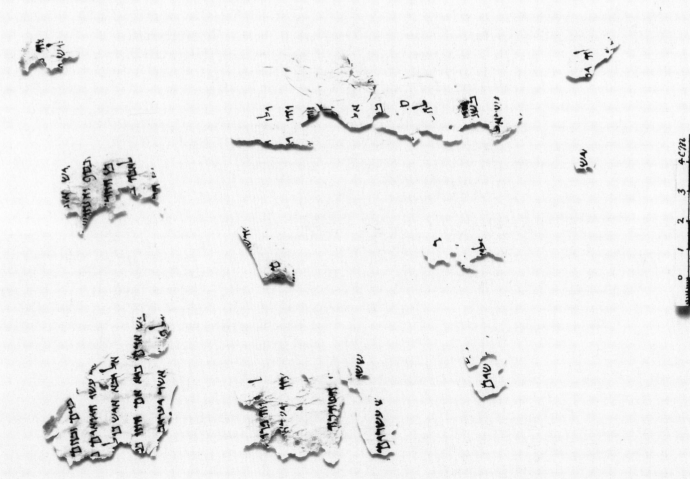

PLATE 1335

PLATE 1336

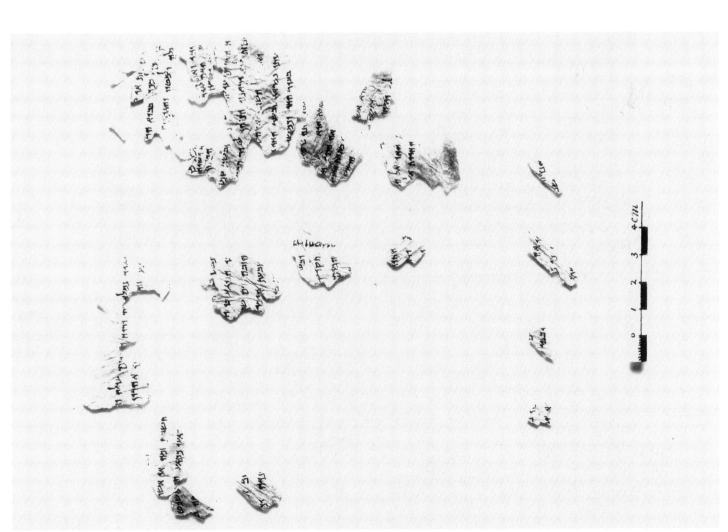

PLATE 1337

PLATE 1338

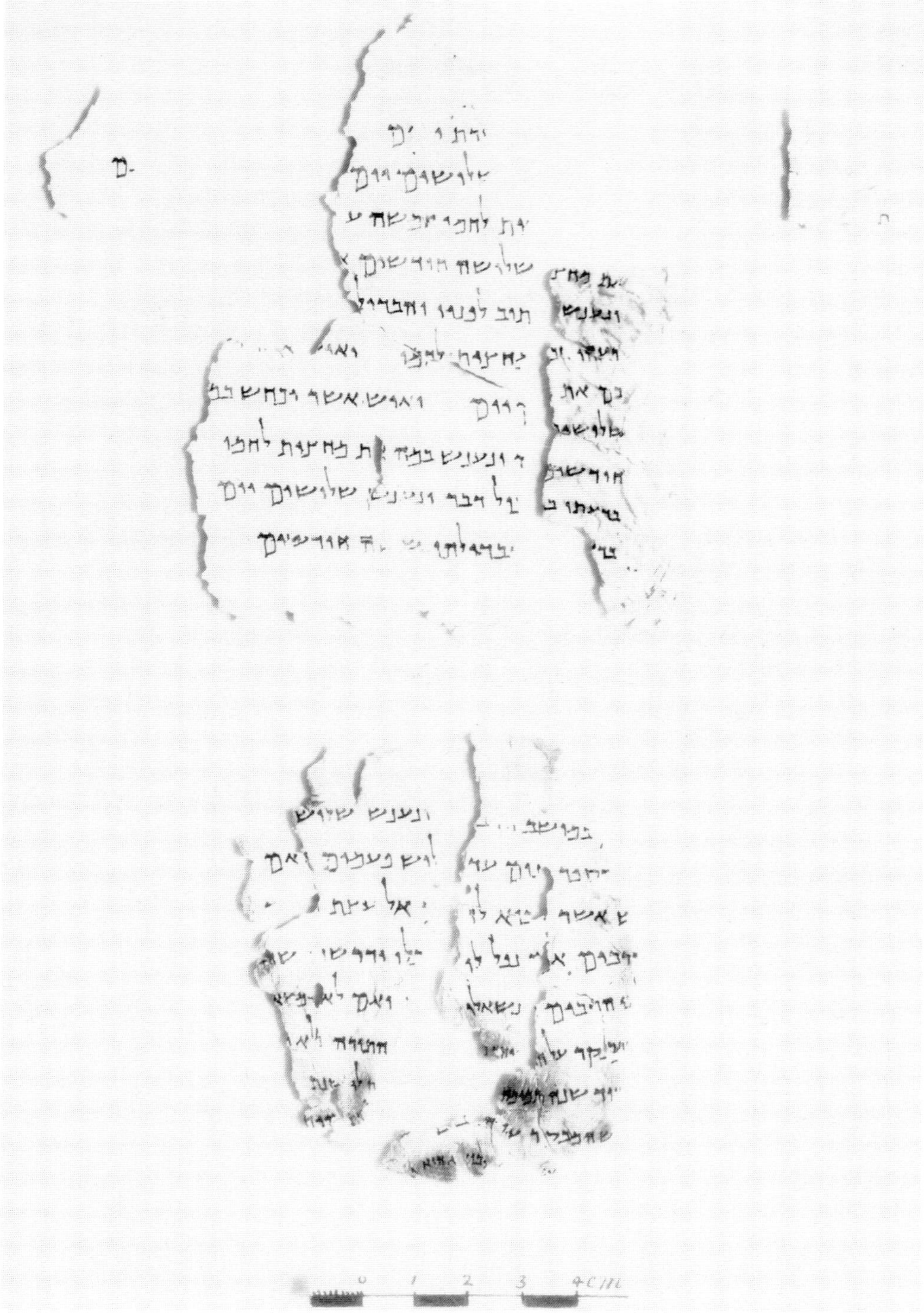

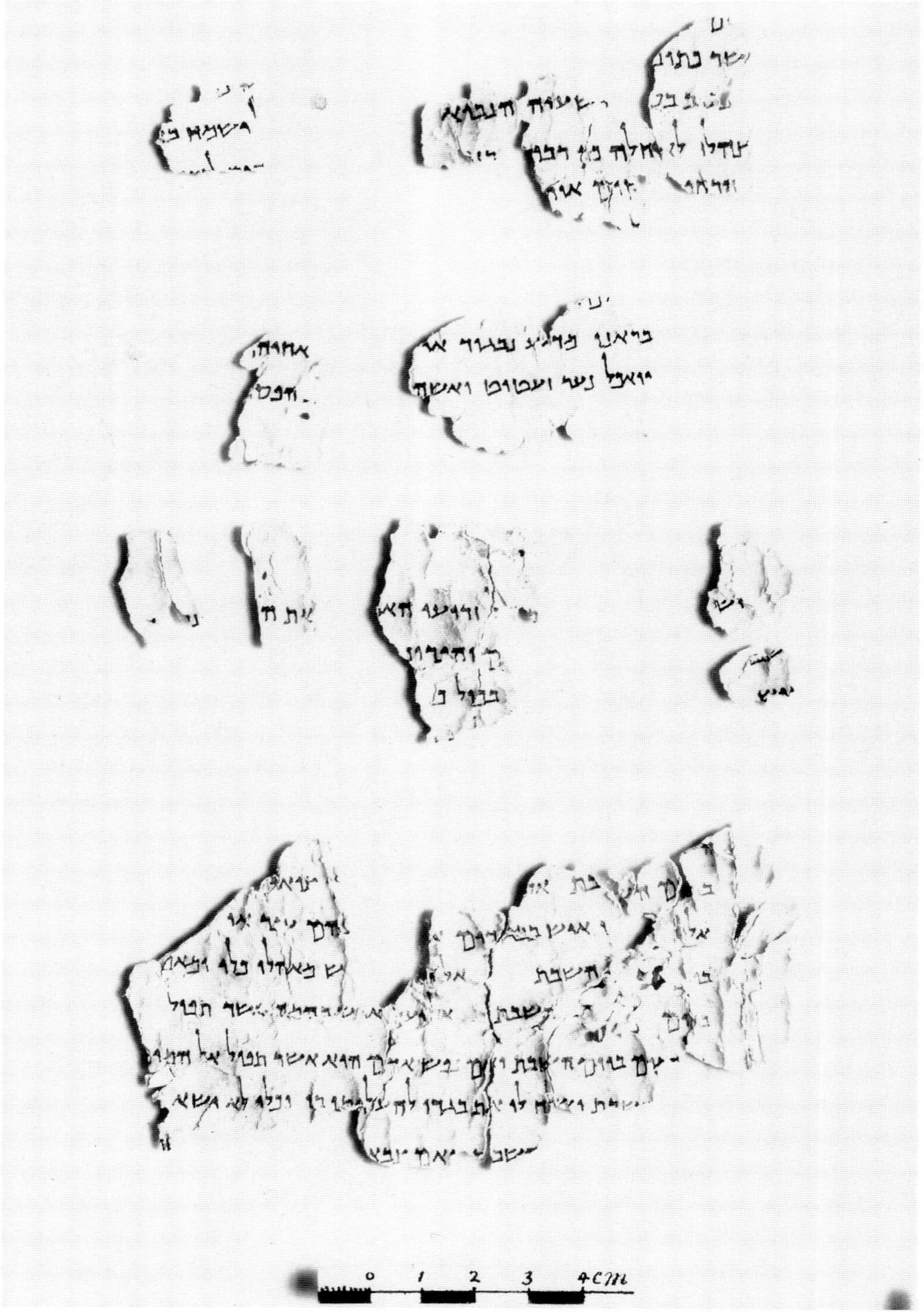

PLATE 1340

PLATE 1339

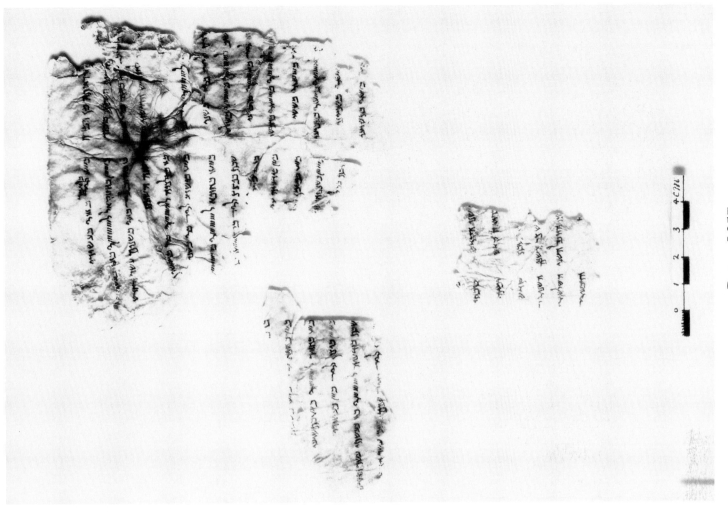

PLATE 1357

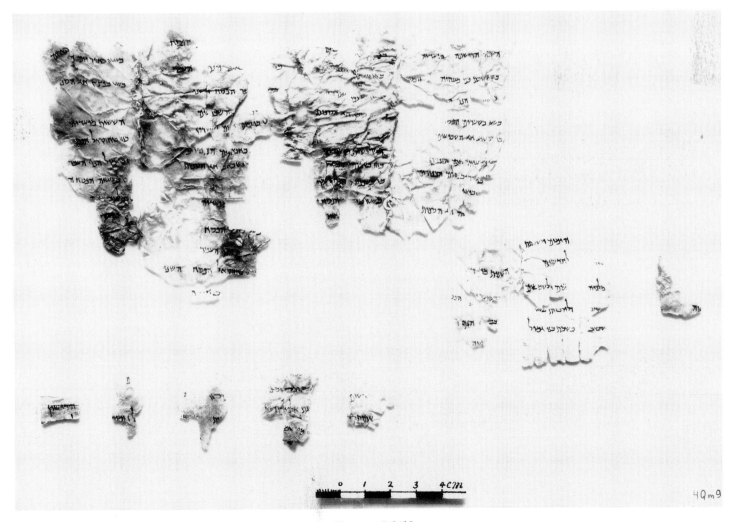

PLATE 1358

4Qm9

PLATE 1360

PLATE 1359

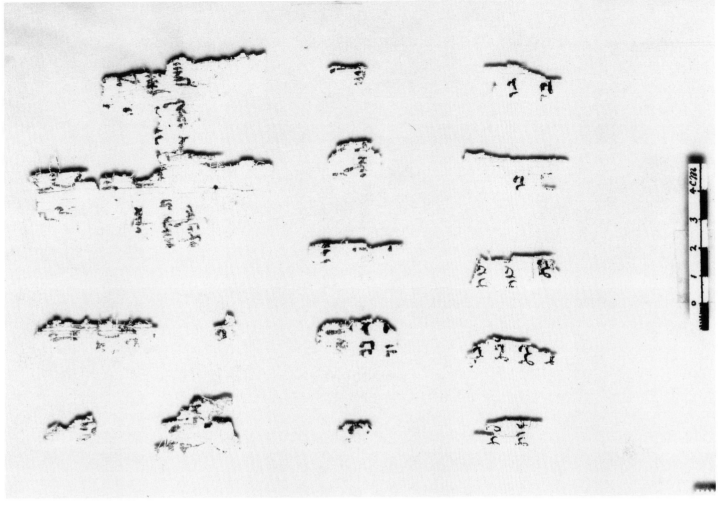

PLATE 1361

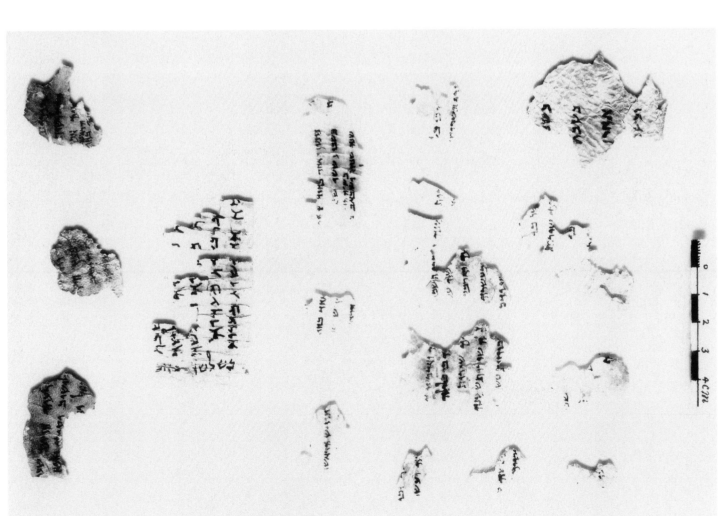

PLATE 1362

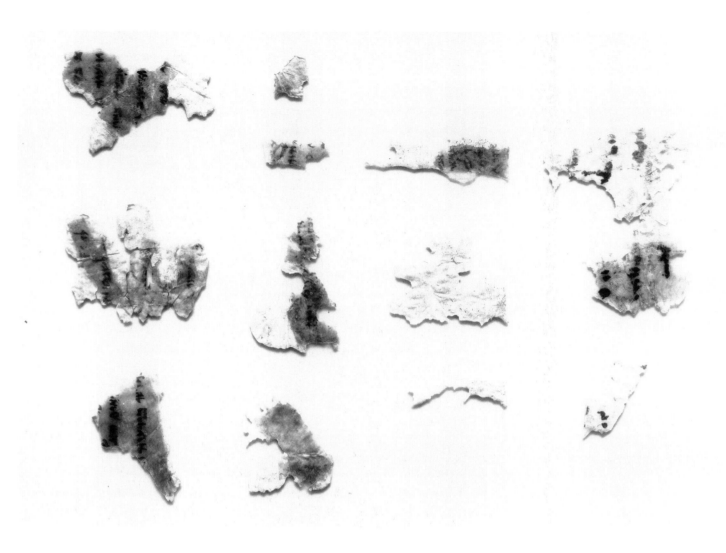

PLATE 1264

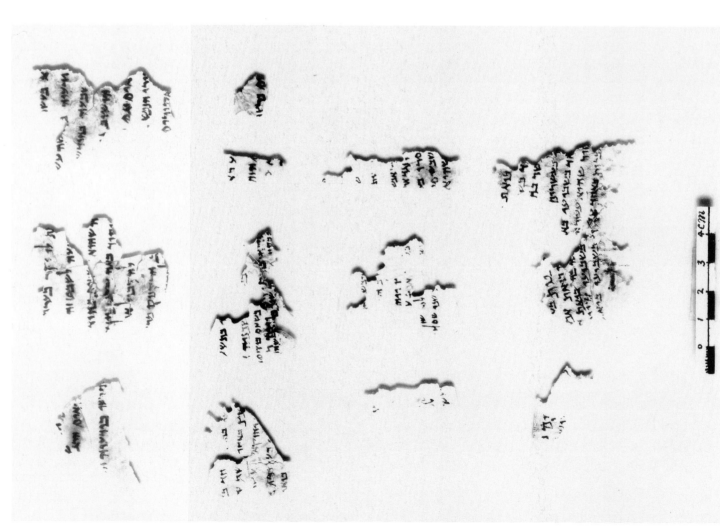

PLATE 1263

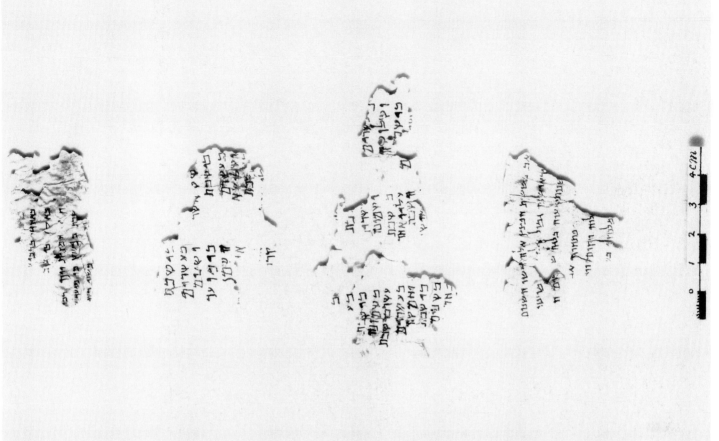

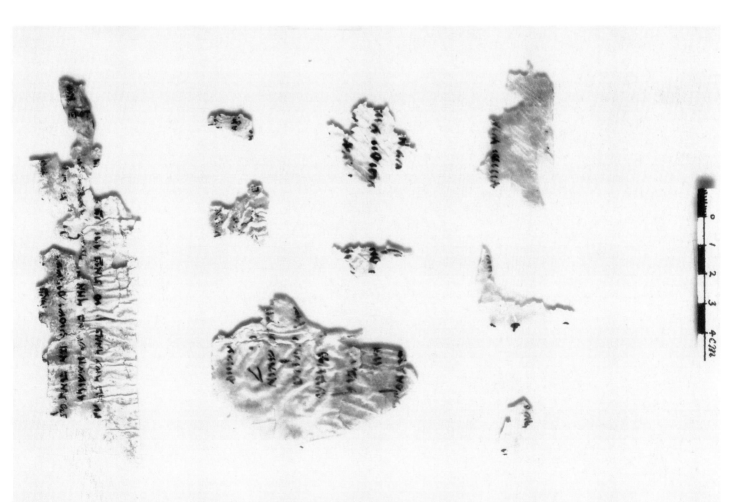

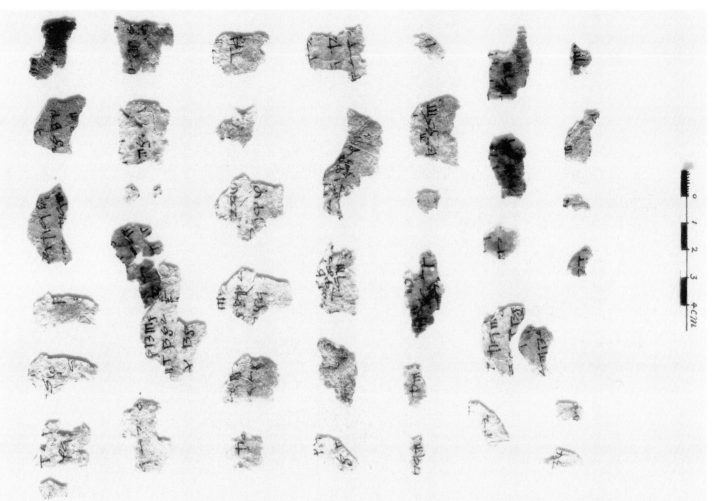

PLATE 1367

PLATE 1368

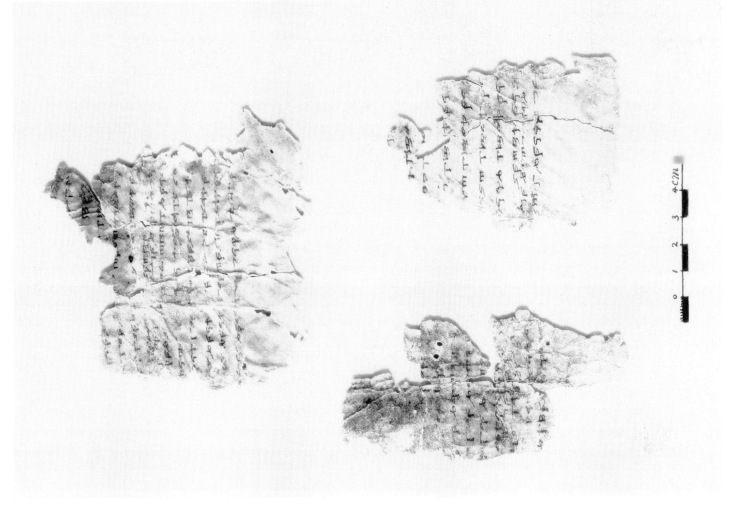

PLATE 1370

PLATE 1369

PLATE 1372

PLATE 1371

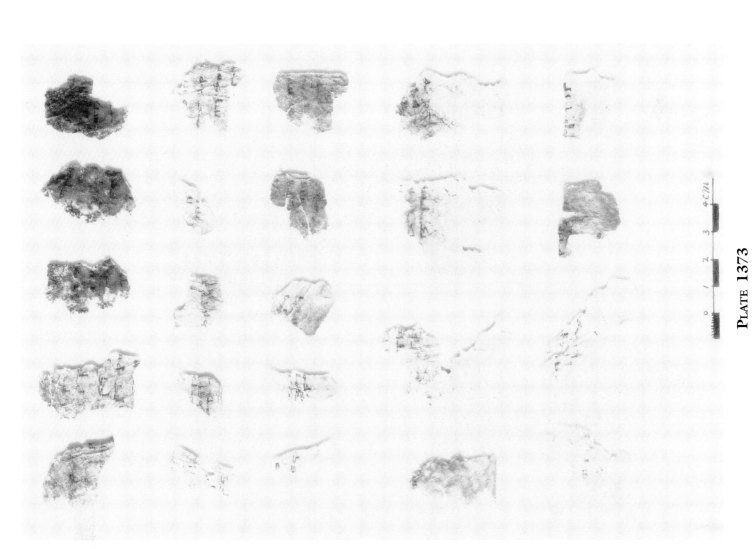

PLATE 1374

PLATE 1373

PLATE 1375

PLATE 1376

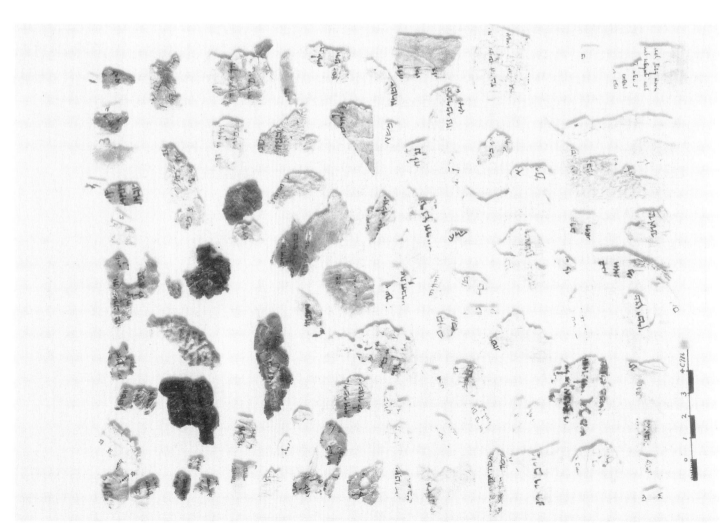

PLATE 1377

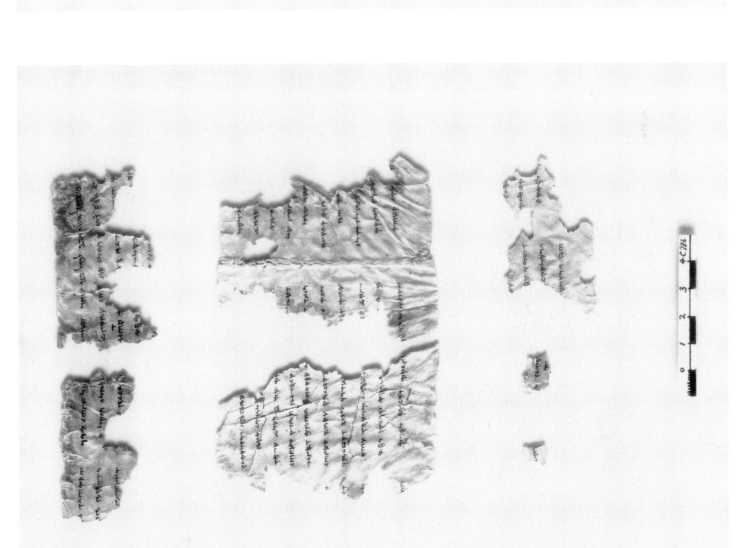

PLATE 1378

PLATE 1379

PLATE 1381

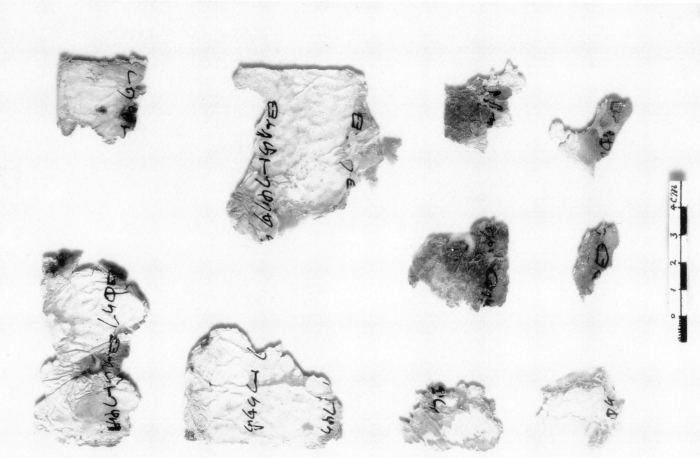

PLATE 1380

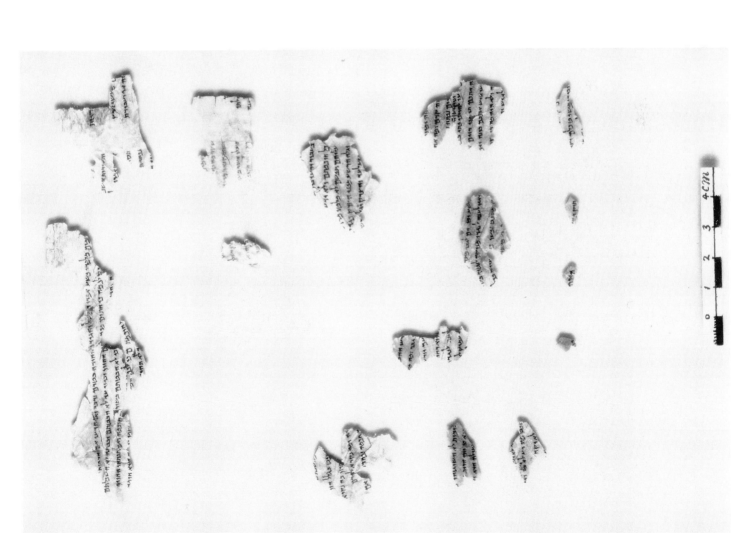

PLATE 1383

PLATE 1382

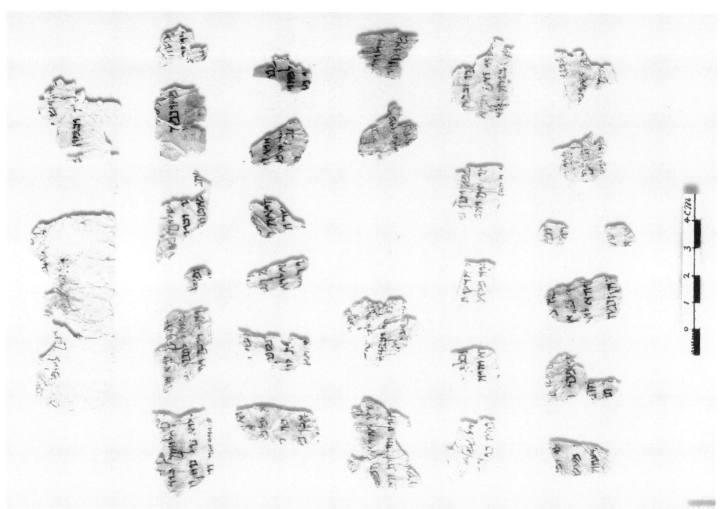

PLATE 1385

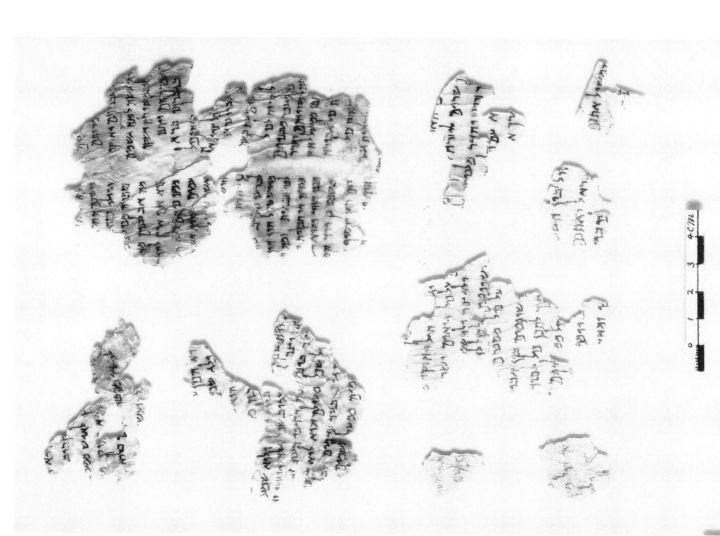

PLATE 1384

PLATE 1387

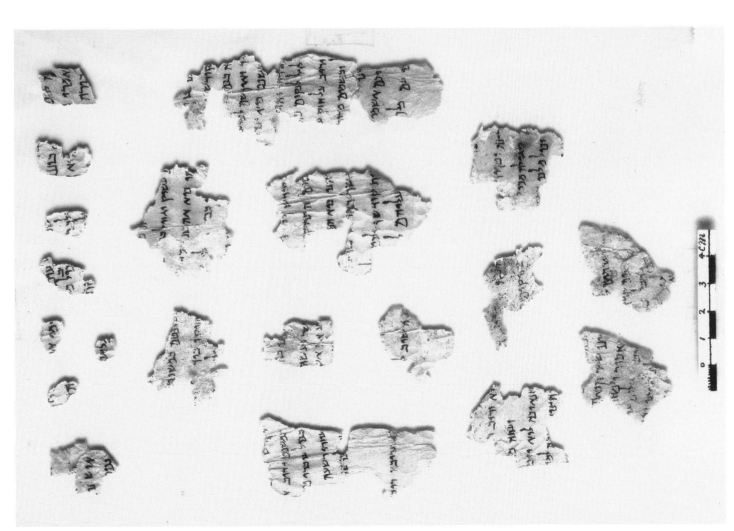

PLATE 1386

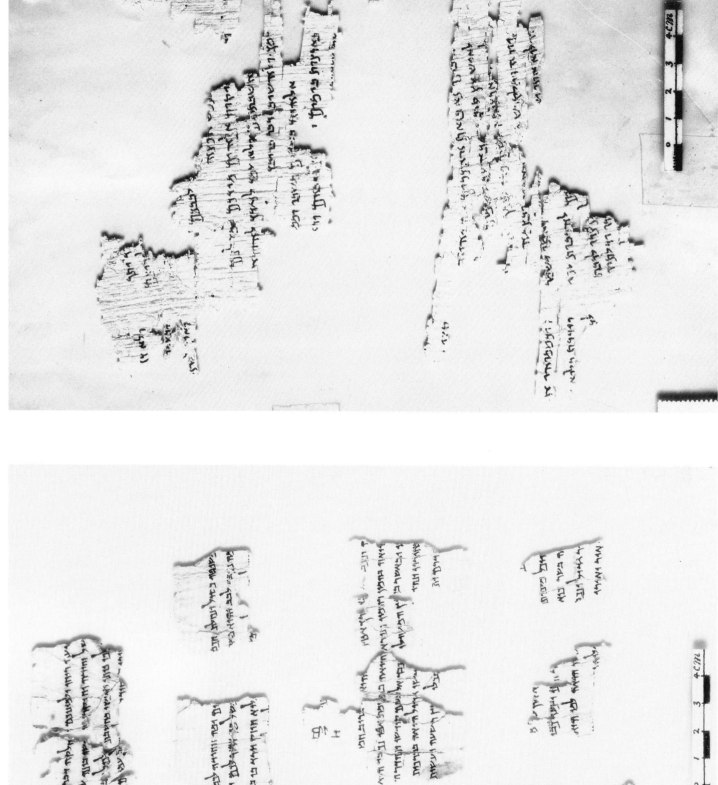

PLATE 1388

PLATE 1389

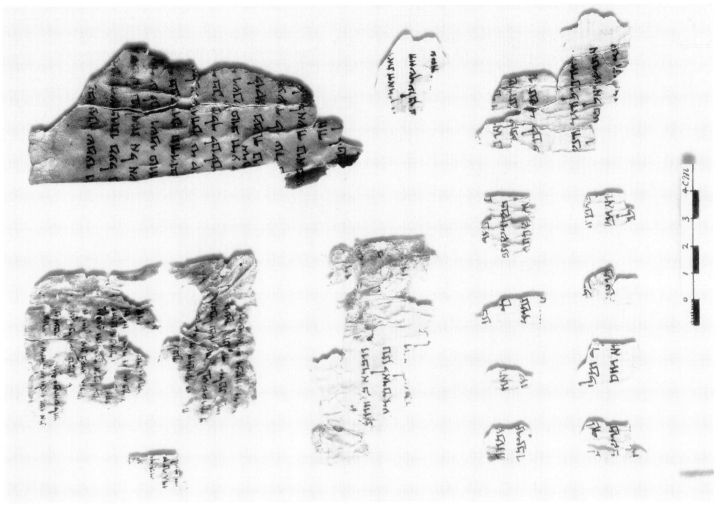

PLATE 1391

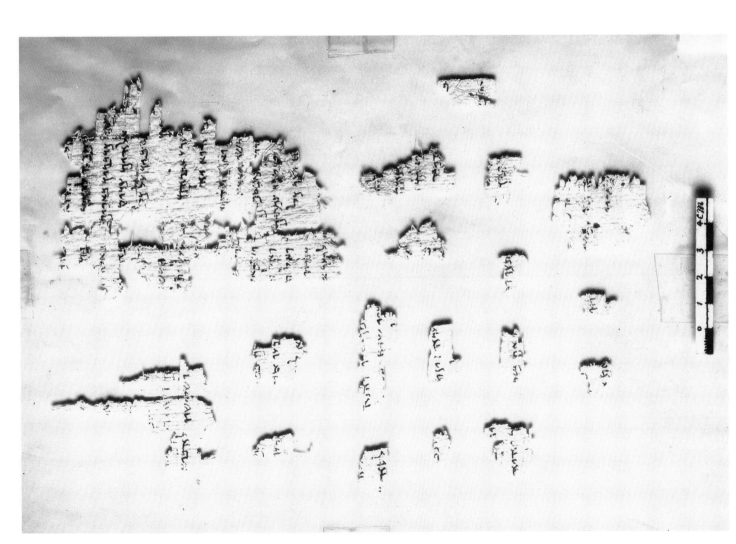

PLATE 1390

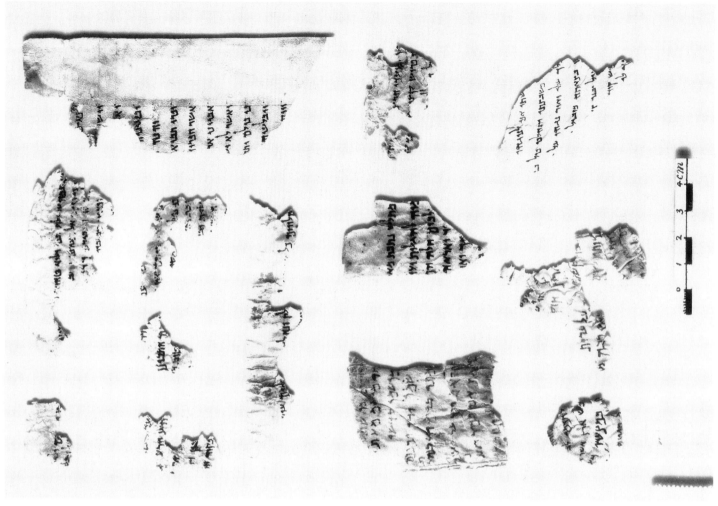

PLATE 1393

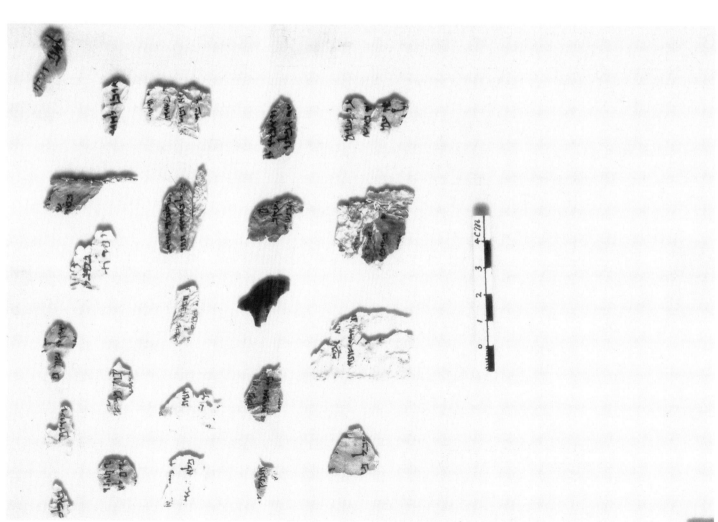

PLATE 1392

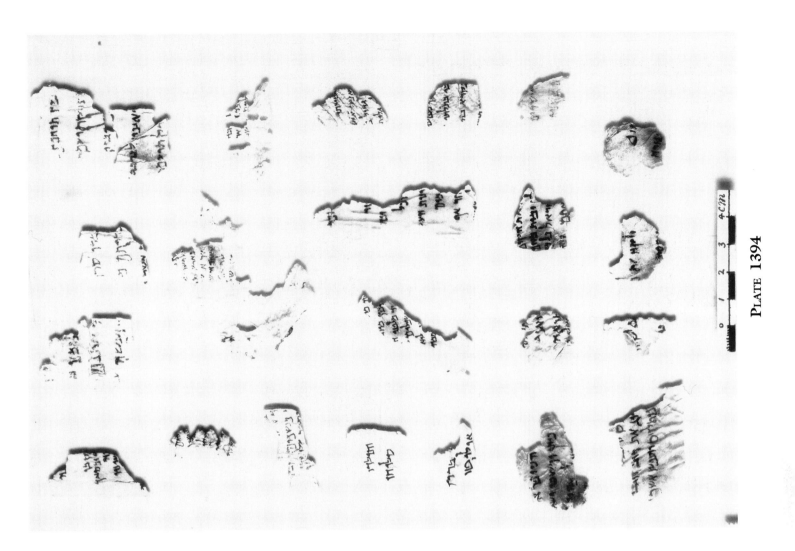

PLATE 1394

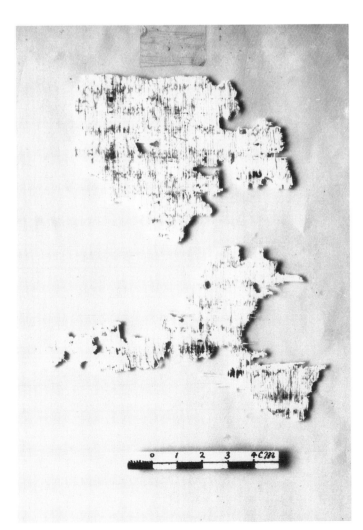

PLATE 1395

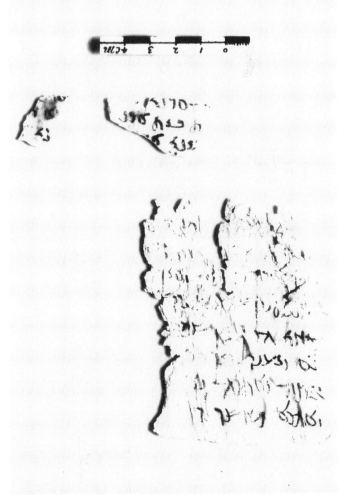

PLATE 1396

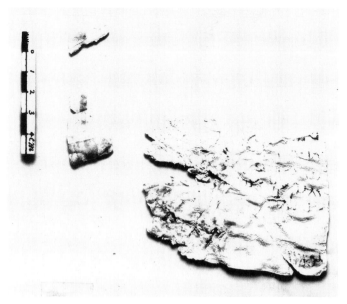

PLATE 1397

PLATE 1398

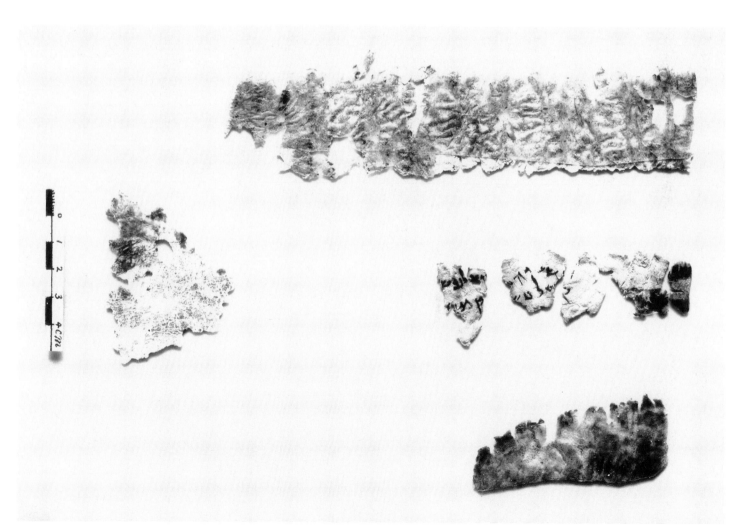

PLATE 1399

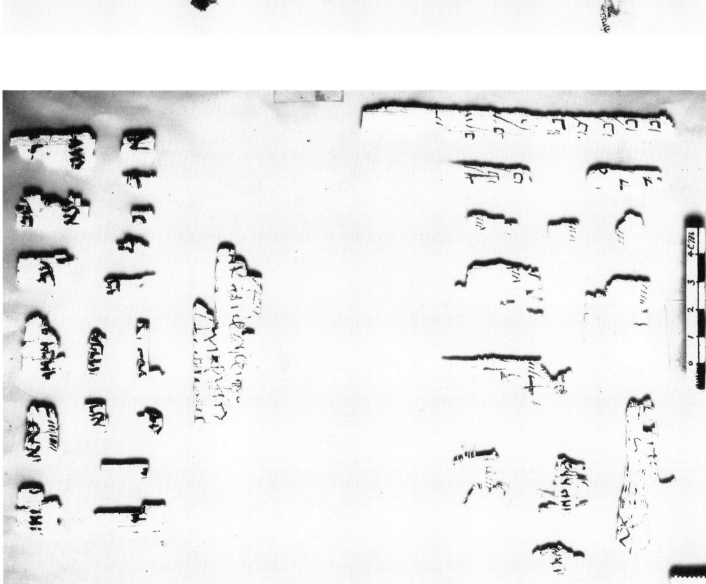

PLATE 1400

PLATE 1401

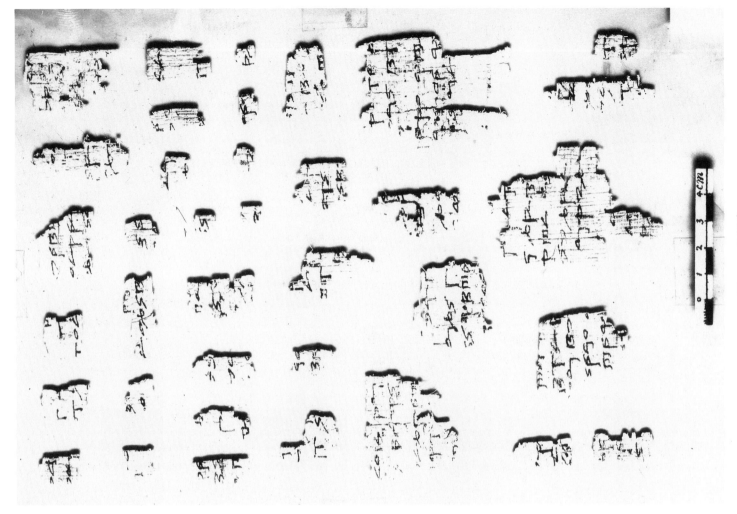

PLATE 1403

PLATE 1402

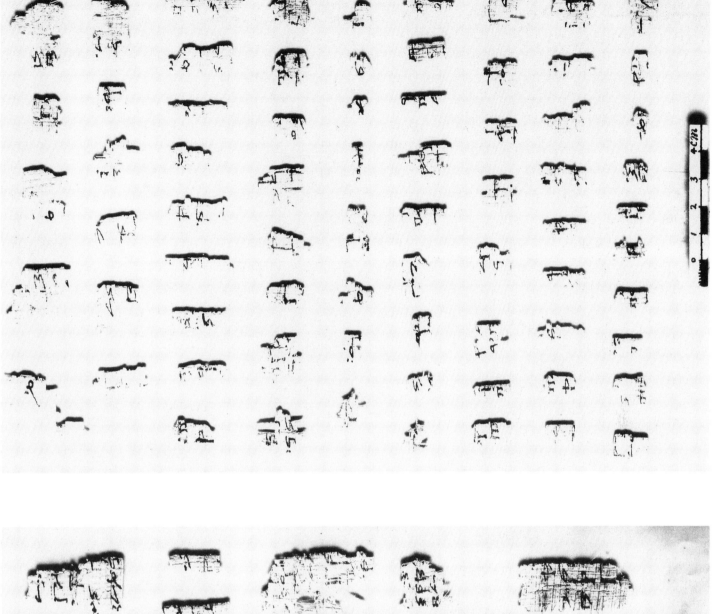

PLATE 1405

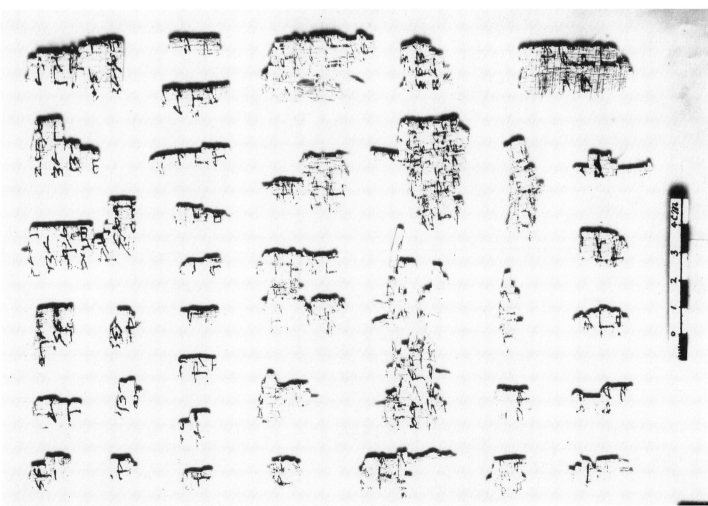

PLATE 1404

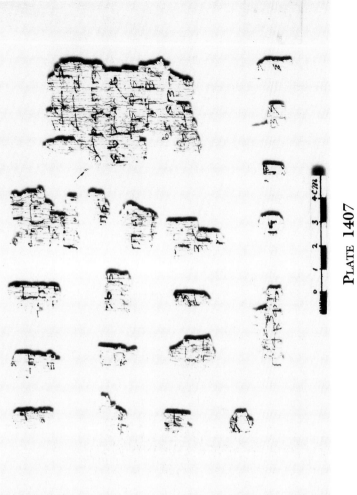

PLATE 1407

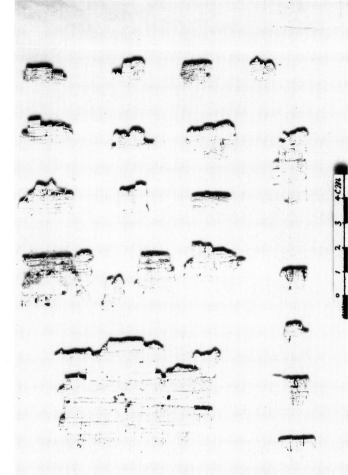

PLATE 1408

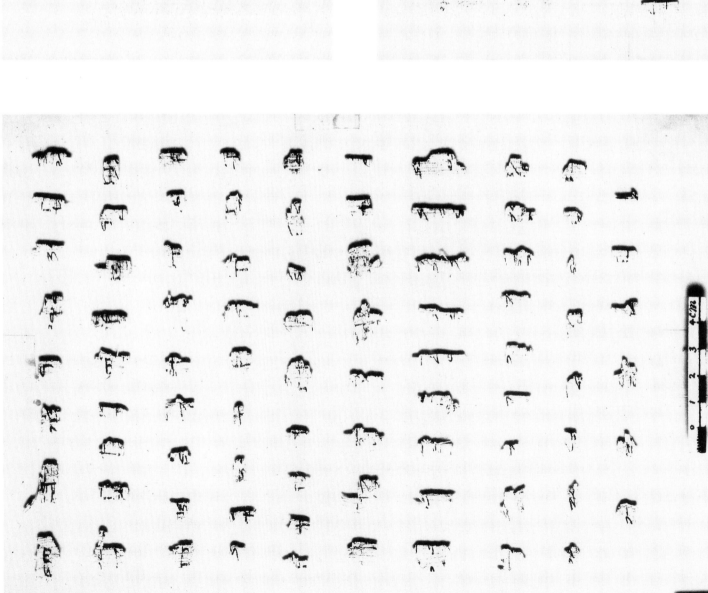

PLATE 1406

PLATE 1436

PLATE 1435

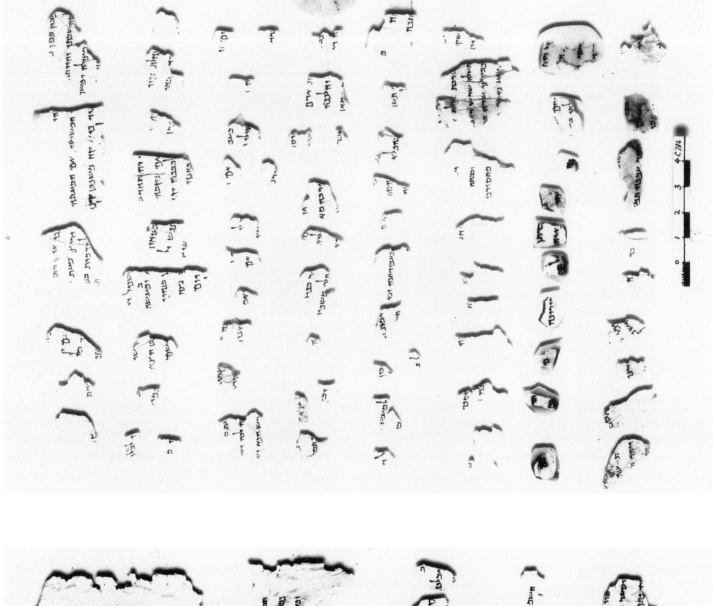

PLATE 1438

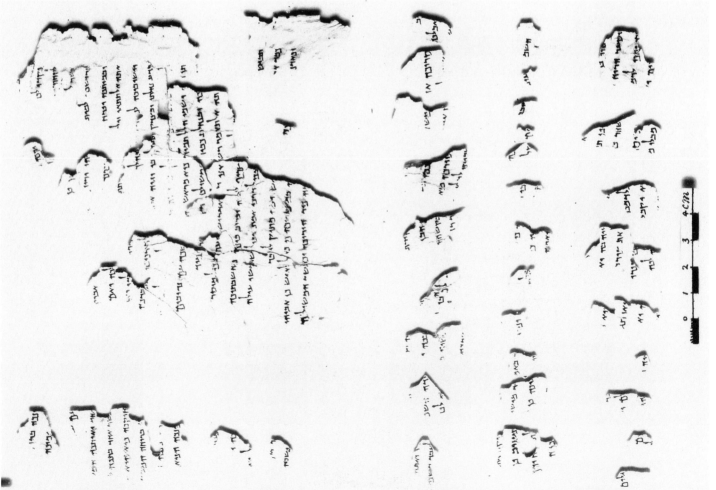

PLATE 1437

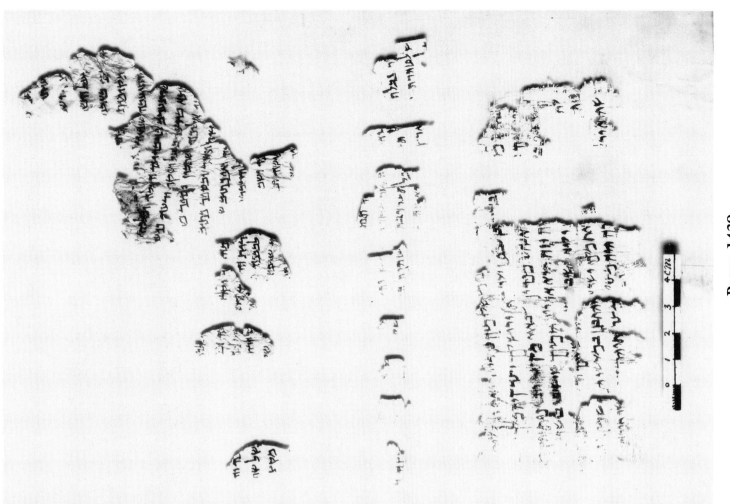

PLATE 1439

PLATE 1440

PLATE 1441

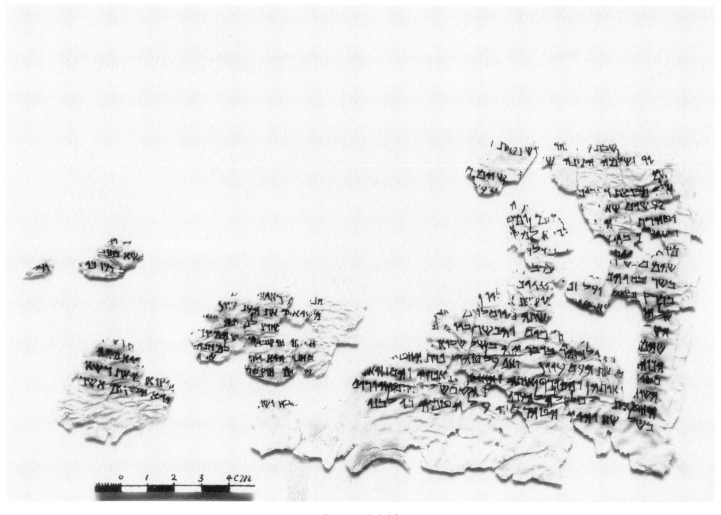

PLATE 1442

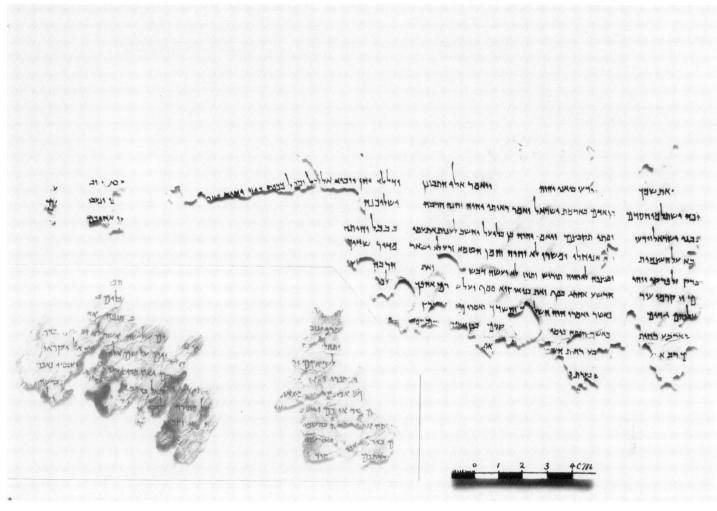

PLATE 1443

PLATE 1444

PLATE 1446

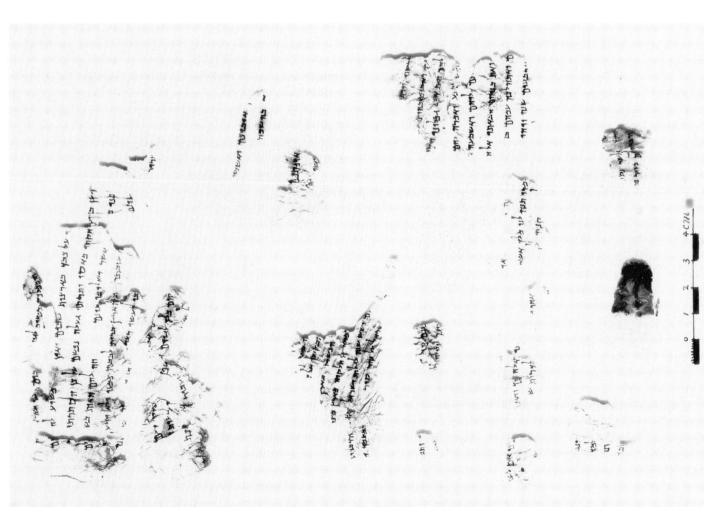

PLATE 1445

PLATE 1448

PLATE 1447

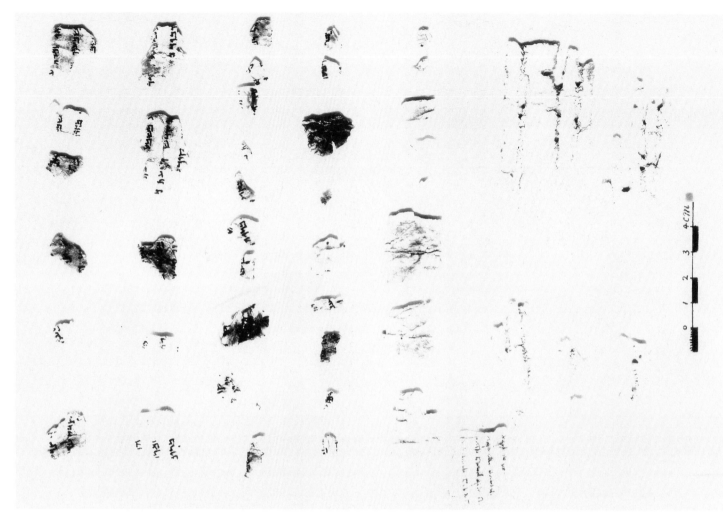

PLATE 1450

PLATE 1449

PLATE 1452

PLATE 1451

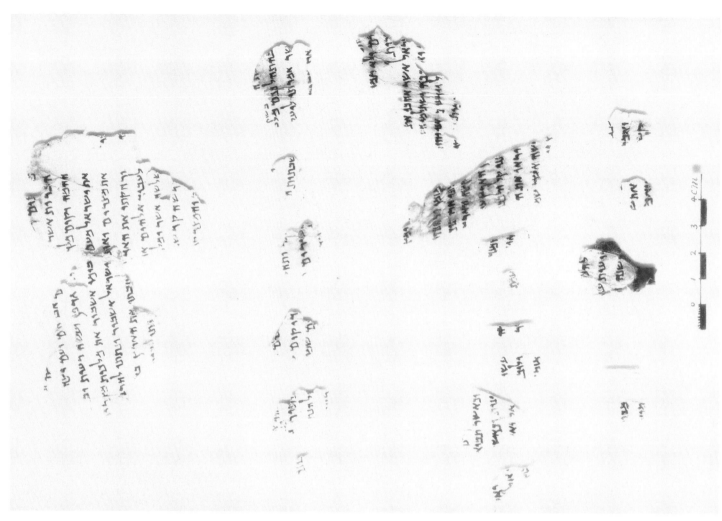

PLATE 1454

PLATE 1453

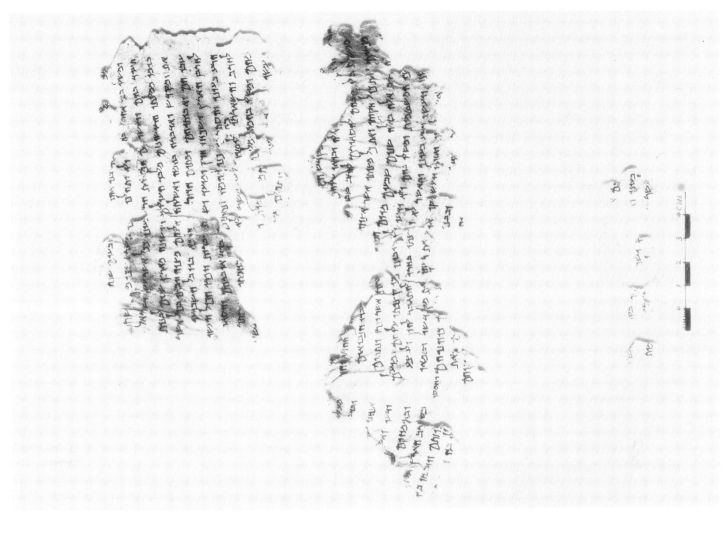

PLATE 1456

PLATE 1455

PLATE 1458

PLATE 1457

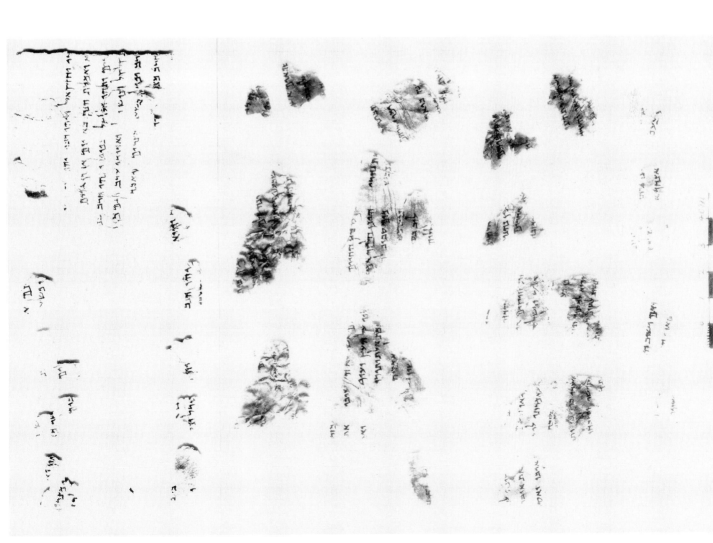

PLATE 1460

PLATE 1459

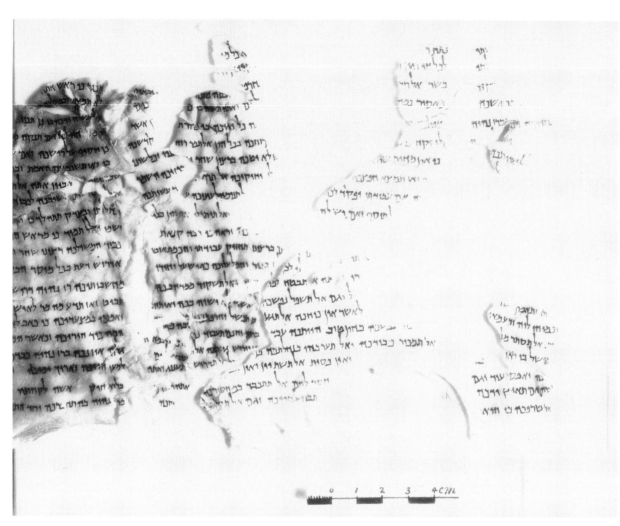

PLATE 1461

PLATE 1462

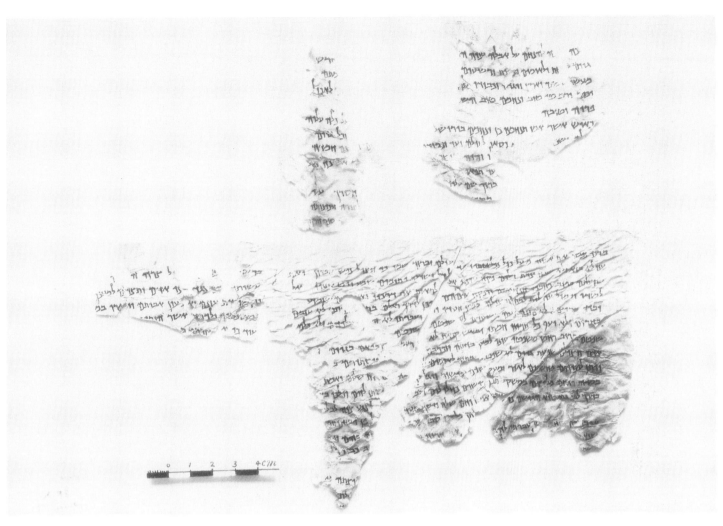

PLATE 1463

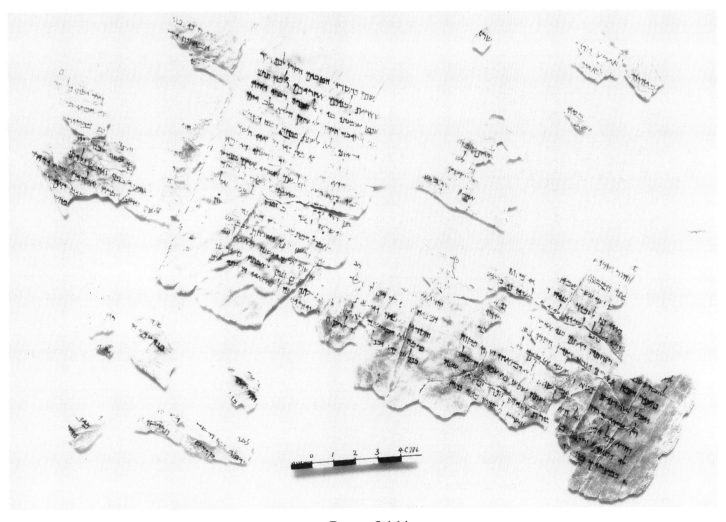

PLATE 1464

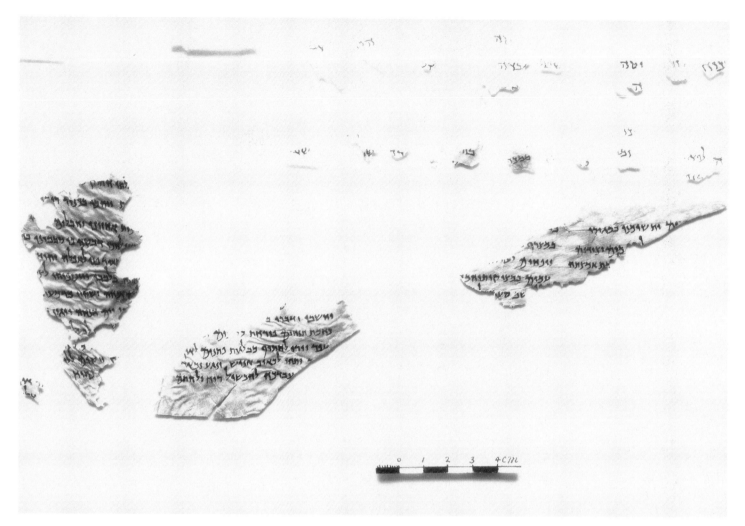

PLATE 1465

PLATE 1466

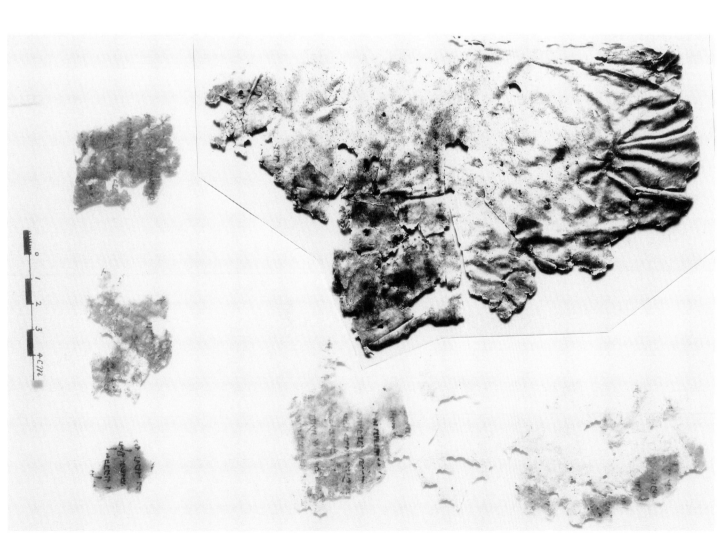

PLATE 1467

PLATE 1468

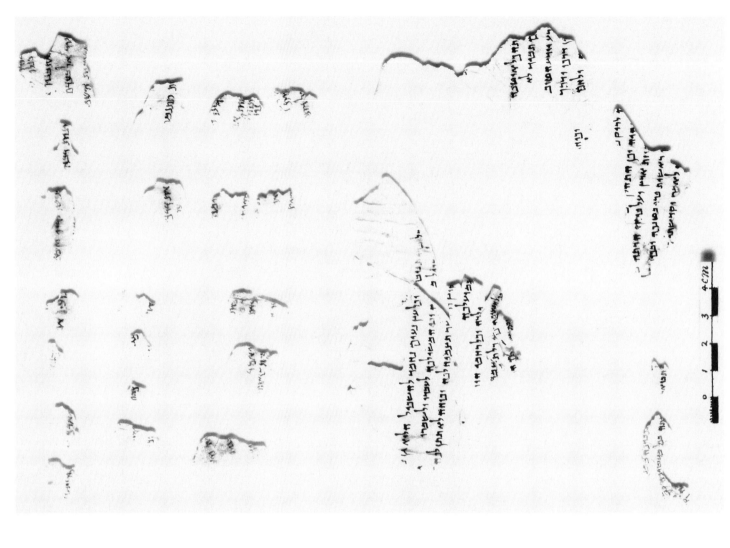

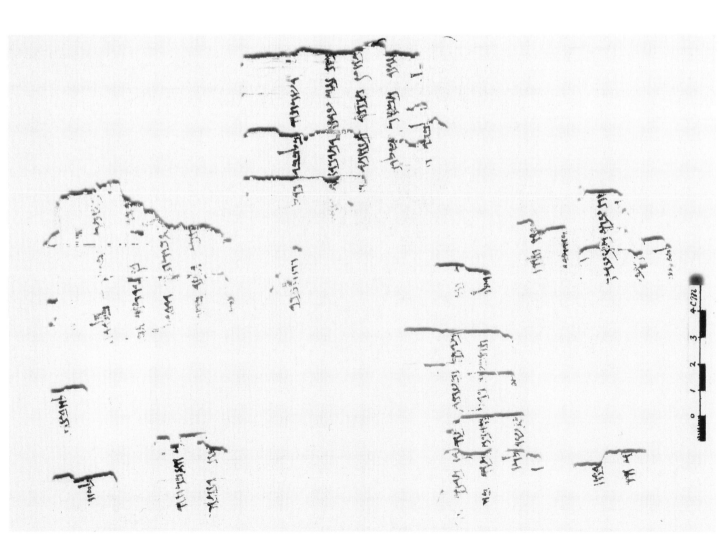

PLATE 1470

PLATE 1469

PLATE 1472

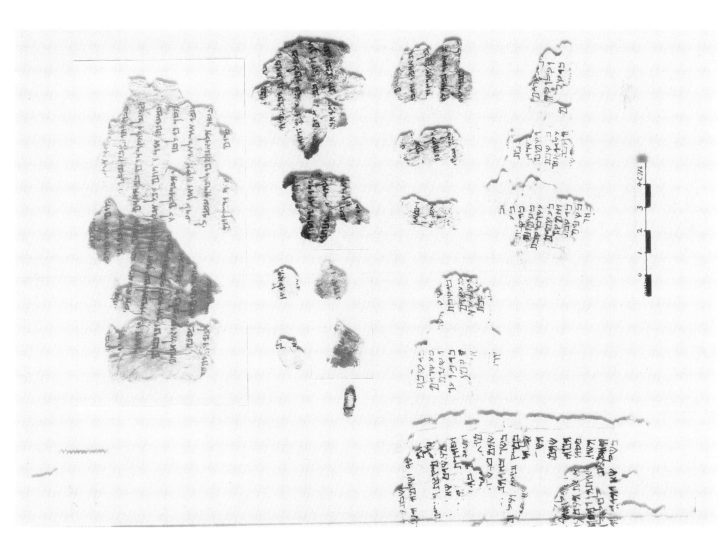

PLATE 1471

PLATE 1474

PLATE 1473

PLATE 1492

PLATE 1491

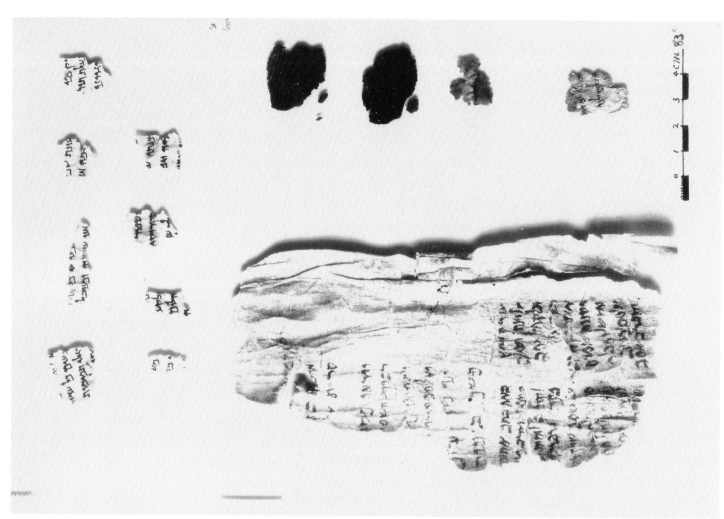

PLATE 1494

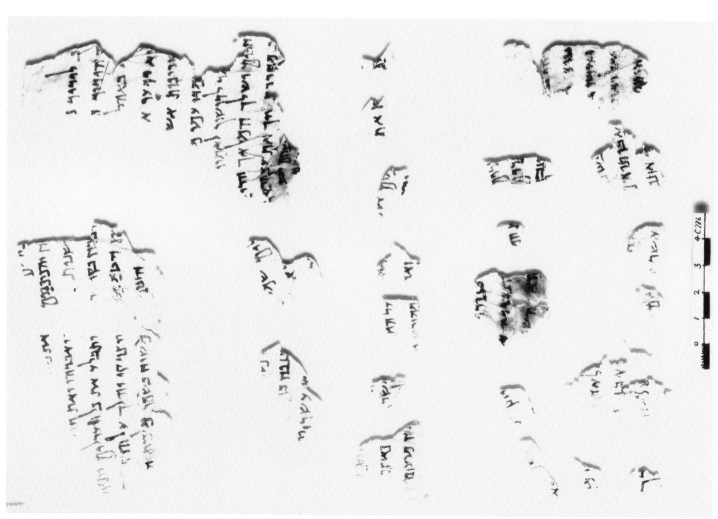

PLATE 1493

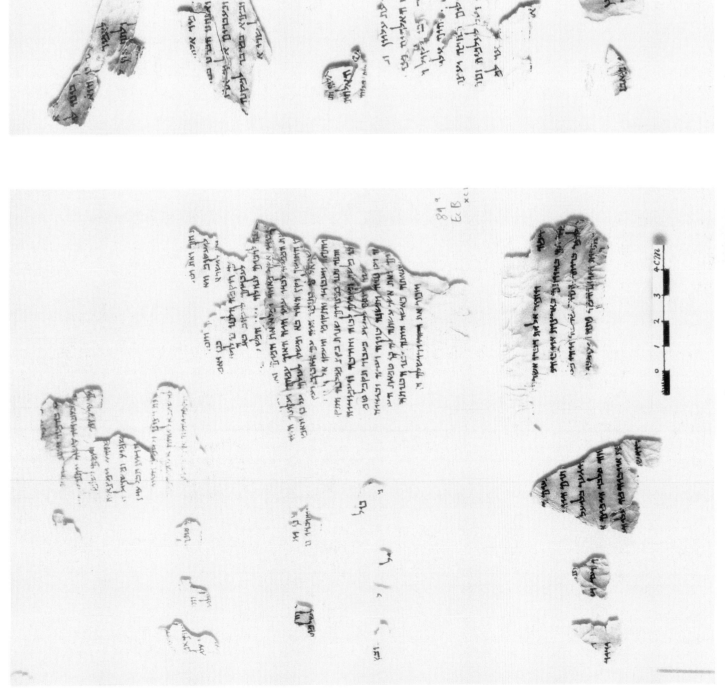

PLATE 1495 PLATE 1496

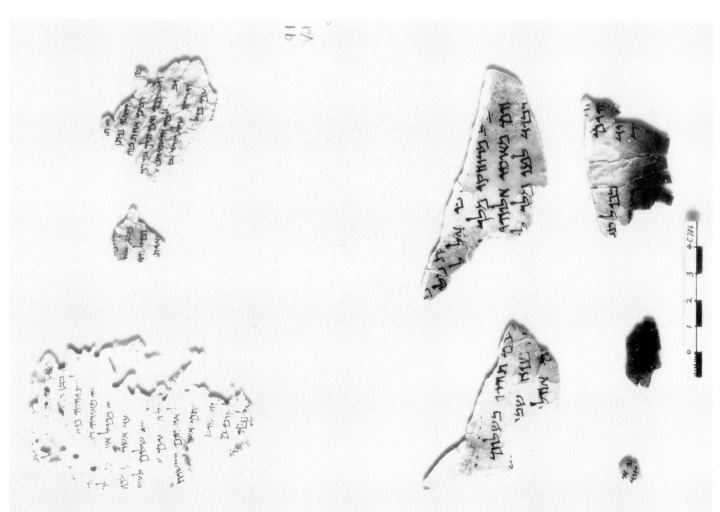

PLATE 1498

PLATE 1497

PLATE 1499

PLATE 1500

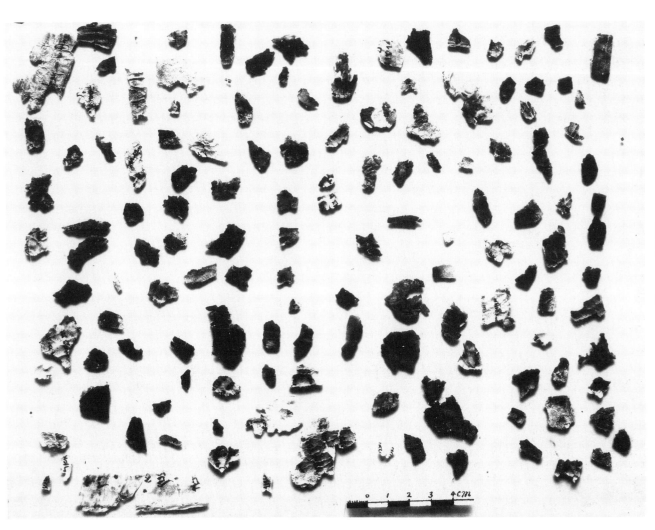

PLATE 1501

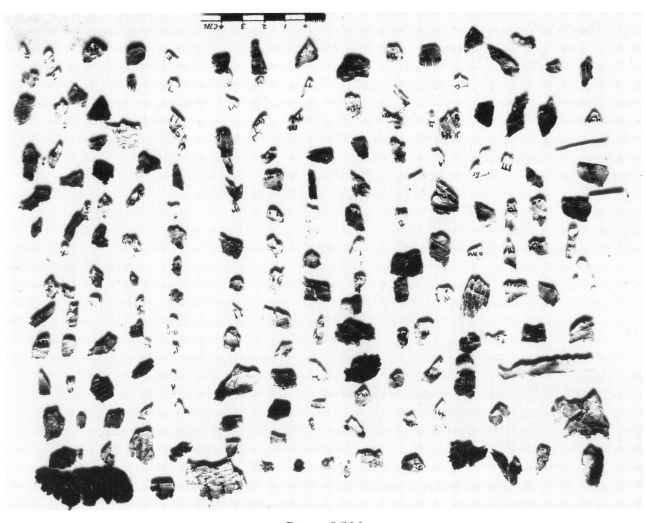

PLATE 1502

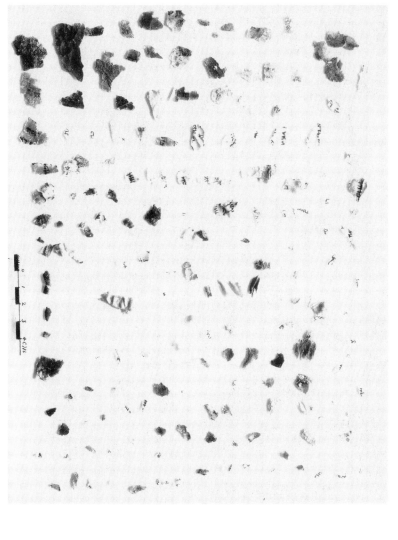

PLATE 1503

PLATE 1504

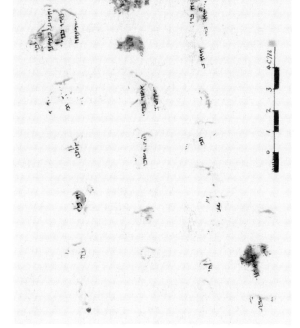

PLATE 1505

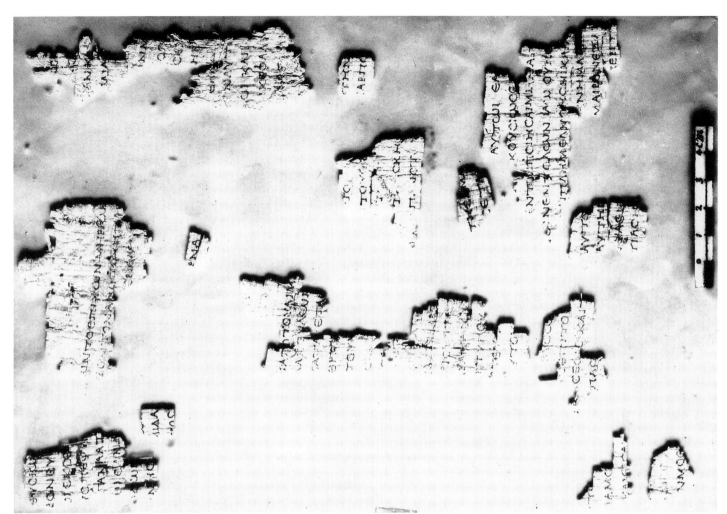

PLATE 1507

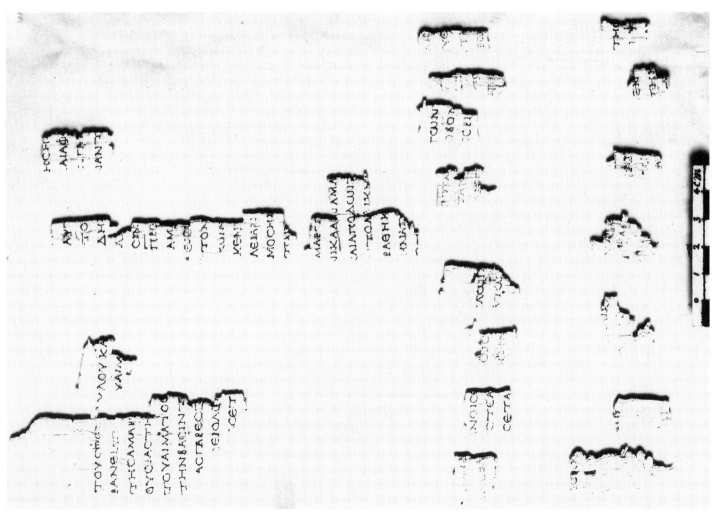

PLATE 1506

PLATE 1509

PLATE 1508

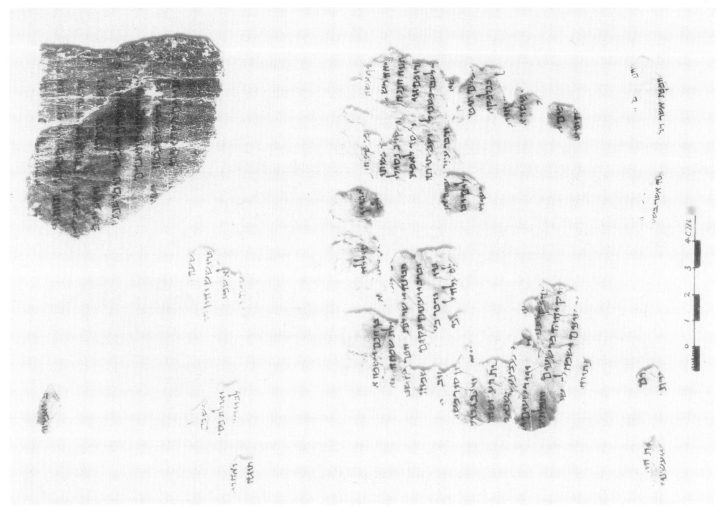

PLATE 1511

PLATE 1510

PLATE 1512

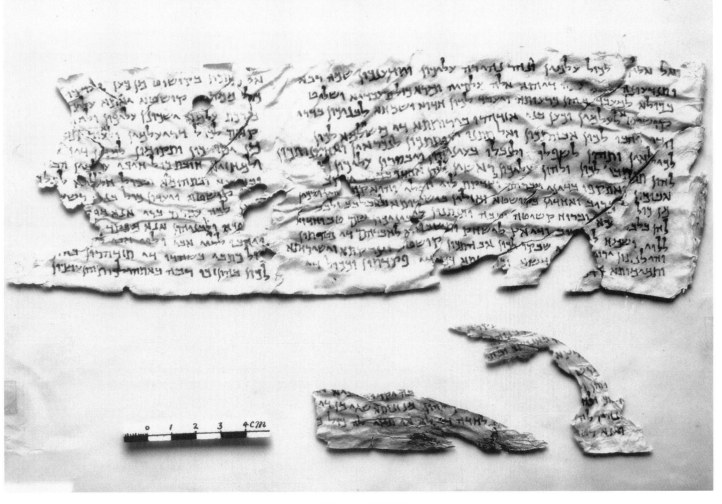

PLATE 1513

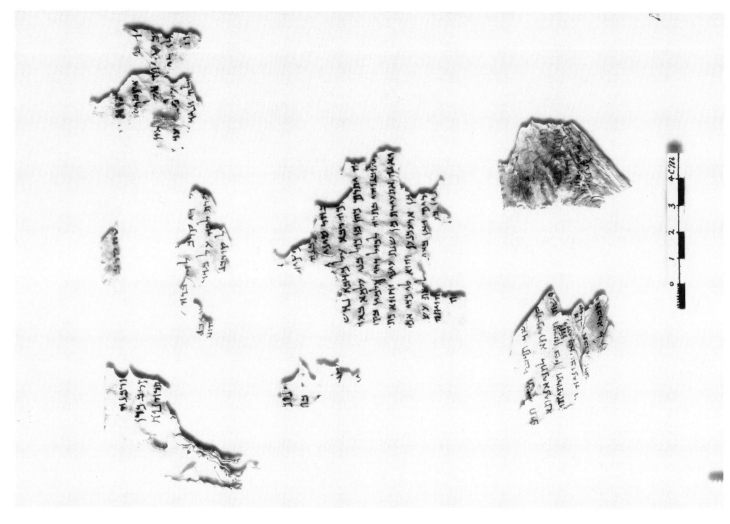

PLATE 1515

PLATE 1514

PLATE 1517

PLATE 1516

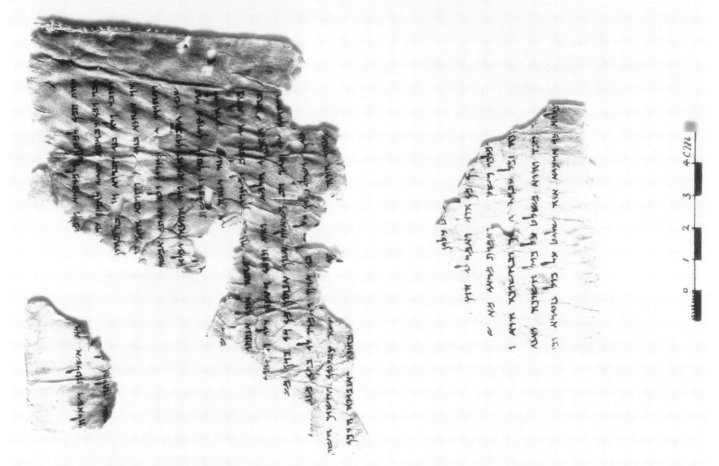

PLATE 1519

PLATE 1518

PLATE 1532

PLATE 1533

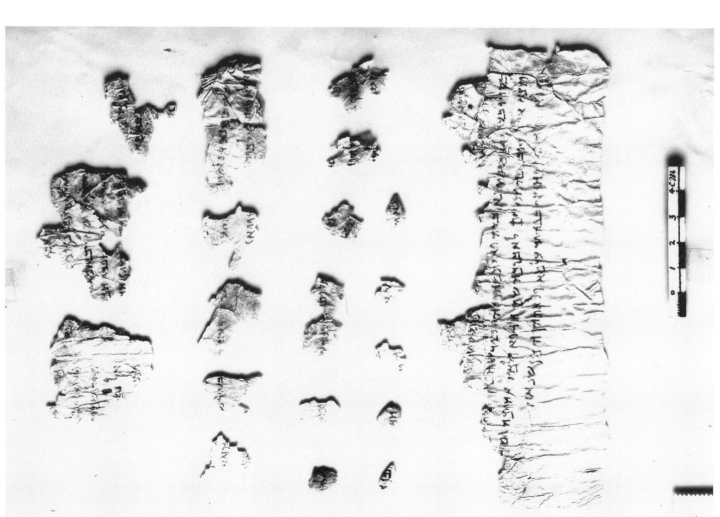

PLATE 1535

PLATE 1534

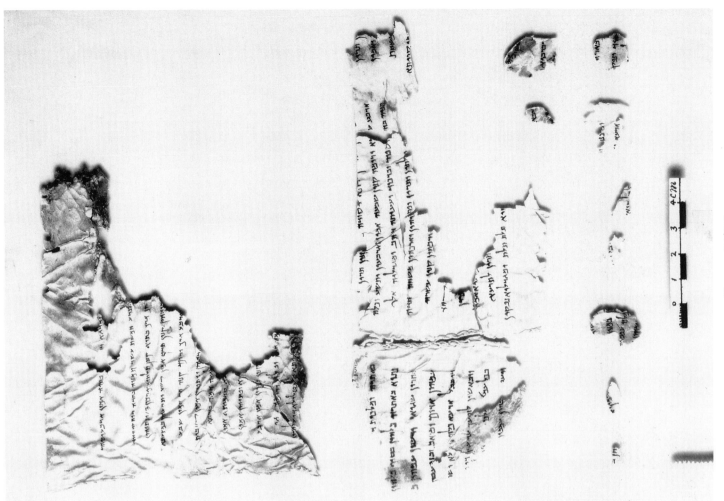

PLATE 1536

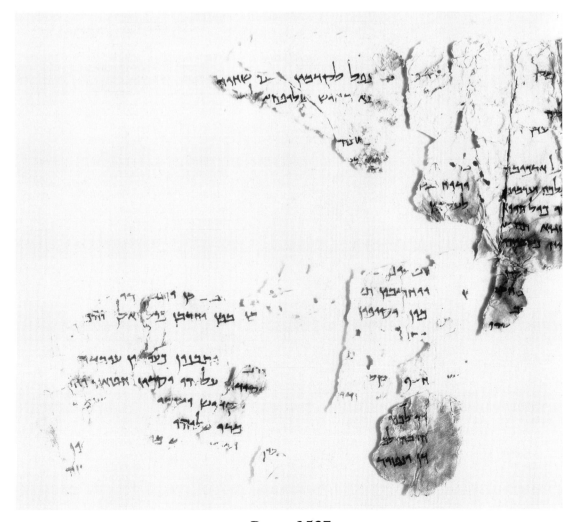

PLATE 1537

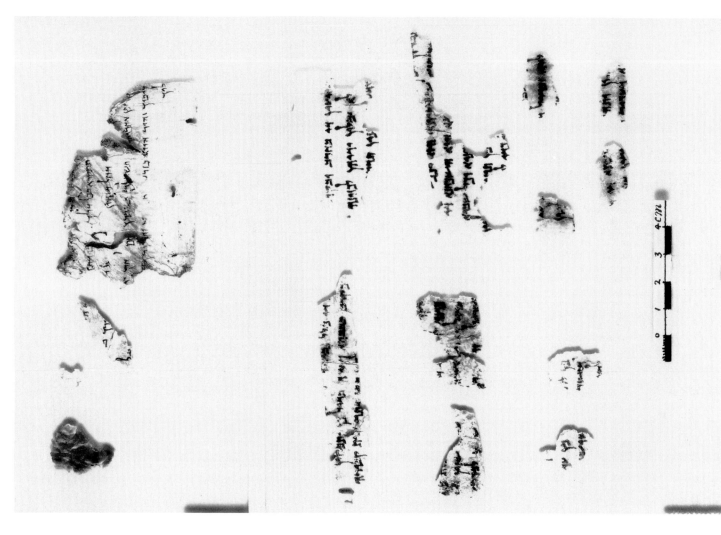

PLATE 1539

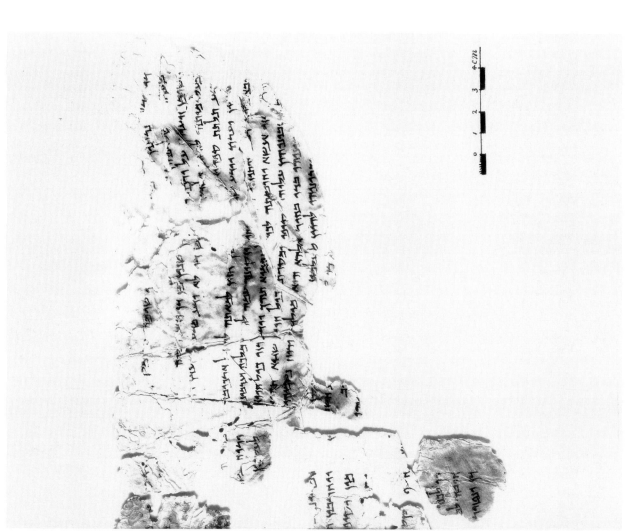

PLATE 1538

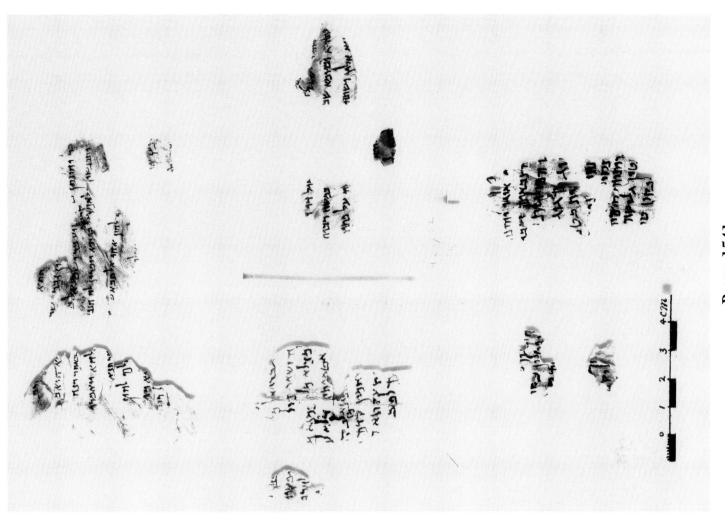

PLATE 1540

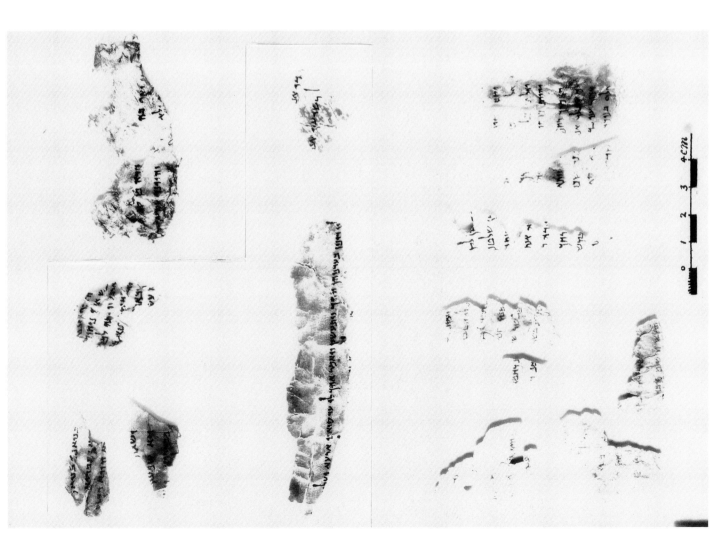

PLATE 1541

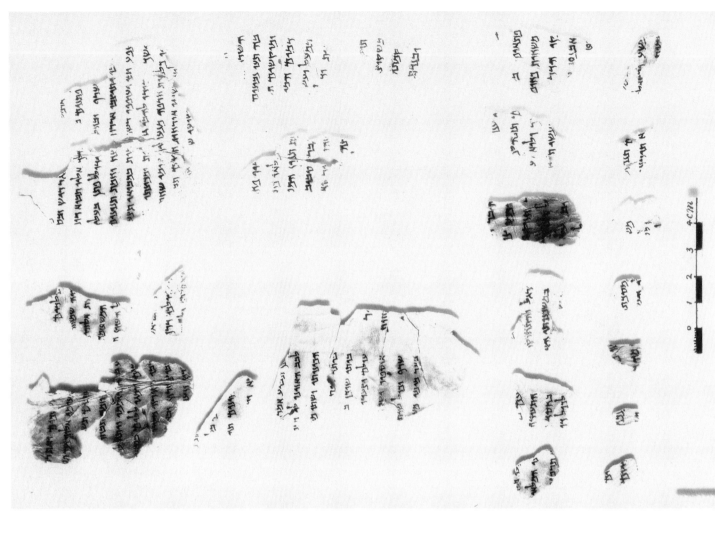

PLATE 1543

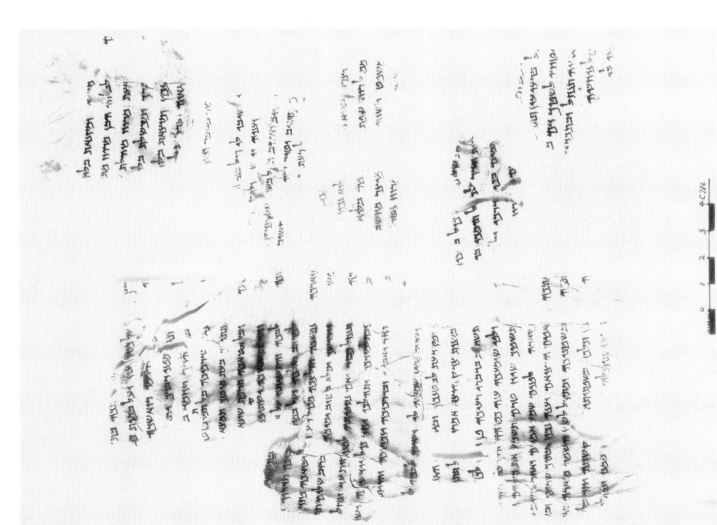

PLATE 1542

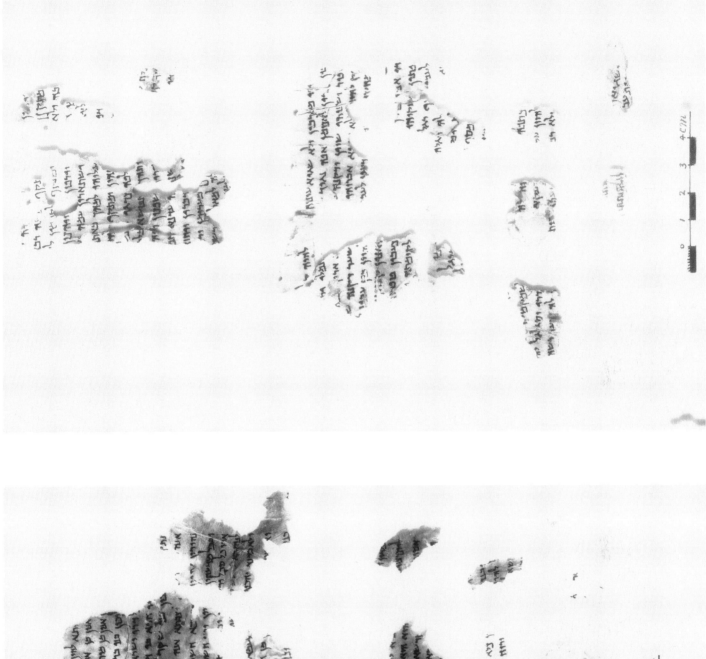

PLATE 1545

PLATE 1544

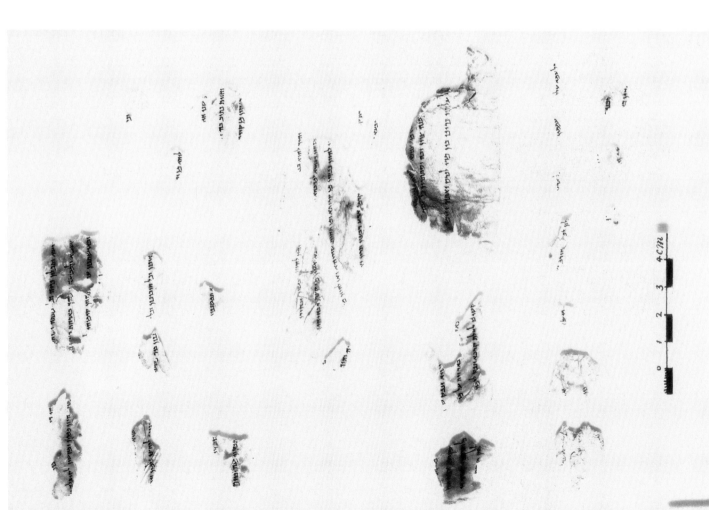

PLATE 1547

PLATE 1546

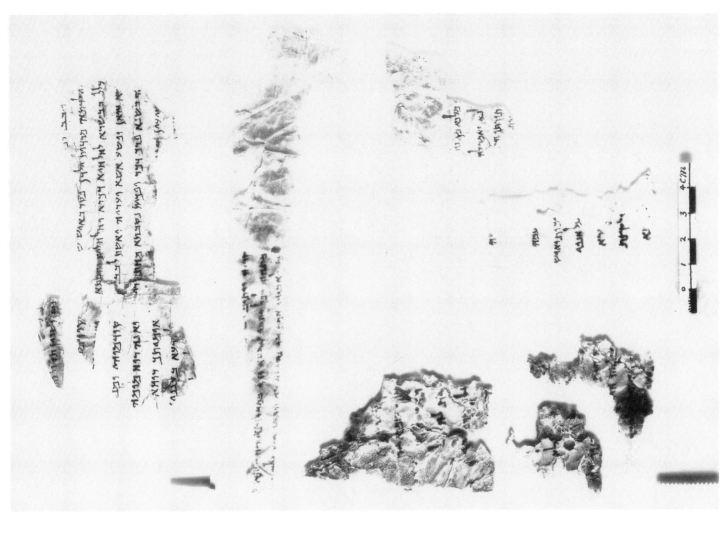

PLATE 1549

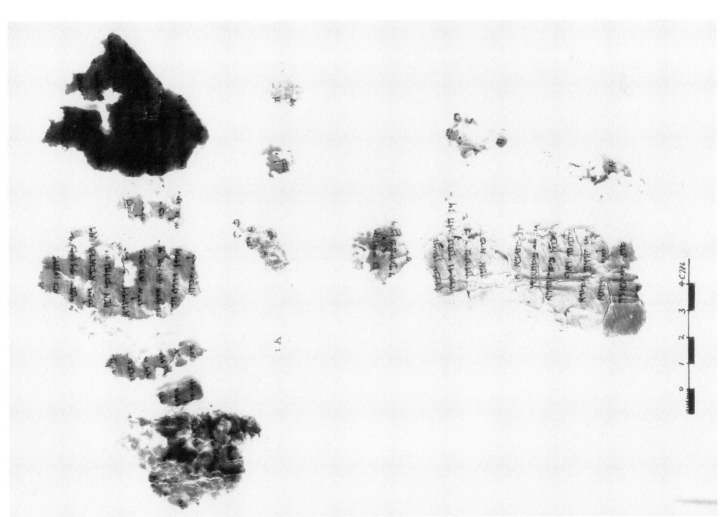

PLATE 1548

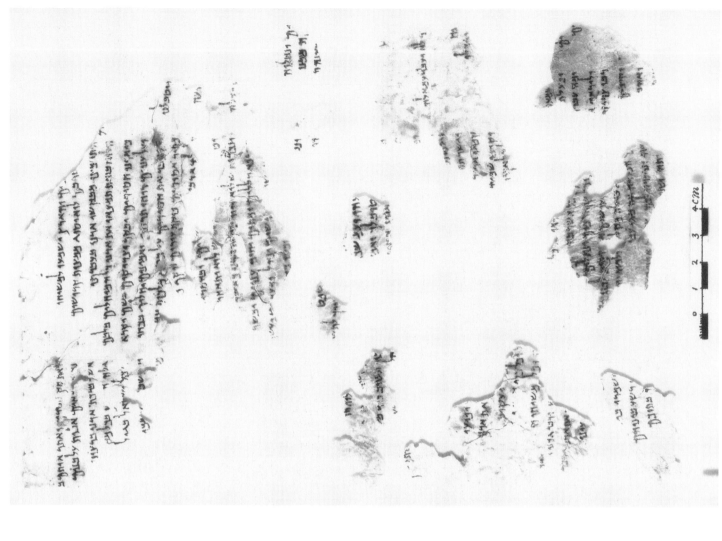

PLATE 1551

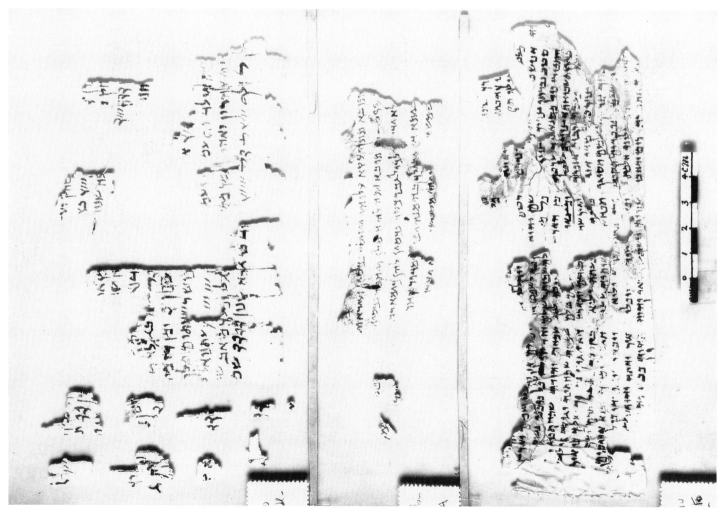

PLATE 1550

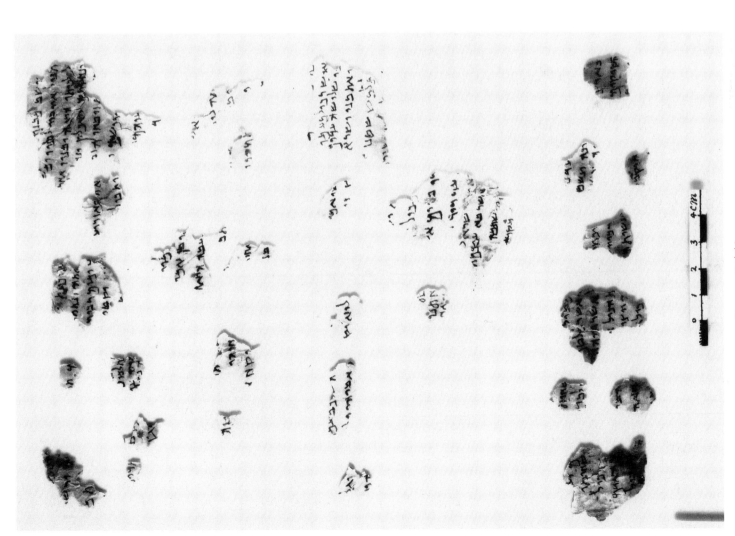

PLATE 1552

PLATE 1553

PLATE 1555

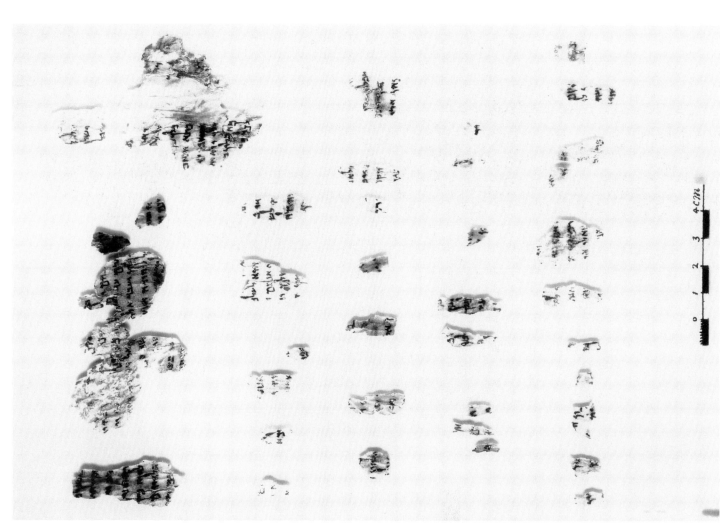

PLATE 1554

PLATE 1556

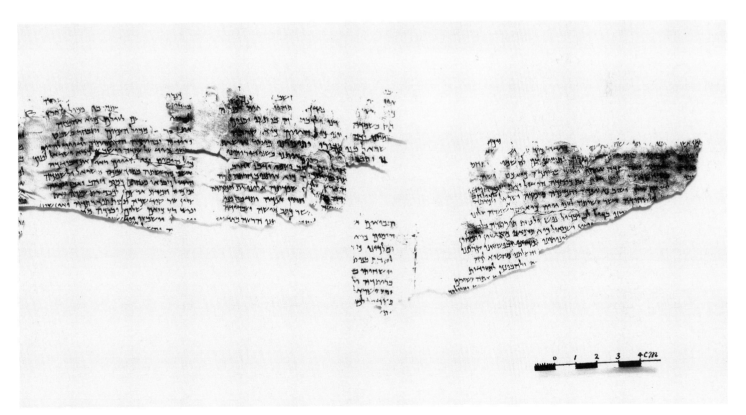

PLATE 1557

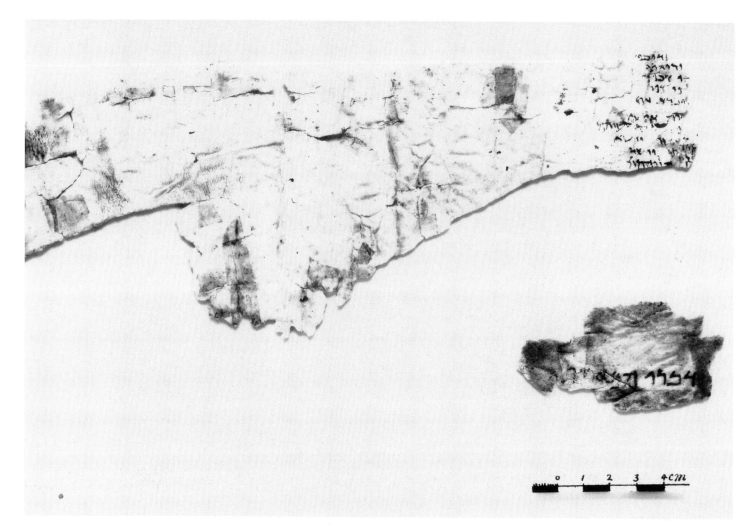

PLATE 1558

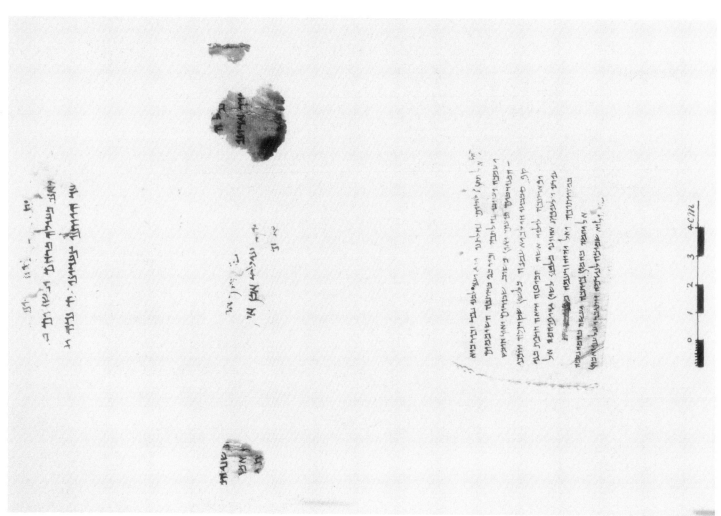

PLATE 1559

PLATE 1560

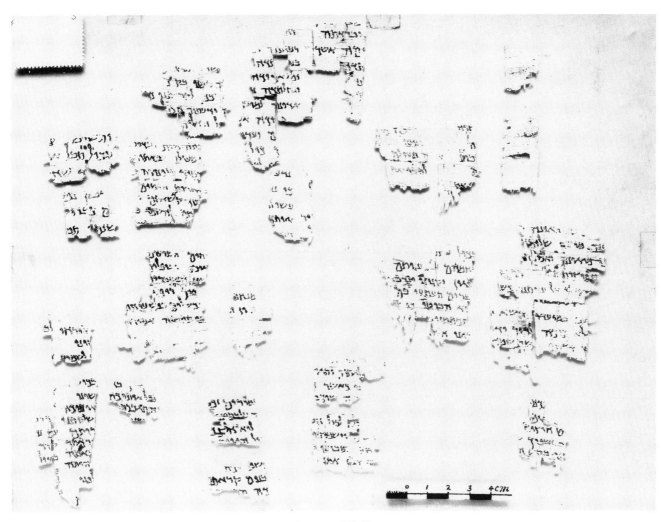

PLATE 1561

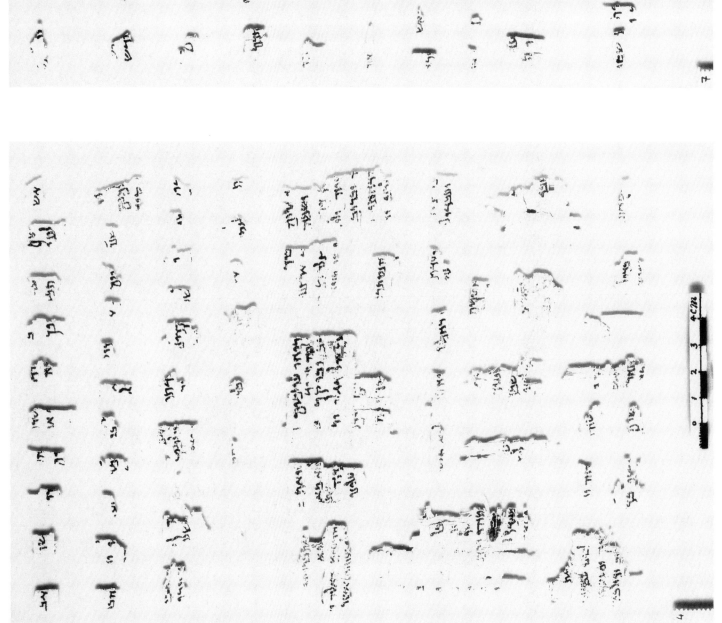

PLATE 1563

PLATE 1562

PLATE 1565

PLATE 1564

PLATE 1566

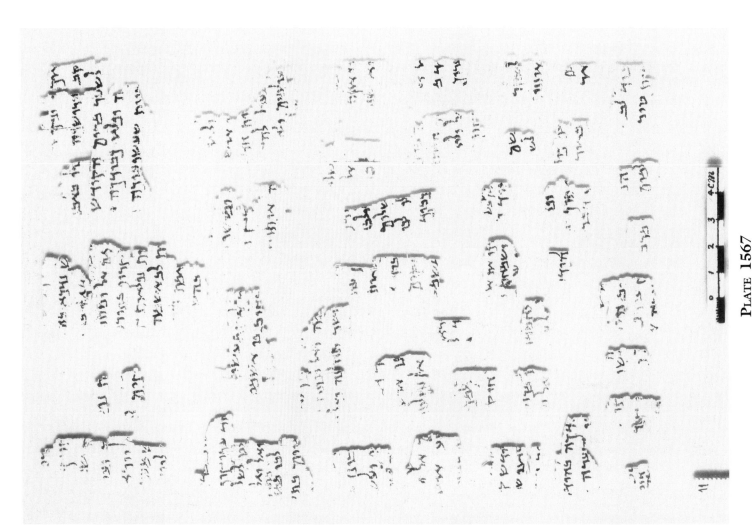

PLATE 1567

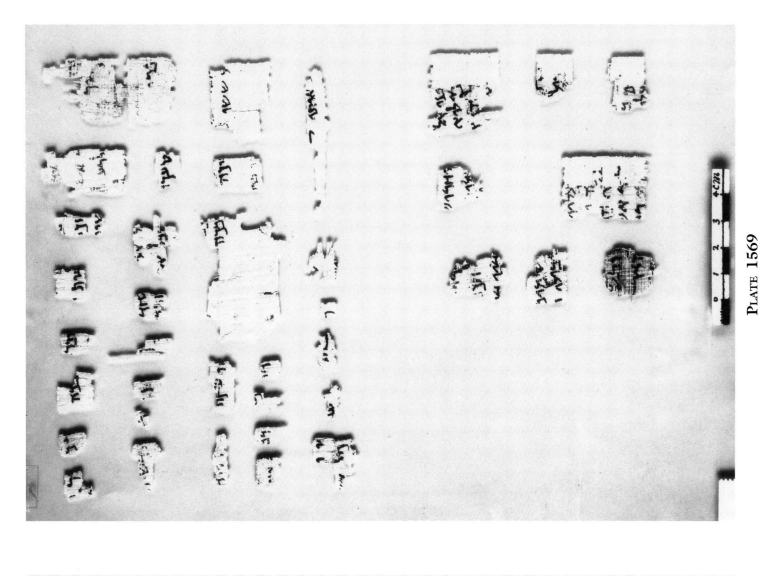

PLATE 1569

PLATE 1568

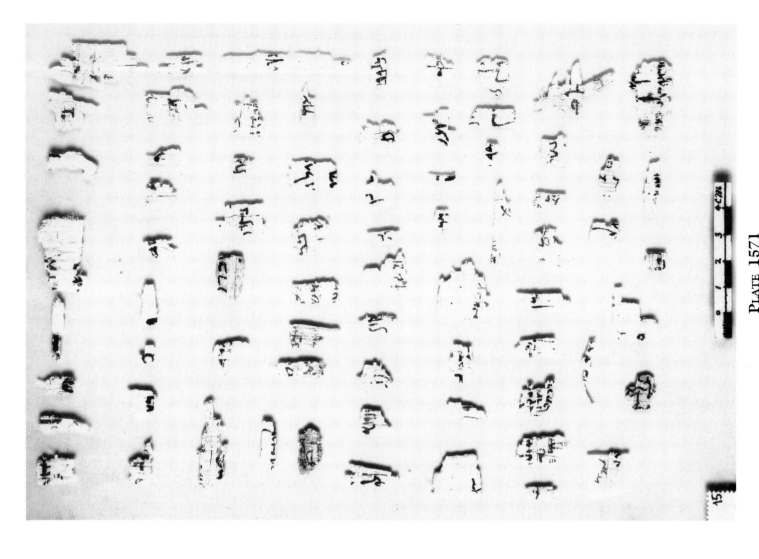

PLATE 1571

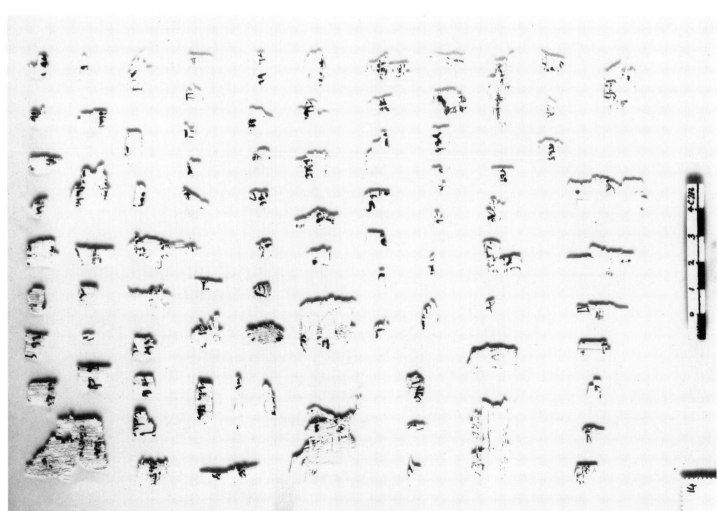

PLATE 1570

PLATE 1573

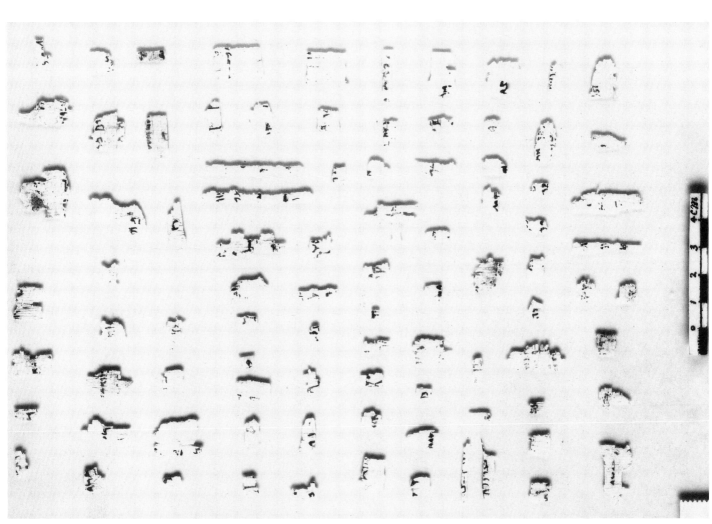

PLATE 1572

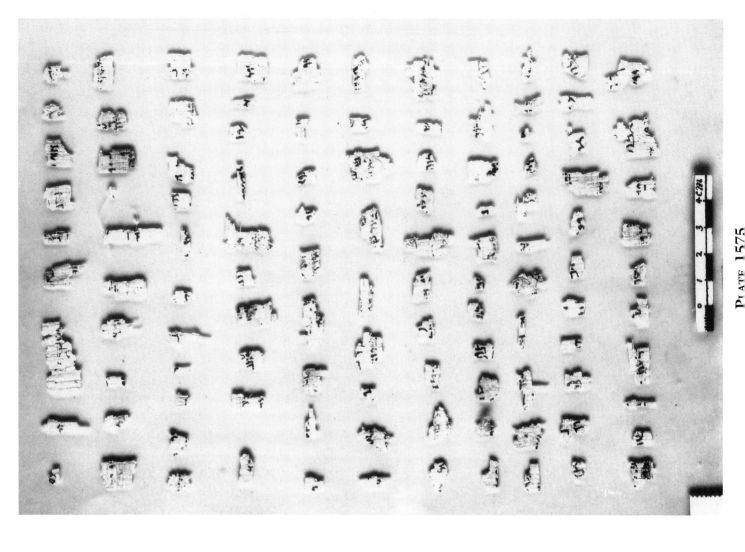

PLATE 1575

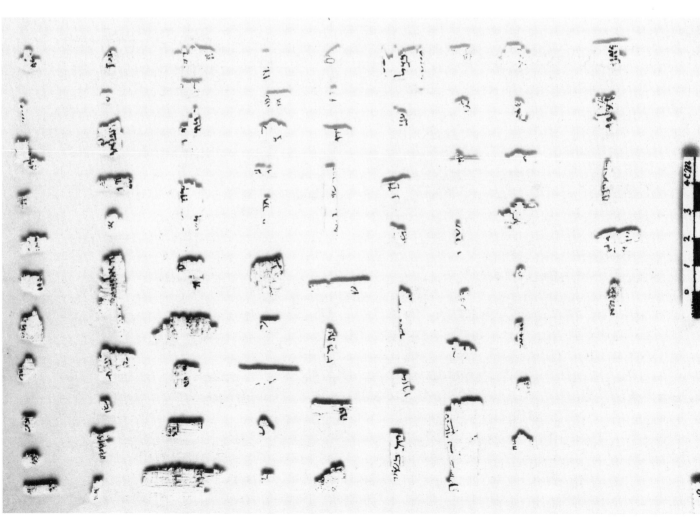

PLATE 1574

PLATE 1577

PLATE 1576

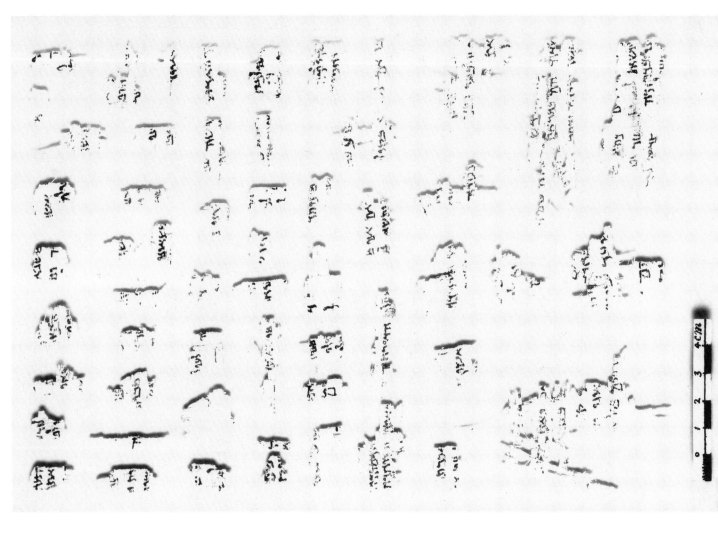

PLATE 1579

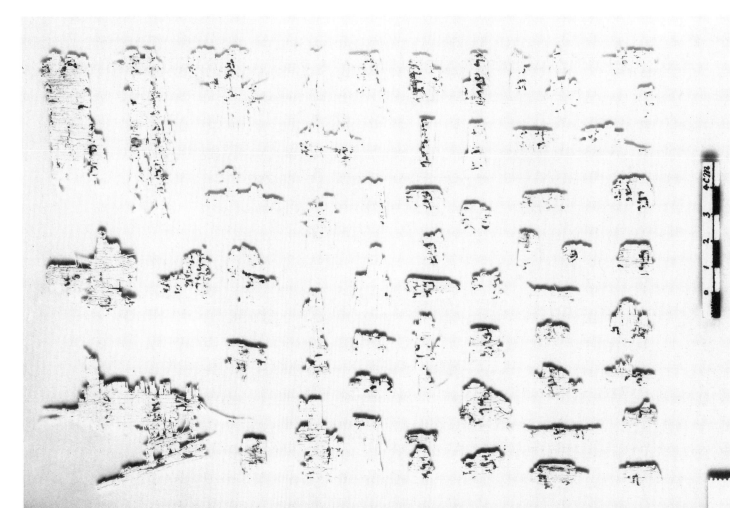

PLATE 1578

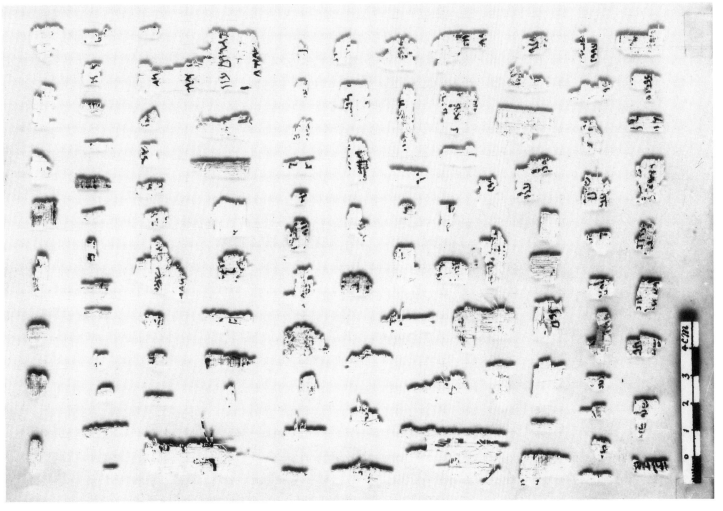

PLATE 1581

PLATE 1580

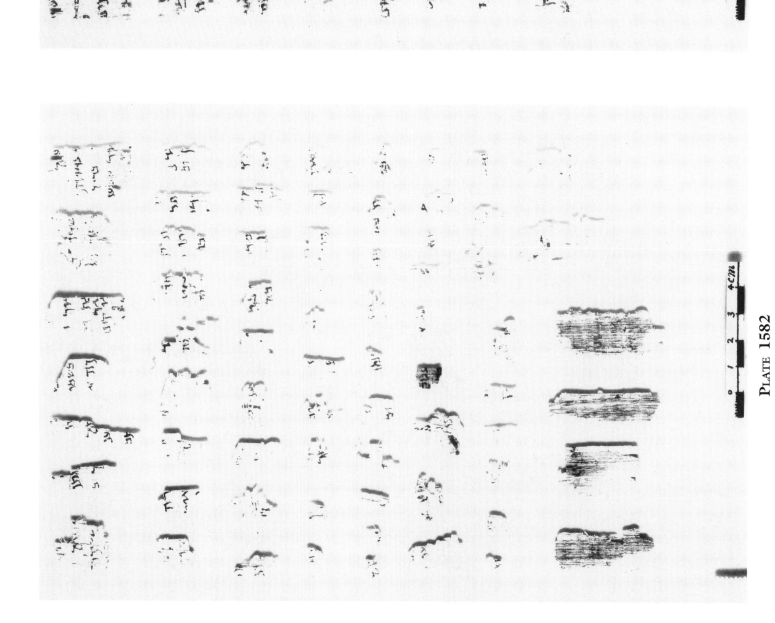

PLATE 1582   PLATE 1583

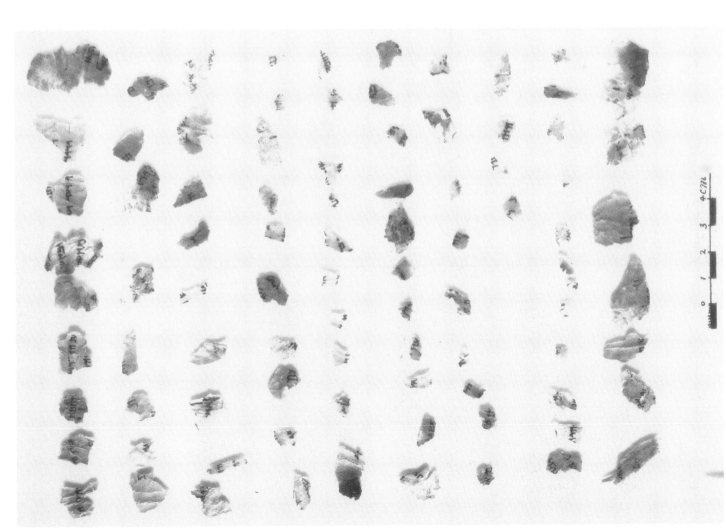

PLATE 1593

PLATE 1592

PLATE 1595

PLATE 1594

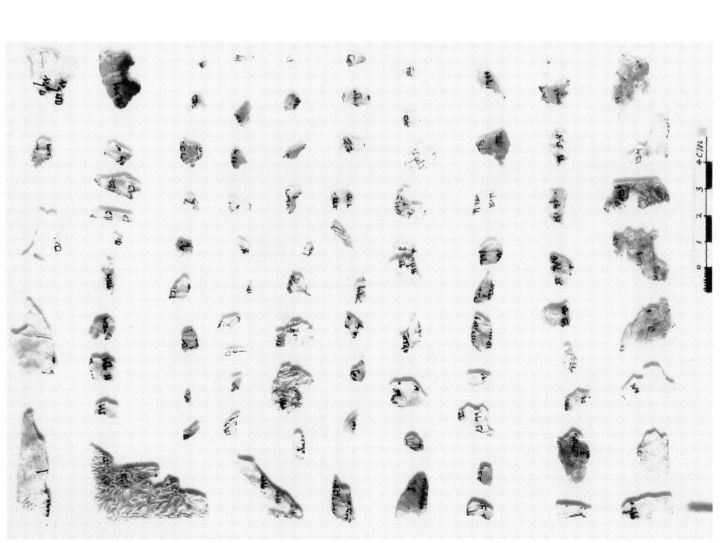

PLATE 1596   PLATE 1597

PLATE 1599

PLATE 1598

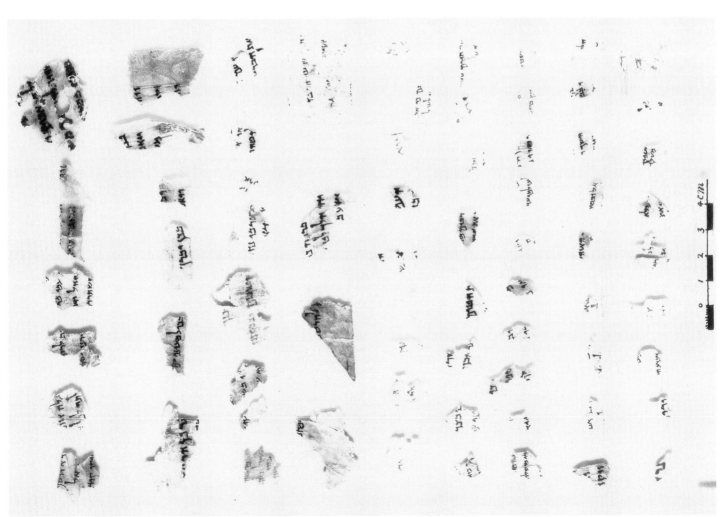

PLATE 1601

PLATE 1600

PLATE 1603

PLATE 1602

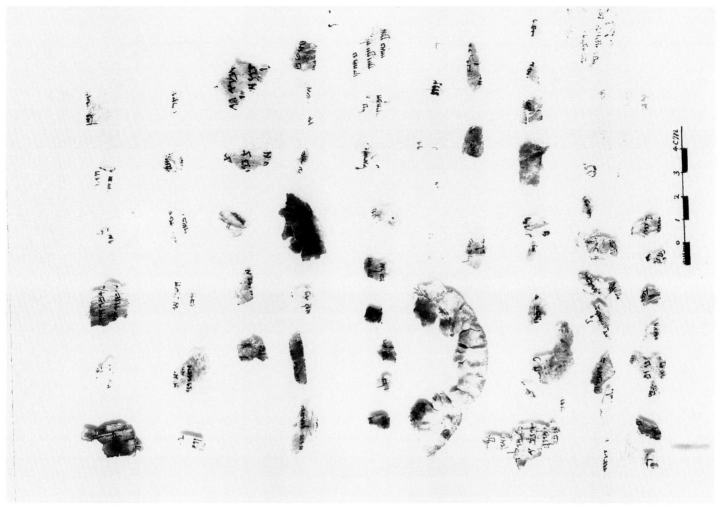

PLATE 1605

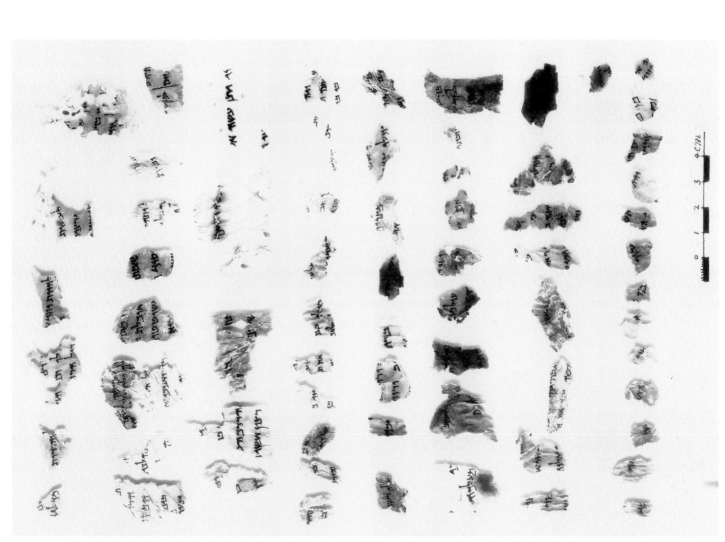

PLATE 1604

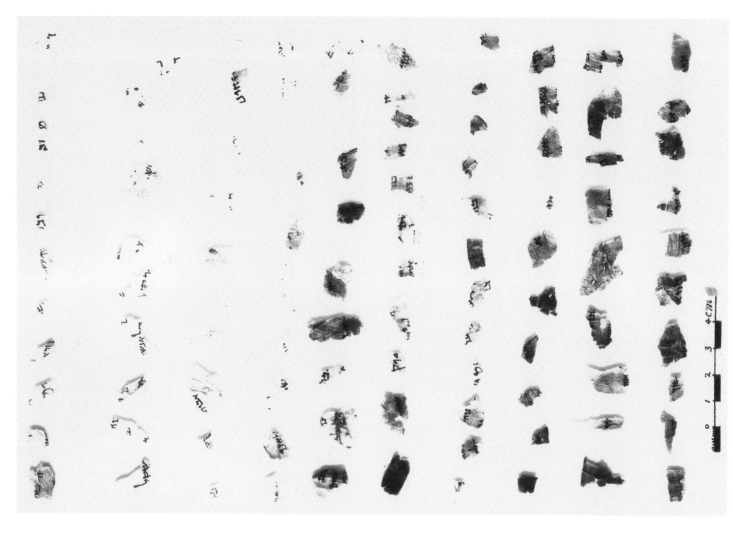

PLATE 1607

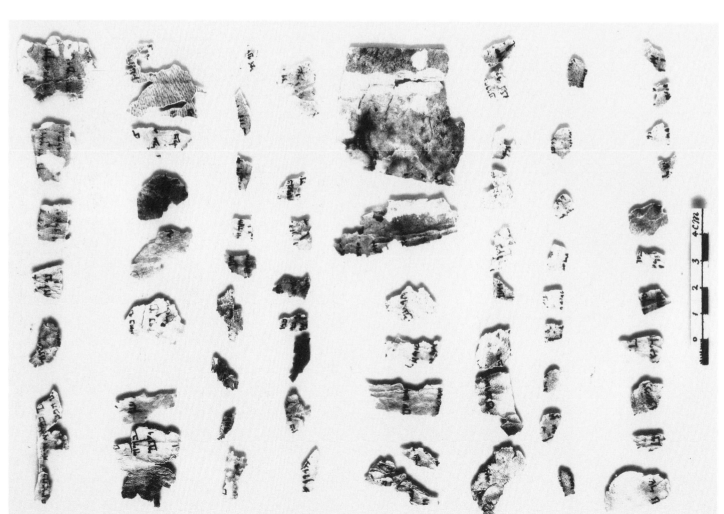

PLATE 1606

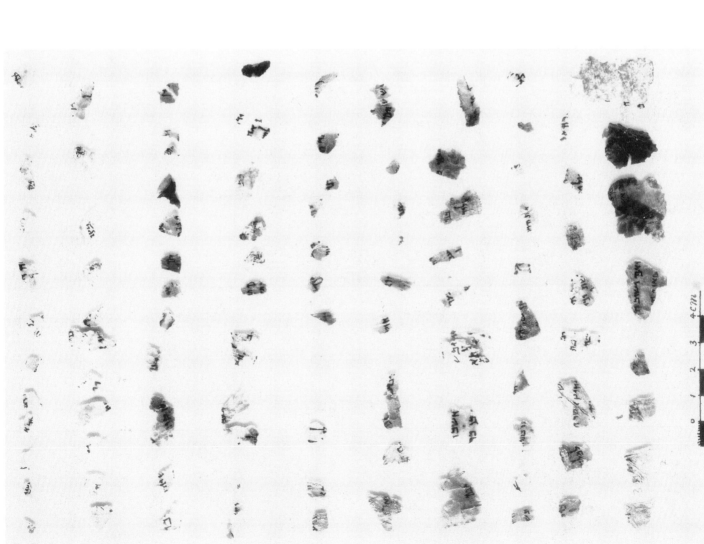

PLATE 1609

PLATE 1608

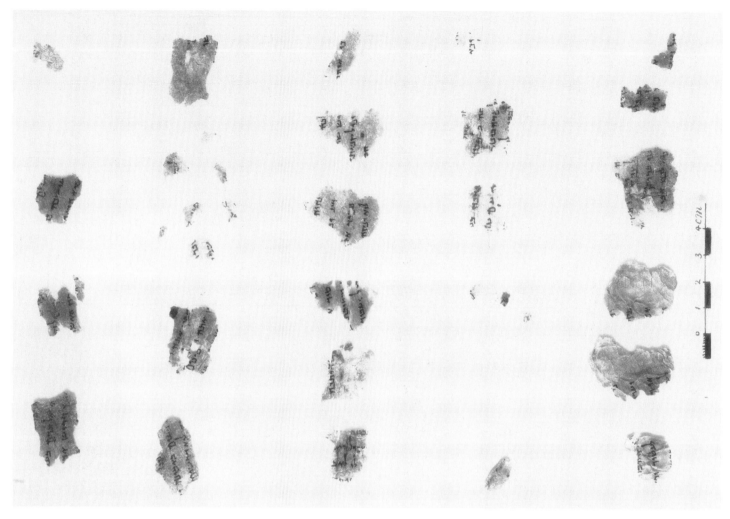

PLATE 1611

PLATE 1610

PLATE 1612

PLATE 1613

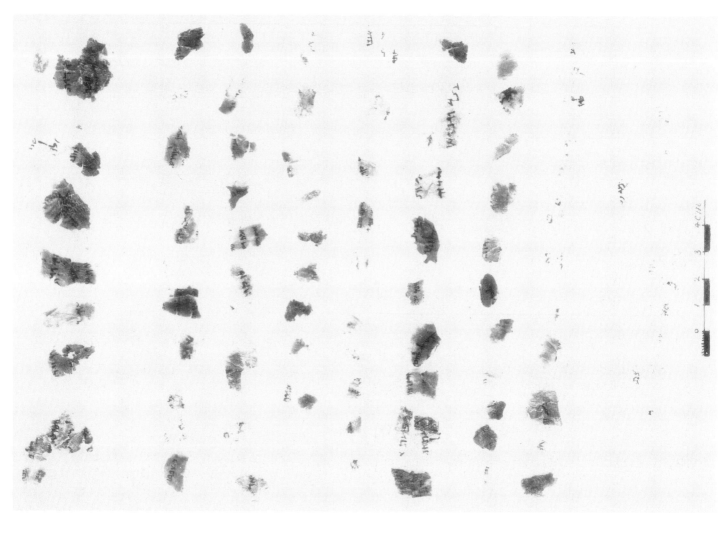

PLATE 1615

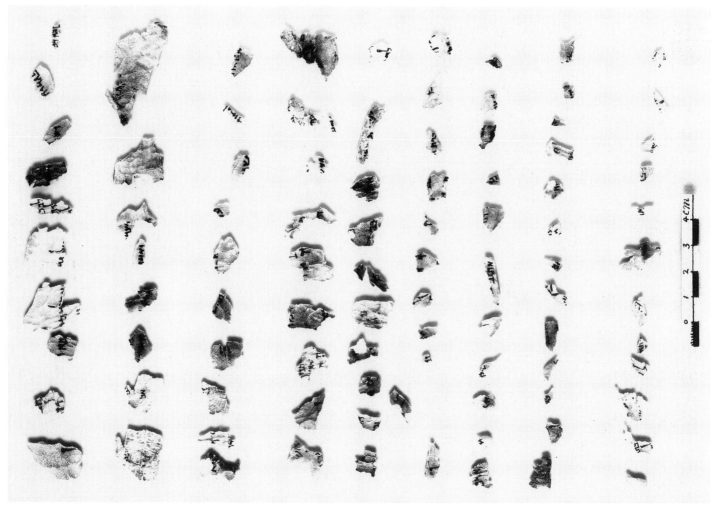

PLATE 1614

PLATE 1617

PLATE 1616

PLATE 1619

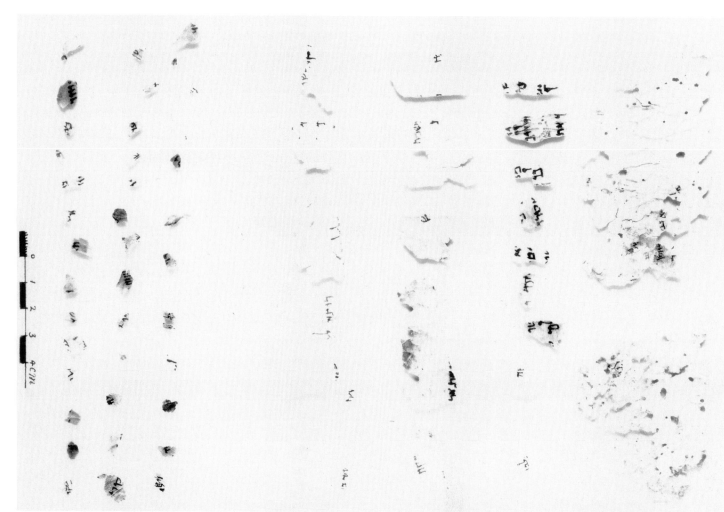

PLATE 1618

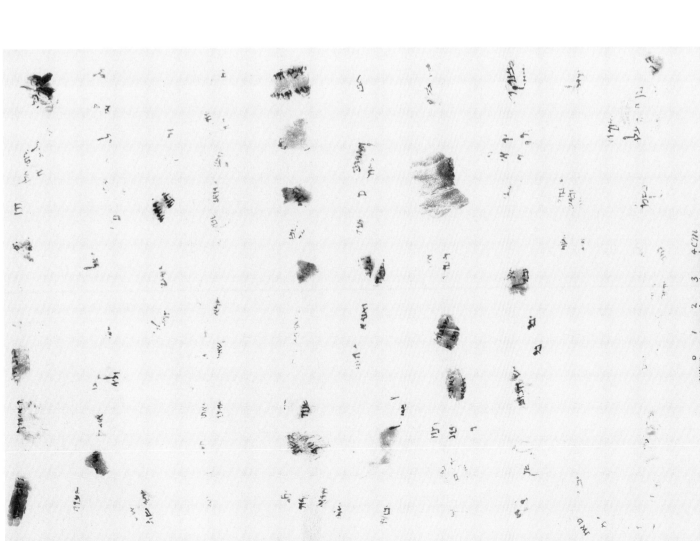

PLATE 1621

PLATE 1620

PLATE 1623

PLATE 1622

PLATE 1625

PLATE 1624

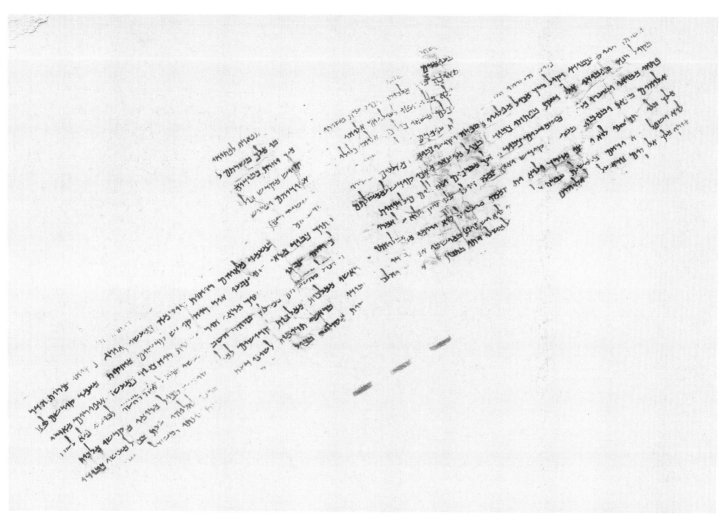

PLATE 1626

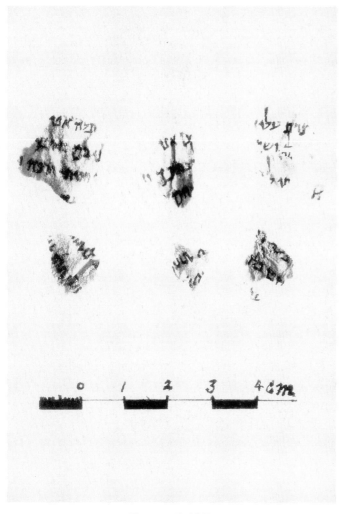

PLATE 1627

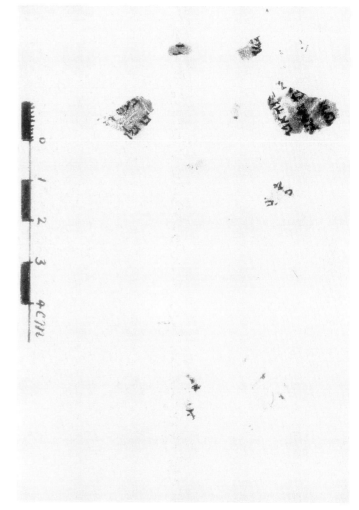

PLATE 1628

PLATE 1629

PLATE 1630

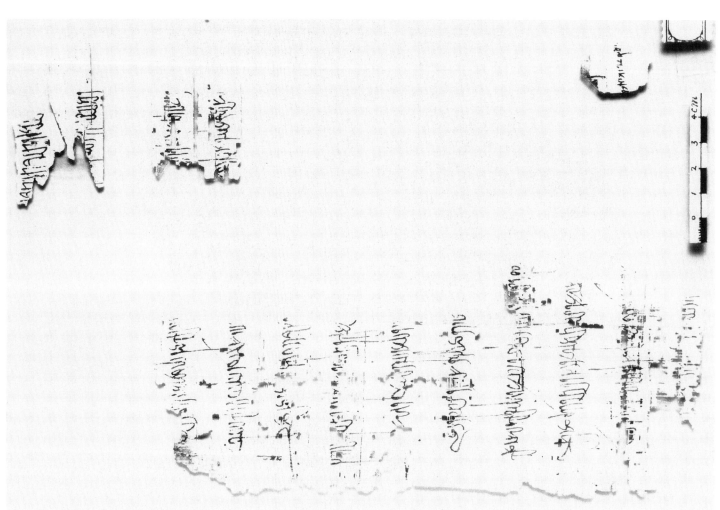

PLATE 1631

PLATE 1632

PLATE 1633

PLATE 1634

PLATE 1635

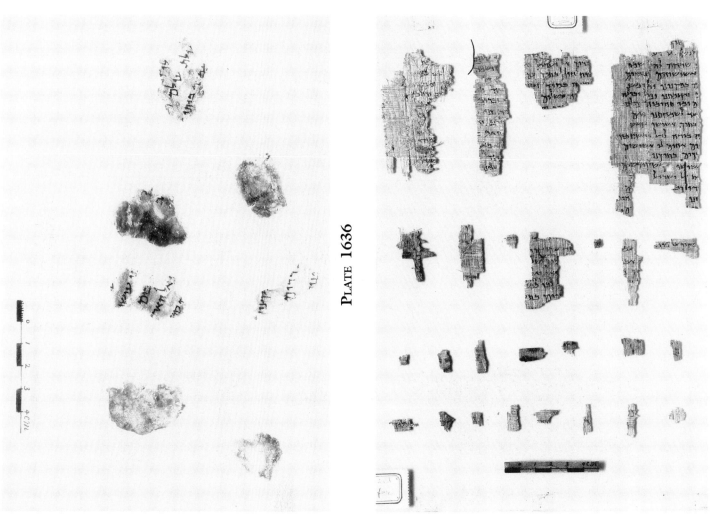

PLATE 1636

PLATE 1637

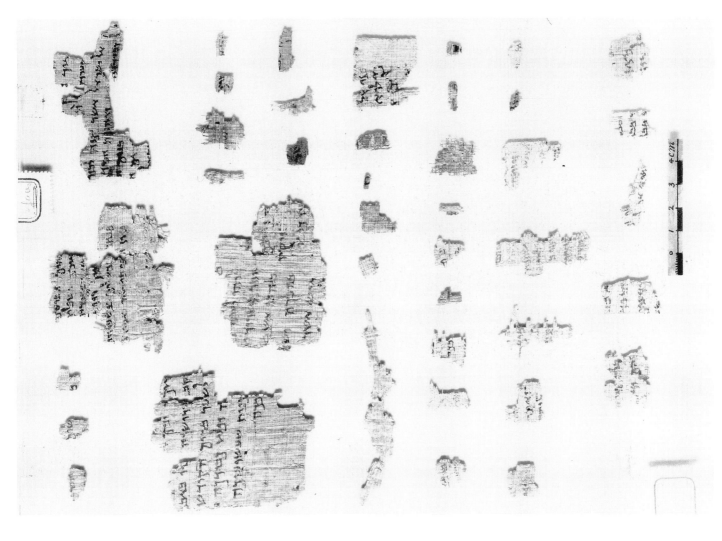

PLATE 1639

PLATE 1638

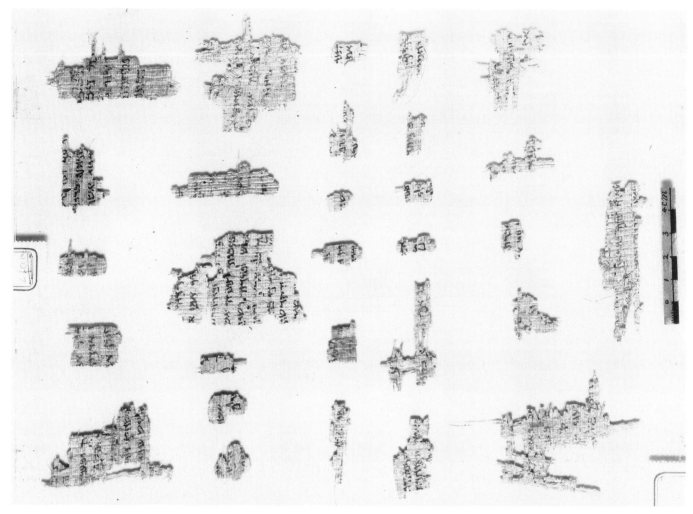

PLATE 1641

PLATE 1640

PLATE 1669

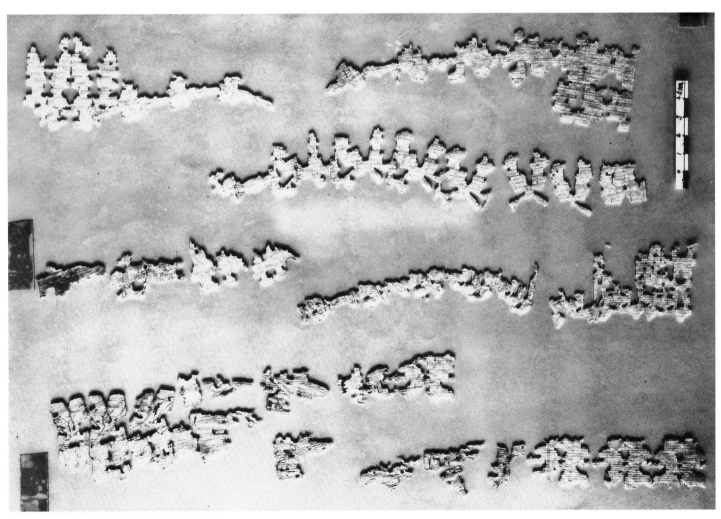

PLATE 1668

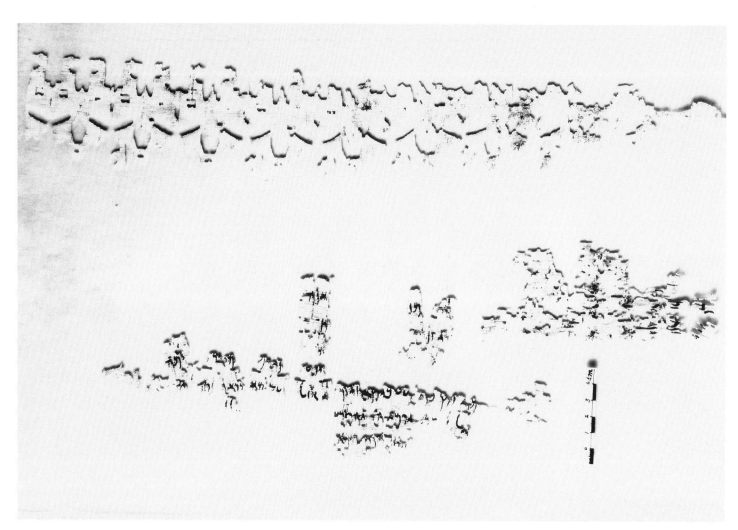

PLATE 1670

PLATE 1671

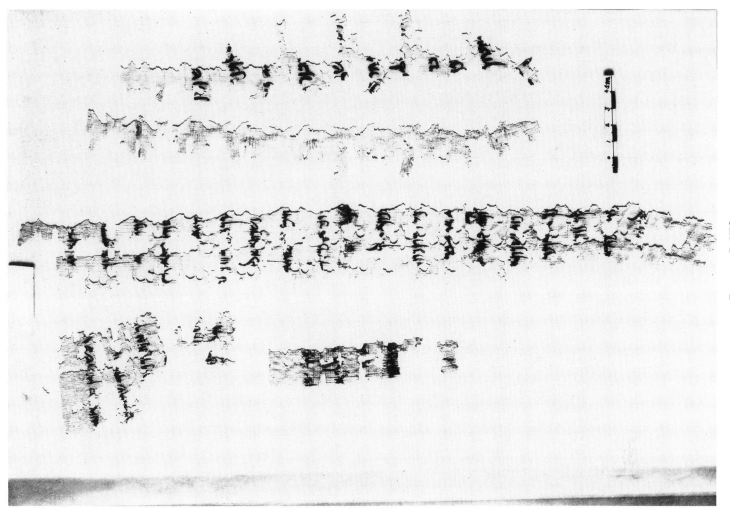

PLATE 1673

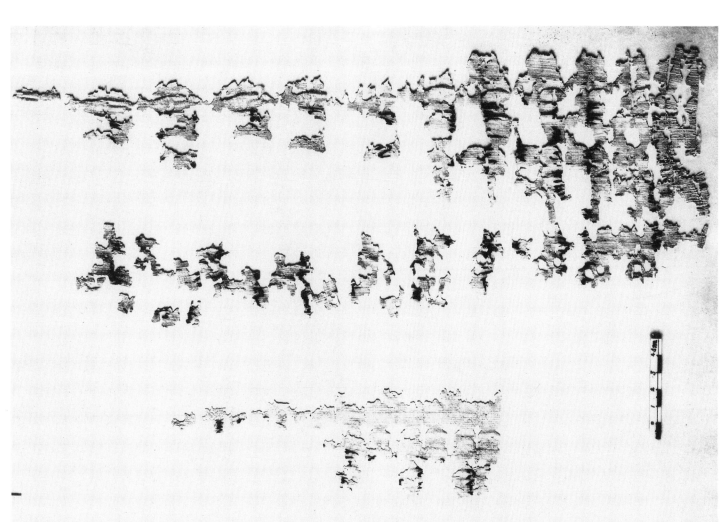

PLATE 1672

PLATE 1675

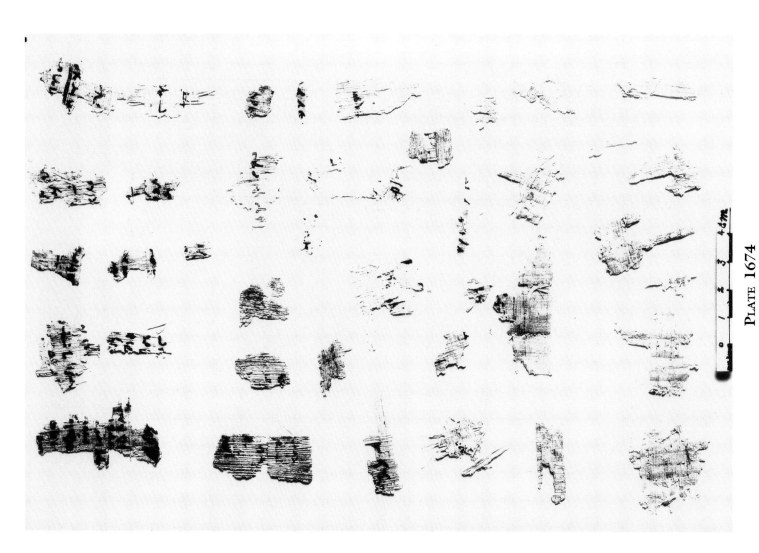

PLATE 1674

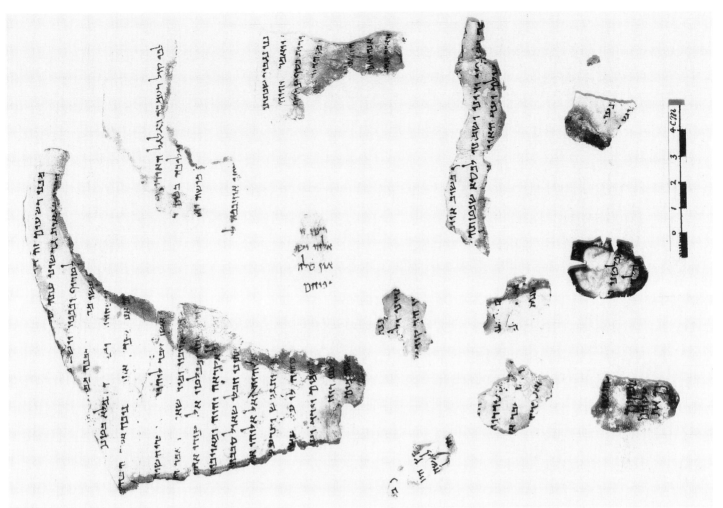

Plate 1689

Plate 1690

PLATE 1691

PLATE 1692

PLATE 1693

PLATE 1694

PLATE 1695

PLATE 1696

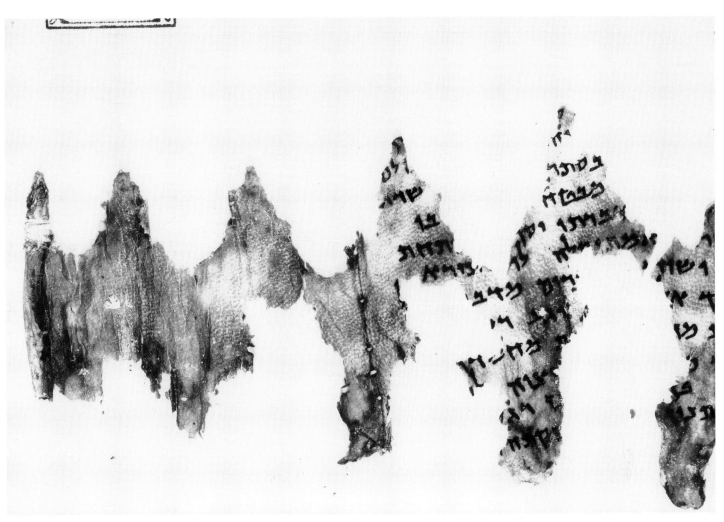

PLATE 1697

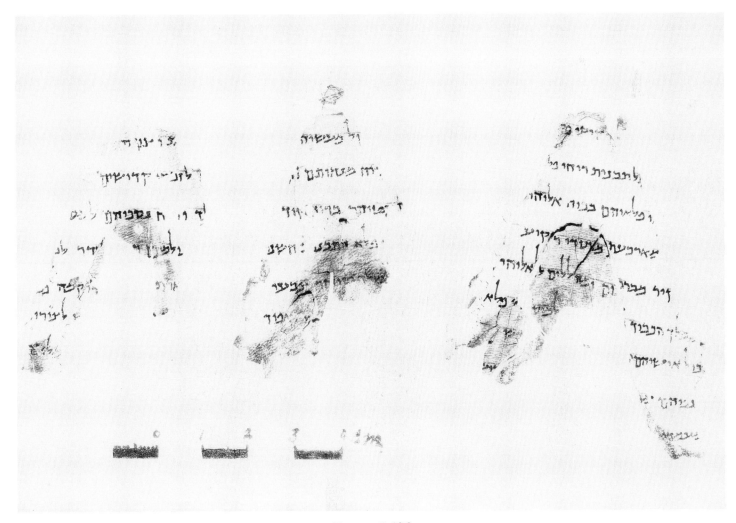

PLATE 1698

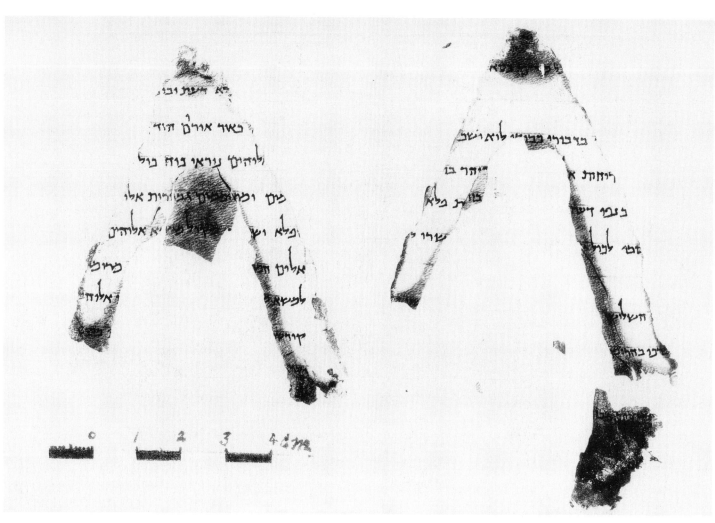

PLATE 1699

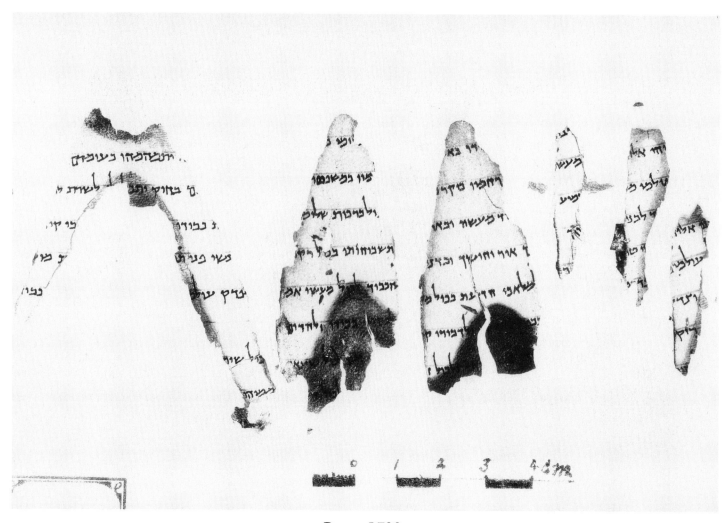

PLATE 1700

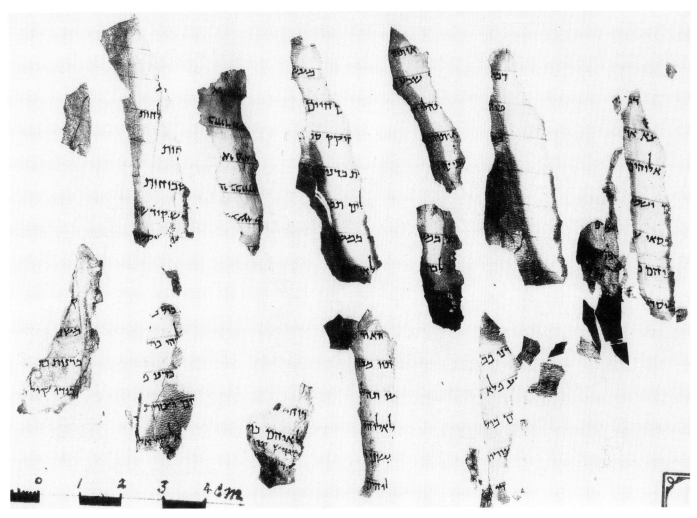

PLATE 1701

PLATE 1702

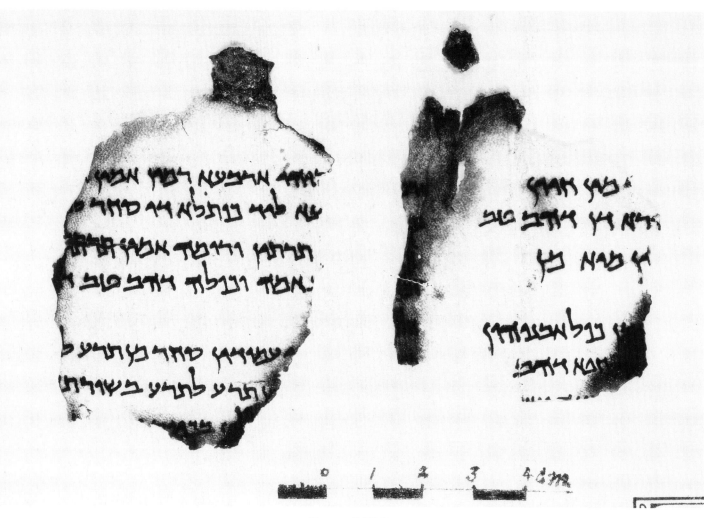

PLATE 1703

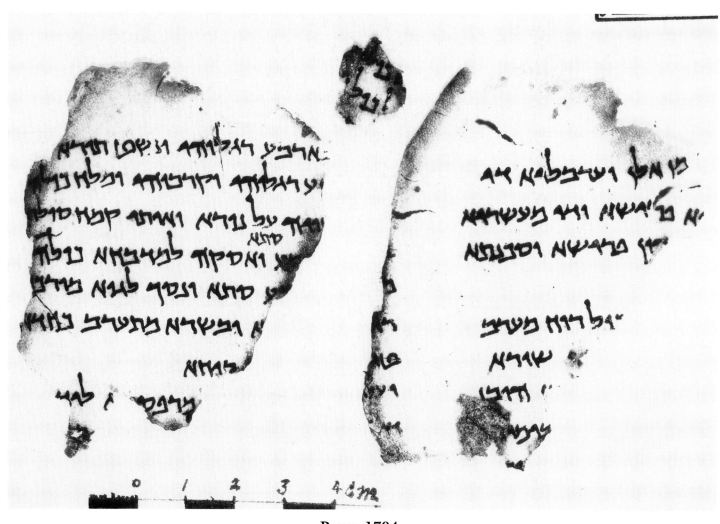

PLATE 1704

PLATE 1705

PLATE 1706

PLATE 1707

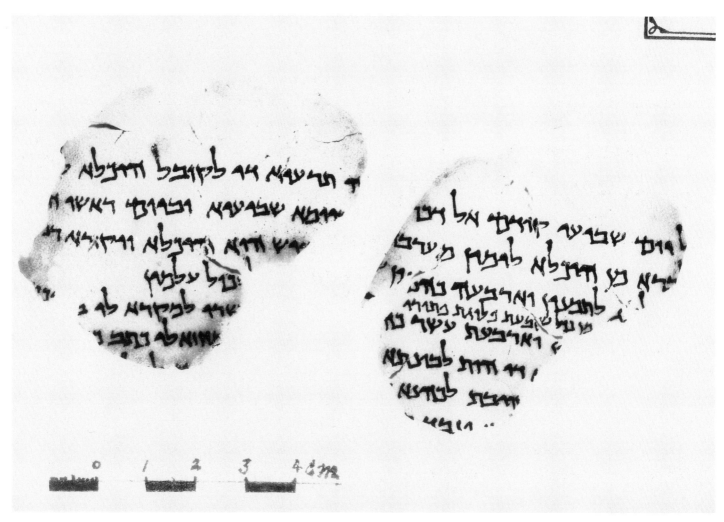

PLATE 1708

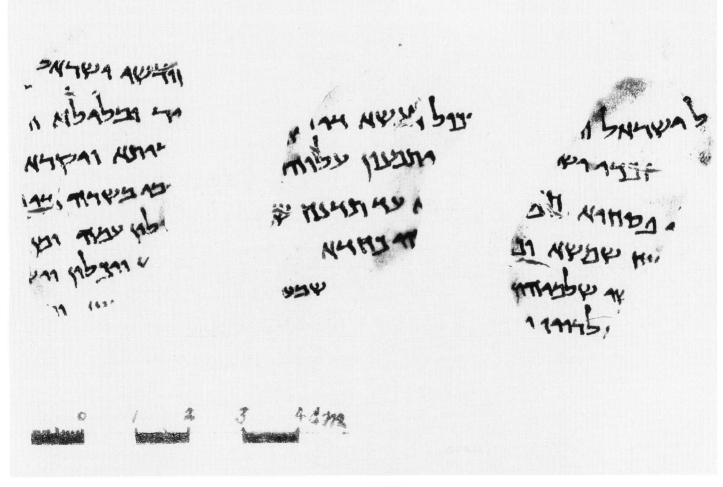

PLATE 1709

PLATE 1710

PLATE 1711

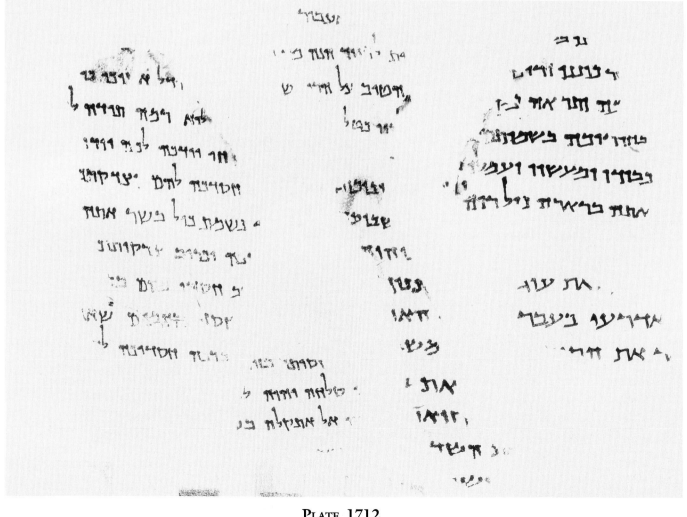

PLATE 1712

PLATE 1713

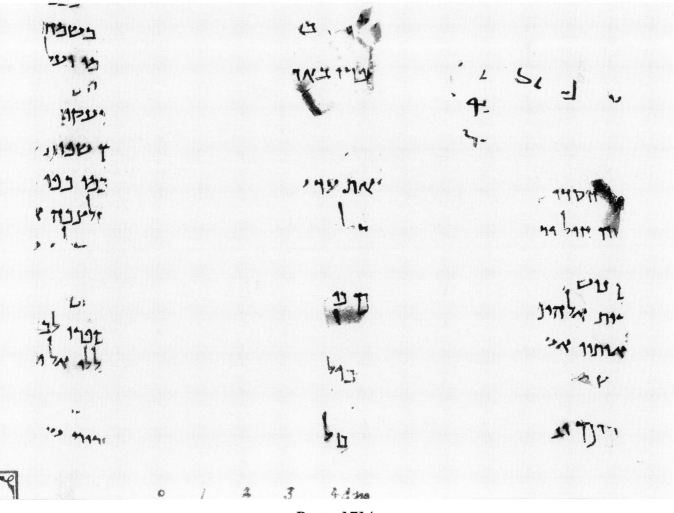

PLATE 1714

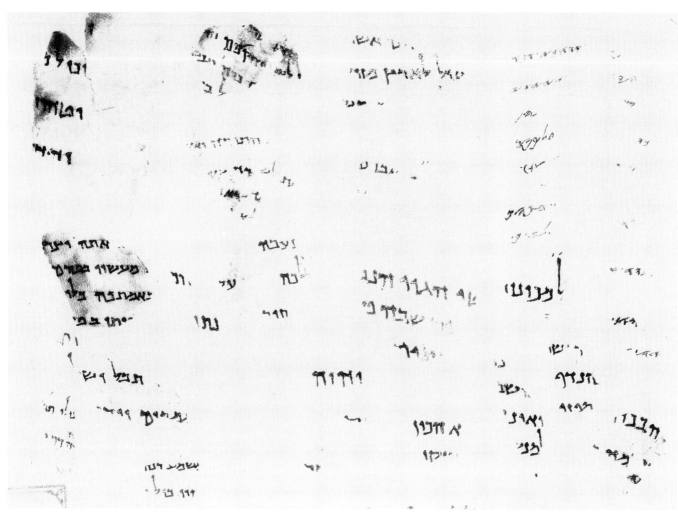

PLATE 1715

PLATE 1716

PLATE 1750

PLATE 1749

PLATE 1752

PLATE 1751

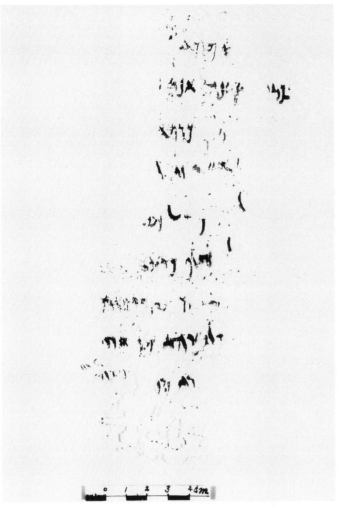

Plate 1753

Plate 1754

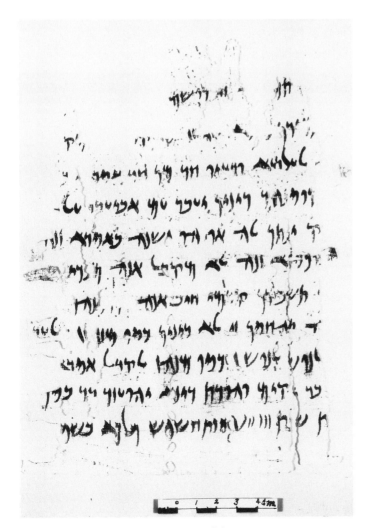

Plate 1755

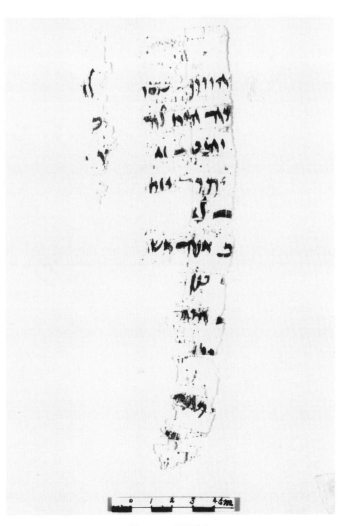

Plate 1756

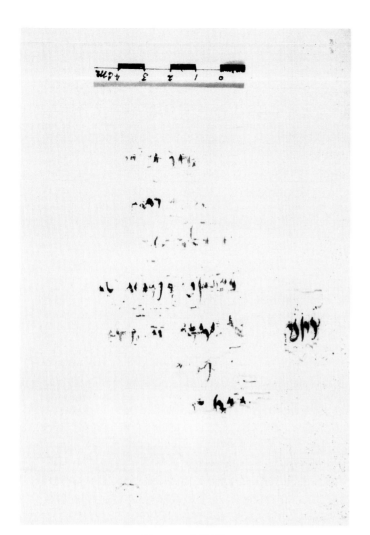

PLATE 1757

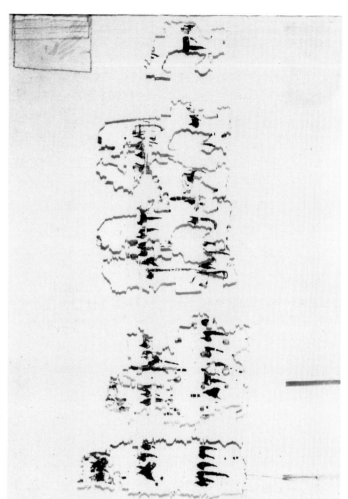

PLATE 1758

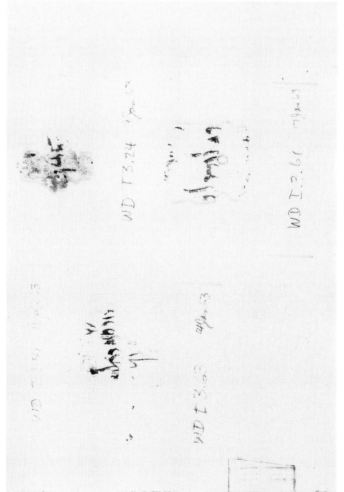

PLATE 1759

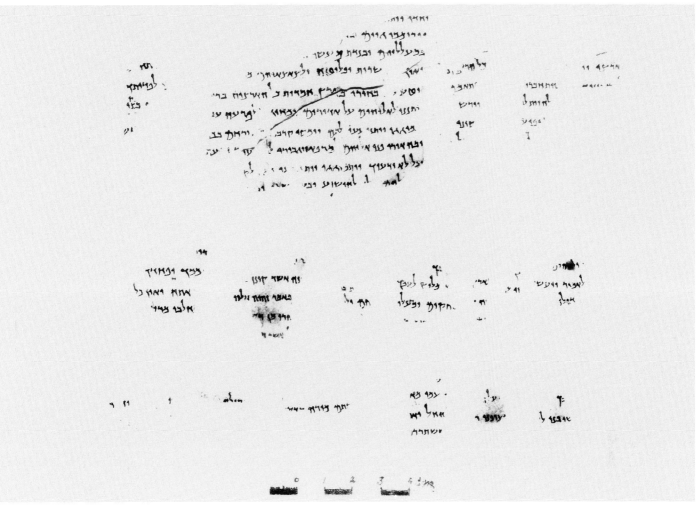

PLATE 1760

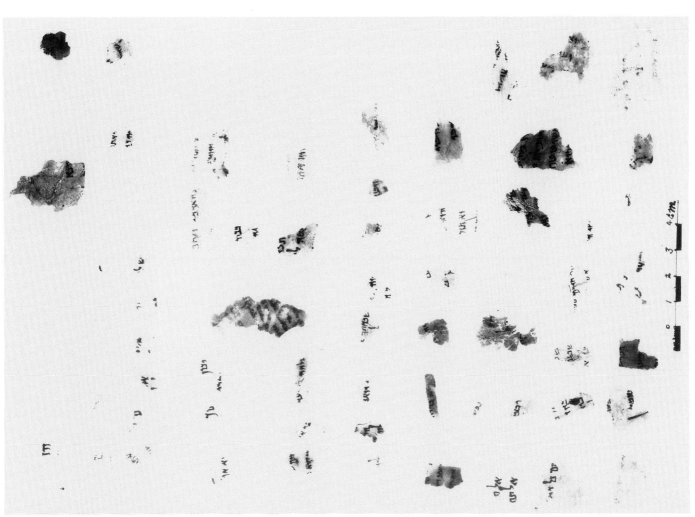

PLATE 1761

PLATE 1763

PLATE 1762

PLATE 1764

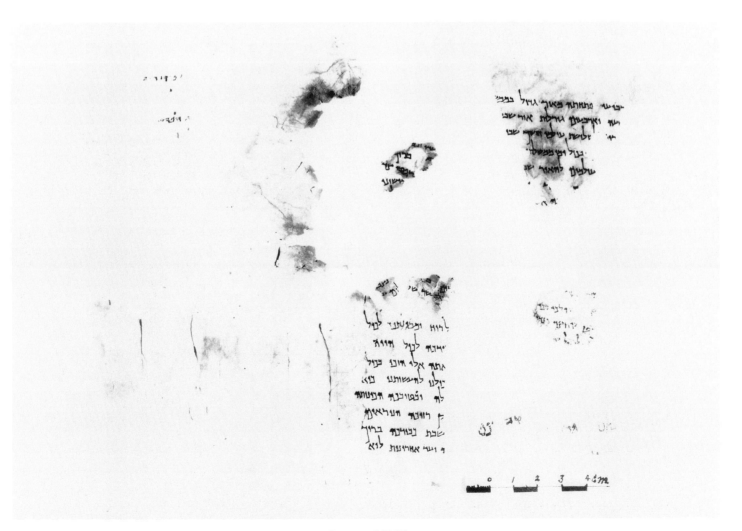

PLATE 1765

PLATE 1767

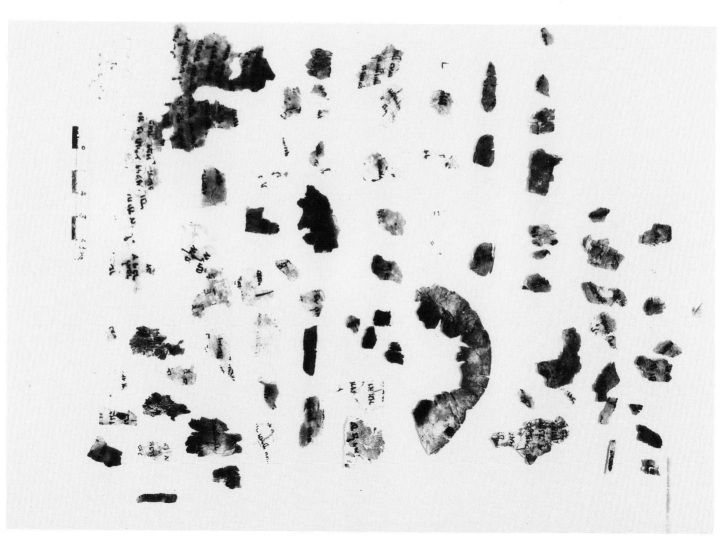

PLATE 1766

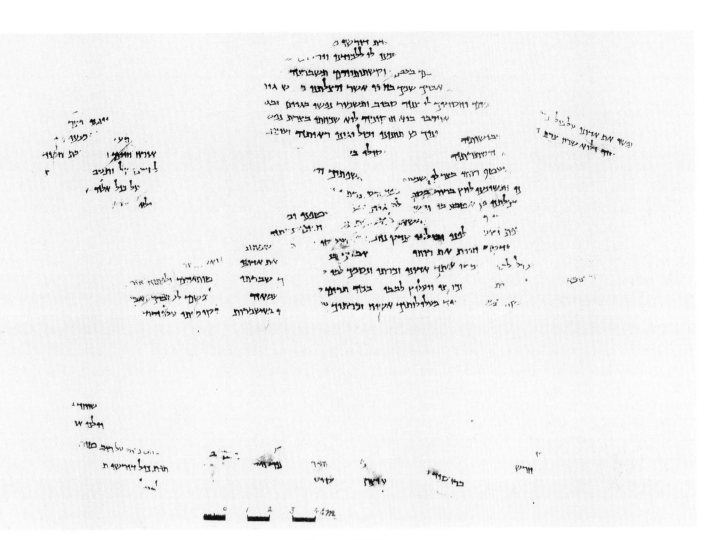

PLATE 1768

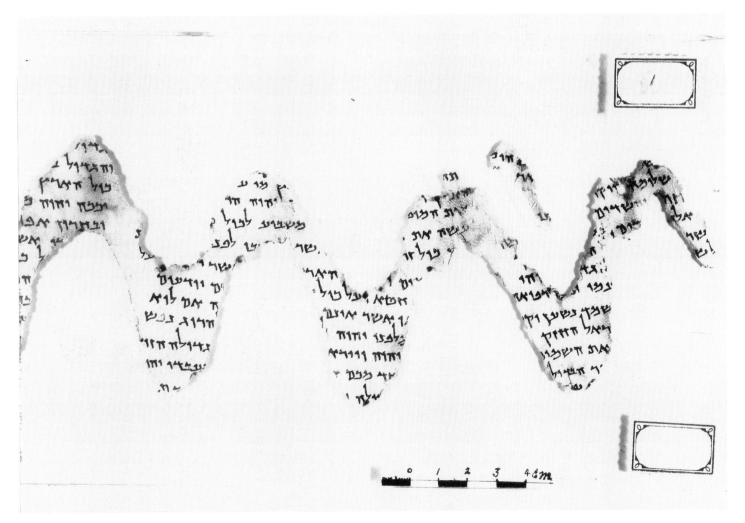

PLATE 1769

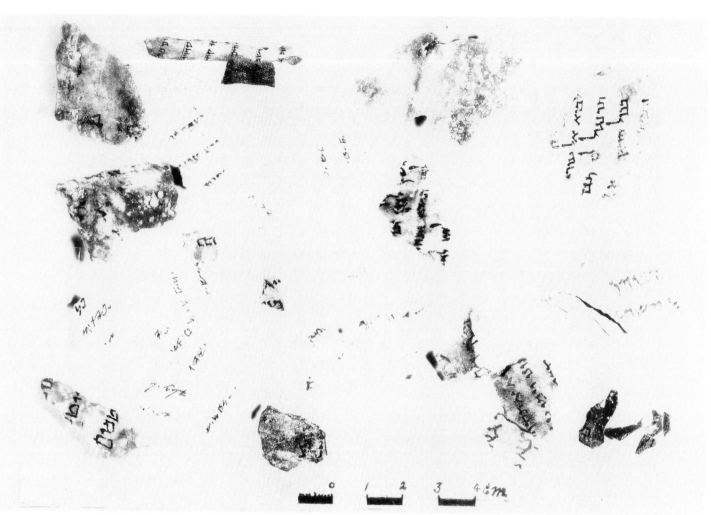

PLATE 1770

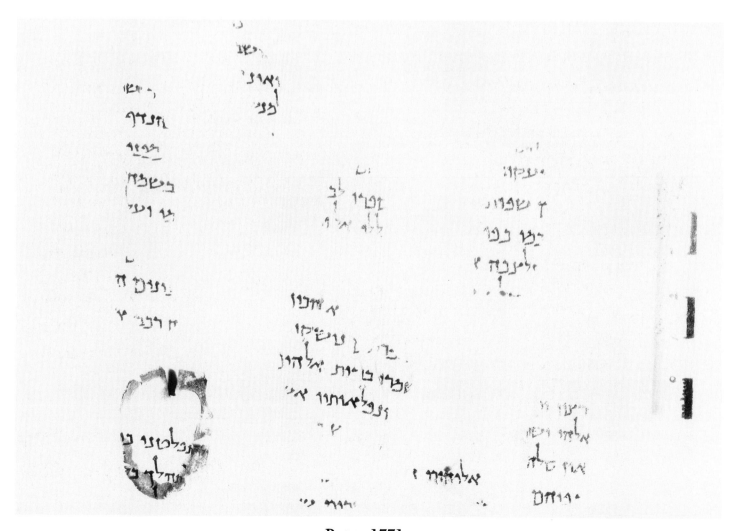

PLATE 1771

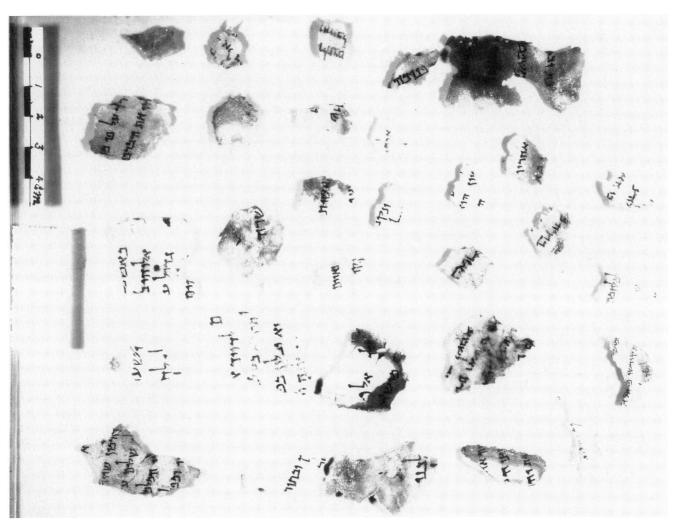

PLATE 1772

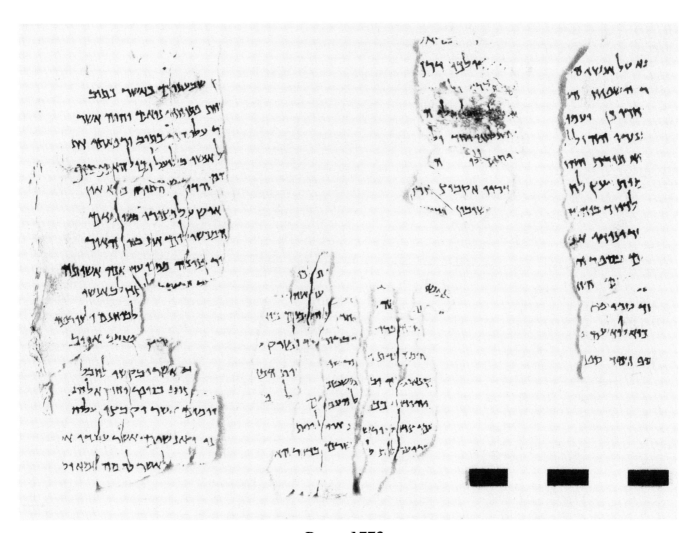

PLATE 1773

Plate 1774

Plate 1775

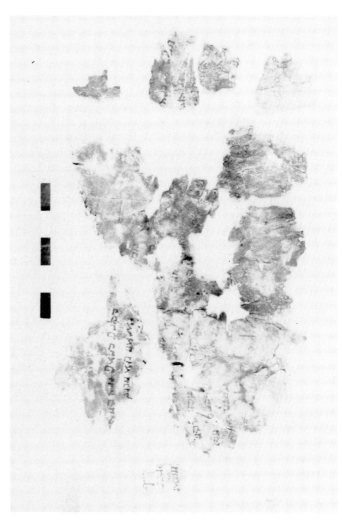

Plate 1776

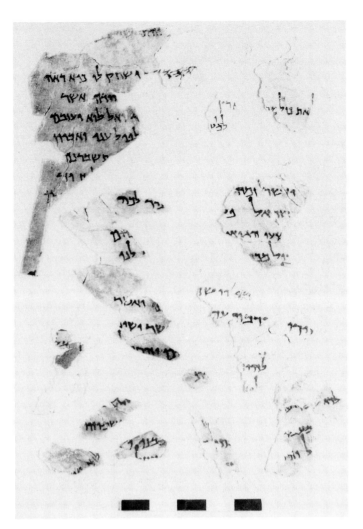

PLATE 1777

PLATE 1778

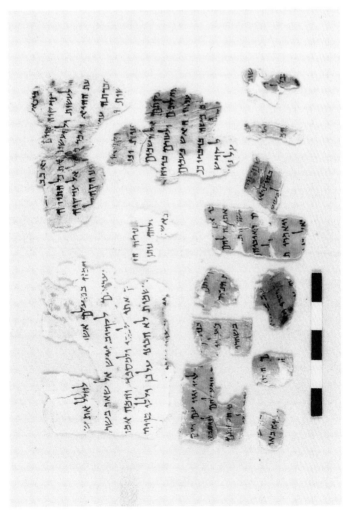

PLATE 1779

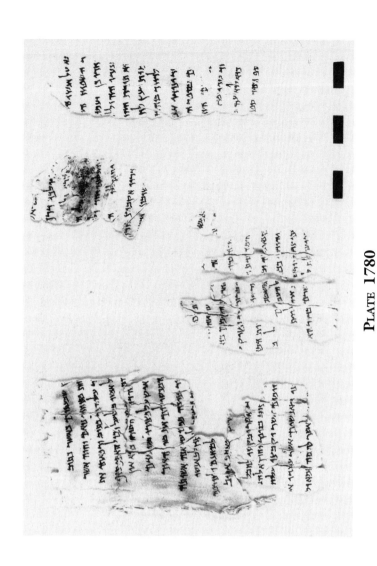

PLATE 1780

PLATE 1781

PLATE 1782

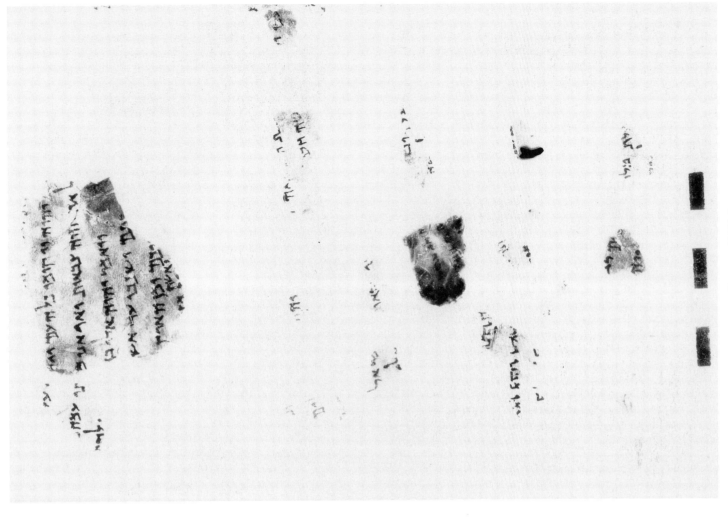

PLATE 1784

PLATE 1783

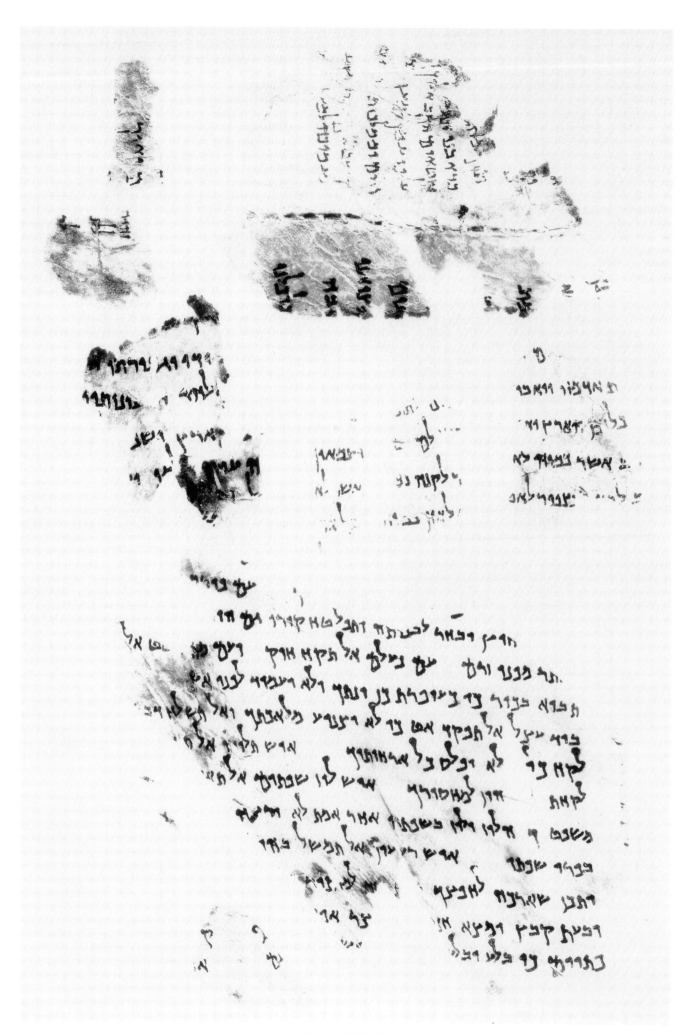

PLATE 1785